Trends in Financial Sector in India

Trends in Financial Sector in India

EDITORS

Arindam Gupta
Samir Ghosh
Kalpataru Bandopadhyay

ALLIED PUBLISHERS PVT. LTD.

Noida • Mumbai • Kolkata • Chennai • Bangalore

ALLIED PUBLISHERS PRIVATE LIMITED

D-5, Sector-2, **Noida**–201 301
Ph. Nos.: 0120-4320295/2542557/4352866
E-mail: delhi.books@alliedpublishers.com

17 Chittaranjan Avenue, **Kolkata**–700072
Ph.: 033-22129618 • E-mail: cal.books@alliedpublishers.com

15 J.N. Heredia Marg, Ballard Estate, **Mumbai**–400001
Ph.: 022-42126969 • E-mail: mumbai.books@alliedpublishers.com

No. 25/10, Commander-in-Chief Road, Ethiraj Lane (Next to Post Office)
Egmore, **Chennai**–600008
Ph.: 044-28223938 • E-mail: chennai.books@alliedpublishers.com

P.B. No. 9932, No. 15, 3rd Floor (Next to Vijaya Bank), 5th Cross, Gandhinagar, Karnataka,
Bangalore–560009. Ph.: 080-41530285/22386239
E-mail: bngl.books@alliedpublishers.com

Website: www.alliedpublishers.com

ISBN: 978-93-89934-60-1

Published by Sunil Sachdev and printed by Ravi Sachdev
at Allied Publishers Pvt. Ltd., D-5, Sector-2, Noida–201 301

ASBM UNIVERSITY

Foreword

As a member of the commerce and management fraternity for more than four decades, I had the privilege of having a close relationship with the Department of Commerce of Vidyasagar University. I am very happy to write the foreword of the book "Trends in Financial Sector in India" which has been edited by three professors of the Department whose expertise in the field of finance is well known. This edited book presents the dynamism of the financial sector and its emerging trends. The chapters of this aptly timed book highlight the important issues and research findings relating to the financial sector.

In an era marked by rapid changes and technological advancements, this publication enriches the literature of the financial sector. The coverage of the themes of various chapters throw light on key areas of the financial sector that include digital banking, IPOS, corporate social responsibility, sustainability issues, effect of technology on financial services, fintech, climate finance, insurance penetration trends, financial inclusion, dividend policy-performance relationship and leverage-performance connectedness. These issues are contemporary and therefore always find place for discussion among academicians and researchers in different academic platforms. This book is praiseworthy for bringing together such relevant issues in a single pack that will help readers to get a comprehensive understanding of the real- life issues bothering the financial sector. Through the insights of leading researchers of finance in this book, readers will gain a deeper understanding of the complex financial issues.

I strongly believe that academicians and researchers who have interest in the financial system and financial sector will be immensely benefitted from the rich contents of this academic contribution. I hope, this book will serve as a valuable resource for those looking to navigate the complexities of the financial landscape. I take this opportunity to congratulate all the editors for bringing out such a commendable publication.

(Prof. Ranjan Kumar Bal)
Vice-Chancellor

Shiksha Vihar, **Post :** ASBM University, Bhola, Chandaka, Bhubaneswar-754 012, India
Phone : +91 674 2374801-05 | **Fax :** +91 674 2374900 | **E-mail :** info@asbm.ac.in | **Website :** www.asbm.ac.in

Preface

The financial sector is a dynamic and ever-evolving field, influencing and reflecting broader economic trends, technological advancements, and societal shifts. This book, Trends in Financial Sector in India, aims to comprehensively examine contemporary issues and developments that are reshaping financial markets, institutions, and practices.

As editors, we recognize the critical role that scholarly discourse plays in advancing our understanding of financial trends. This collection brings together contributions from esteemed researchers and practitioners who offer diverse perspectives on the myriad factors affecting the financial landscape. Each chapter presents in-depth analyses, empirical research, and theoretical insights that contribute to the ongoing conversation about the future of finance.

The book is organized into several thematic sections, reflecting the multifaceted nature of the financial sector. Topics covered include the impact of fintech innovations, sustainable finance practices, demographic influences on financial behavior, and the evolving regulatory environment. By addressing these themes, we hope to illuminate the complexities and challenges that professionals and academics face in this rapidly changing domain.

We extend our gratitude to the contributing authors for their expertise, dedication, and passion for the subject matter. Their commitment to rigorous research and thoughtful analysis has enriched this volume. We also acknowledge the support of Allied Publishers Pvt. Ltd. for their role in bringing this project to fruition. Furthermore, we are deeply grateful to the faculty members of our department for their wholehearted support, without which this book would not have been possible. In conclusion, we invite readers to engage with the ideas presented in this book and reflect on how they might apply in their own contexts—whether in academia, industry, or policy-making. As the financial sector continues to evolve, ongoing research and dialogue are essential for navigating the challenges and opportunities that lie ahead.

Contents

Customers' Perception on Security Problems of Digital Retail Banking: A Study in West Bengal

Biswajit Dey[1] and J.K. Das[2]

ABSTRACT: Digital innovation has been increasing the scope and reach of digital banking in India. Accessibility and availability of banking services through online as well as offline to both digitally active and inactive public have increased to achieve inclusive financial banking network. Along with this, the strategy and techniques of innovative digital banking frauds and scams have also been originated by using the loopholes of different digital banking services leading to the decay of confidence and trust of customers and creating security problems. It is observed that from 2019 to 2021, there is above 342% and 130% increase in number of credit/debit card frauds and online banking frauds respectively. From the empirical analysis on survey result on 211 respondents it is found that there is moderate level of perception of respondents on the security problems of digital retail banking and Age, Occupation and Use frequency of digital banking have significant impact on such perception at 5% level of significance. Banks need to be high alert on security aspect and also the customer's perception on it and banks should try to reduce moderate level of perception to lower level.

Keywords: Digital Innovation, Digital Retail Banking, Banking Frauds, Security Problems.

Background of the Study

The effort of banks to make entire banking system digital is beyond imagination in India. Digital is the expected layer of banking service and online payment has now become the core retail banking services. With the increase in number of smart phone and internet availability, Indian retail banking has seen a sharp increase in digital retail payment adoption and usage by the different classes of people and it is perceived to be virtual banking in near future.

The more retail banking becomes easily accessible, the more it is prone to be exposed to the negative side of digital insecurity. The entire banking operation

[1] PhD Research Scholar, University of Calcutta & WBA&AS Officer, Department of Finance, Government of West- Bengal, India. E-mail: phdbiswajit96@gmail.com

[2] Professor and Dean, Department of Commerce, University of Calcutta, India. E-mail: jadabkdas@gmail.com

has been data driven and technology centric. For making financial inclusion, banking becomes open integrated and its loopholes benefits are leveraged by the fraudsters and hackers leading to the fear of digital insecurity and financial losses. Banks are comprehensively giving effort to mitigate the extent of such risk to minimum level. In current times, cashless society much requires the digital protection and cyber security in online banking from fraudulent activities and the primary objectives of cyber security or digital security in online banking is to safeguard the people's banking assets and data (Srinivasulu, 2023).

Technological innovation has created the innovative fraudulent activities with online banking leading to the loss of faith by the people on banking. During the past few years mainly after the demonetisation period in which digital banking takes the surge, cyber-crimes involving online banking frauds have increased a lot. Deep (2023) in his article in 'The Hindu' has brought a fact that over 3500 complaints about financial frauds targeting mainly senior citizens and widowers, are received by the Central Government's Cyber Crime portal. The Hindu (2023)[23] has also conducted a survey which asserted that in India, 39% of the families have experienced financial frauds and of them only 24% have got back their defrauded funds from the bank. The majority of the frauds are related to the debit and credit card frauds as per the survey. The following table shows the different categories of cyber frauds relating to digital banking during 2019-2021.

Table 1: Number of Different Cyber Frauds in India

Year	*Credit/Debit Card Fraud*	*ATM Fraud*	*Online Banking Fraud*	*OTP Fraud*	*Others Fraud*
2019	367	2067	2093	549	1157
2020	1194	2160	4047	1093	1901
2021	1624	1899	4823	2028	3633

Source: National Crime Record Bureau publication (www.ncrb.gov.in)

It is seen from the above table that except ATM frauds, all other frauds are increasing from 2019 to 2021. The number of online banking frauds of 4823 in 2021 is the highest among the other. Over 342% in frauds cases observed with cards from 2019-2021 whereas 130.43% is increased in online banking cases.

Every innovation in digital banking services for financial inclusion's purpose can contribute to the origination of new sort of banking frauds. There are several eye-catching banking frauds occurred that have shaken the very purpose of easy accessibility of financial services made by the digital banking innovation and

[3] The Hindu (2023). https://www.thehindu.com/news/national/39-indian-families-claim-to-be-victim-of-online-financial-fraud-survey/article66802997.ece

leading to newer type of security problem. Recently in India, AePS related frauds have taken the night sleep of the general public. According to NPCI, Aadhaar-enabled Payment System (AePS) is introduced with an objective of providing digital banking financial services to those customers who are digitally inactive (Bhakta, 2023). AePS is one of the digitally enabled banking services through which a digitally inactive customer can withdraw cash upto Rs. 10,000 from his bank account by using his Aadhaar number and biometric authentication like finger print or Iris scan (Rawat, **2023**). AePS frauds are made by stealing Aadhaar number and Finger prints from different sources like property registration documents (Akram, 2023). Many innocent people have become the victim of such scams and such frauds are violating the very purpose of the introduction of AePS in India.

Due to such scams and frauds, a negative perception on banking security control is generated forcefully into the minds of people and a negative image is created. Such perception barrier creates a larger security problem that ought to be resolved by the robust security features by the banking authority.

Review of Literature

Shanab and Matalqa (2015) have suggested in their study to take necessary steps at every levels to curb security flaws since e-banking still remains untrusted for many people. Vimala (2016) has found that 50% of the respondents have faced hacking and phishing attacks. It is also recommended for hi-tech security measures like internet scam protector, hacking detector etc. must be taken by the banks. Tabiaa *et al.* (2017) have made a descriptive study on digital banking security risks and asserted that the need of digital security will be grown along the development of more sophisticated online banking systems. They proposed that banks should strive to the better security management as a major aspect of administration offerings. Milosavljević and Njagojević (2019) have stated customers need to be familiar with the internet banking security but the study found that customers are not really familiar with the this security and major threats emanating from such security problems. It is also found that customers are also not concerned with such security of the online banking. Vishnuvardhan *et al.* (2020) have examined the different security attacks on mobile banking. Descriptively analysed all these security threats on mobile banking and these include wireless attacks, DDoS attacks, Malware attacks, TCP/IP Spoofing, server compromise etc. Nayar and Rathod (2021) have stated that banks must have rigid cyber hygiene regimen to safeguard the customers and must make customers aware of the different cyber frauds. Thus study also proposes for insurance coverage for cyber-attacks. Eleyan *et al.* (2022) have found out in their study that age and educational level have affected the awareness level of people towards cyber risks on their bank accounts.

Research Gap and Objectives of the Study

In recent times, online banking scams and frauds have risen at a significant rate. After extensive reviewing of past studies, very few of them have focussed on current picture of banking frauds and its impact on customers' perception. Therefore, the present study will meet up this gap and focussed on the following research objectives:

- To understand the present picture of digital banking frauds in India;
- To study customers' perception on digital banking's security;
- To find out different demographic factors affecting such perception.

Research Methodology

The present study is descriptive and empirical in nature. For meeting the objective, both primary and secondary data have been collected. Secondary data is collected from different websites like NCRB, RBI and different e-news are also used for factual information. Primary data is collected from the survey on 211 respondents in West Bengal. Primary data is collected on the basis of five-point Likert scale and according to the central limit theorem on large sample size, parametric statistical tests are conducted. Descriptive statistics like Mean, SD, Skewness and Kurtosis are used. One way ANOVA test is also applied.

Analysis and Findings

This segment shows the customers' perception on security of digital banking.

Demographic Characteristics of Respondents

The following table shows the demographic features of respondents i.e. Age, Location, Gender, Education, Occupation and Used Frequency of Digital Banking.

Table 2: Demographic Characteristics of Respondents

Age	*Frequency*	*%*	*Occupation*	*Frequency*	*%*
18–26 years	68	32.2	Government employee	43	20.4
26–34 years	57	27	Private employee	39	18.5
34–42 years	35	16.6	Students	56	26.5
42–50 years	26	12.4	Business	7	3.3
Above 50 years	25	11.8	Professional	7	3.3
Total	**211**	**100**	**Self Employed**	**17**	**8.1**

Age	*Frequency*	*%*	*Occupation*	*Frequency*	*%*
Education	Frequency	%	Retired	9	4.3
Class 10	8	3.8	Unemployed	33	15.6
Higher Secondary	35	16.6	Total	211	100
Graduation	81	38.4	Gender	Frequency	%
Post Graduation	77	36.5	Female	114	54
Professional study	10	4.7	Male	97	46
Total	**211**	**100**	**Total**	**211**	**100**
Use Frequency	Frequency	%	Location	Frequency	%
Rarely	53	25.2	Rural	33	15.6
Sometimes	65	30.8	Semi Urban	34	16.2
Frequently	52	24.6	Urban	144	68.2
Very frequently	41	19.4	Total	211	100
Total	**211**	**100**			

Source: Primary Data

From the above table 2, it is found that majority of respondents (32.2%) are young aged i.e. 18–26 years and graduate respondents are in majority i.e. 38.4%. Since majority respondents are young aged, thus students occupy the majority respondents i.e. 26.5%. Majority of respondents are female i.e. 54% and majority comes from urban locality which accounts for 68.2%. It is also found that majority of respondents are using digital banking sometimes.

Customers' Perception on Security Problems

Table 3: Reliability of Security Problems Statements

Reliability Statistics	
Cronbach's Alpha	No. of Items/ Attributes
0.850	5

Source: Computed by authors

It is found from the above table 3 that, Cronbach's Alpha value is 0.850 which shows high reliability and internal consistency of 5 security problem statements.

It is found from the above table 4 that Mean values of all five attributes are ranging from 2.588 to 2.953 which is between '2 to 3' revealing that respondents have moderate level of perception on the security problems of digital retail banking. SD of all the five attributes are ranging from 1.178 to 1.259 suggesting that all the attributes have similar level of variation according to the perception of respondents. The above table also shows that all the five attributes are positively skewed and negatively excess kurtosis and both of which are within normally acceptable range of –2 to +2 (George and Mallery, 2014). It is also observed that majority of respondents have undecided about the 2nd attribute i.e. they are still in dilemma about whether digital retail banking can save them from losing vital banking information or not and due to this reason that Mean value of 2.953 is the highest among the others.

Table 4: Descriptive Statistics of Security Problems Attributes

Attributes	*Frequency (%)*					*Mean*	*S.D.*	*Skew.*	*Kurt.*
	1 (SD)	*2 (D)*	*3 (N)*	*4 (A)*	*5 (SA)*				
Feeling of Less Security	33 (15.6)	58 (27.5)	47 (22.3)	50 (23.7)	23 (10.9)	2.867	1.250	0.106	–1.054
High Chance of Losing Banking Information	27 (12.8)	47 (22.3)	69 (32.7)	45 (21.3)	23 (10.9)	2.953	1.178	0.022	–0.782
Dissatisfaction with digital security	38 (18)	54 (25.6)	54 (25.6)	48 (22.7)	17 (8.1)	2.773	1.217	0.109	–0.985
Bad Experience with Online Banking	41 (19.4)	74 (35.1)	42 (19.9)	39 (18.5)	15 (7.1)	2.588	1.197	0.404	–0.818
It creates Security Threat to Customers	50 (23.7)	49 (23.2)	49 (23.2)	48 (22.7)	15 (7.2)	2.664	1.259	0.152	–1.109

Source: Primary Data

Demographic Factors Affecting Customers' Perception

In this segment, significant demographic factors or characteristics are found out with the help of one way ANOVA. Average score of the five attributes are taken for the test.

Table 5 shows that Age, Occupation and Use Frequency of digital banking by the respondents have significantly affected the customers' perception on security problems. These three demographic factors are significant across which the customers' perception is significantly varying.

Table 5: Variation of Security Problem

Demographic Factors	*F Value*	*P Value*
Age	12.383	0.000*
Location	2.618	0.075
Gender	0.096	0.757
Education	0.809	0.521
Occupation	4.215	0.000*
Use Frequency	16.969	0.000*

*Indicates significant at 0.05 level.
Source: Computation by authors

Concluding Remarks

It is found that the more banking will be digital, the more number of digital banking frauds and scams will be increasing. If the number of such frauds is not controlled, the customers' belief in online banking security will be problematic. Currently as per survey results, customers put moderate perception on security problems in digital retail banking. There is a high chance of increasing negative perception of customers on security aspect since the majority of customers have still remained undecided about the security strength of online banking on one of the security problem attributes i.e. high chance of losing banking information and majority are also dissatisfied with digital security. Thus, banks should take it seriously into accounts to reduce such negative attributes of perception on security problems that still customers are currently facing.

References

[1] Akram, M. (2023). Aadhaar-Enabled Payment Scam Hits Citizens Registering Properties in Karnataka; Police Suspect Intermediaries' Role. *The Indian Express. https://indianexpress.com/article/cities/bangalore/aadhaar-enabled-payment-citizens-karnataka-8990185/.*

[2] Bhakta, P. (2023). NPCI Stepping in to Stop AePS Frauds, Suggests Ways to Banks. *The Economic Times.* https://economictimes.indiatimes.com/tech/technology/npci-stepping-in-to-stop-aeps-frauds-suggests-ways-to-banks/articleshow/104804844.cms.

[3] Deep, A. (2023). Over 3,500 Financial Frauds Reported Online Daily, Says National Cyber Security Coordinator. *The Hindu.* https://www.thehindu.com/news/national/over-3500-financial-frauds-reported-online-daily-says-national-cyber-security-coordinator/article66482305.ece.

[4] Eleyan, D., Yousef, R. AND Eleyan, A. (2022). Assessment of Cybersecurity Awareness among E-Banking in Palestine—Empirical Study from Customer's Perspective. *Journal of Theoretical and Applied Information Technology.* 100 (16). 4952–4962.

[5] George, D. and Mallery, P. (2014). *IBM SPSS Statistics 23 Step by Step-A Simple Guide and Reference* (14th Ed.). Routledge.

[6] Milosavljević, N. and Njagojević, S. (2019). Customers' Perception of Information Security in Internet Banking. *Advances in Economics, Business and Management Research*, 108. 272–277.

[7] Nayar, K. and Rathod, P. (2021). Cyber Security Challenges in Indian Banks. *Shodh Sarita*. 8(29), 167–172.

[8] Rawat, S.S. (2023). AePS Scam: Here are the Things You Need to Do If You Are a Victim of Fraud. *Business Standard.* https://www.business-standard.com/finance/personal-finance/aeps-scam-here-are-the-things-you-need-to-do-if-you-are-a-victim-of-fraud-123110200968_1.html

[9] Shanab, E.A. and Matalqa, S. (2015). Security and Fraud Issues of E-banking. *International Journal of Computer Networks and Applications*, 2(4), 179–187.

[10] Srinivasulu, K. (2023). Cybersecurity threats in digital banking sector. *Economic* Times. https://cio.economictimes.indiatimes.com/news/digital-security/cybersecurity-threats-in-digital-banking-sector/102298156.

[11] Tabiaa, M., Madani, A. and Kamoun, N.E. (2017). E-Banking: Security Risks, Previsions and Recommendations. *International Journal of Computer Science and Network Security,* 17(11), 189–196.

[12] Vimala, V. (2016). An Evaluative Study on Internet Banking Security among Selected Indian Bank Customers. *Amity Journal of Management Research*, 1(1), 63–79.

[13] Vishnuvardhan, B., Manjula, B. and Naik, R.L. (2020). A Study on Digital Banking: Security Issues and Challenges. *Springer*, 163–185.

Post-Listing Performance of Indian IPOs: A Study into the Role of Anchor Investors

Prasenjit Roy[1] and Arindam Gupta[2]

ABSTRACT: In a bid to evaluate post-listing performance of the Initial Public Offerings (IPOs), the study employs a total of 247 IPOs, 156 of which are anchor investor-participated and 91 non-anchor investor-participated, listed in the National Stock Exchange (NSE) during 2009–2020. The results of average abnormal return (AAR) and cumulative average abnormal return (CAAR) provide evidence that anchor investor-participated IPOs outperform non-anchor investor-participated IPOs. The results convey that anchor investors preferred to refrain from flipping activity on conclusion of the lock-in period and thereby obviated excessive dilution of listing gains. Thus, they remain successful in providing credibility to the market participants and in boosting their confidence to invest in Indian IPOs over a longer time frame. The confidence instilled in the investors by the anchor investors is likely to enable the Indian security market to prosper and flourish in the upcoming days which remains also the target of its regulator, SEBI.

Keywords: Anchor Investors, Lock-in Period, Post-listing Performance, IPO-underpricing.

Introduction

Initial public offerings (IPOs) are found be underpriced across countries and stock markets (Loughran *et al.*, 1994). The literature on IPO-underpricing is extensive and well documented. IPO-underpricing refers to the positive difference between the closing price on the listing day and the offer price of an IPO (Gupta & Suri, 2017). In a perfect market, the offer price of an IPO ought to be in equivalence to the closing price on the first trading day (Nafid, 2014). However, investment bankers usually price IPOs at levels that differ from the intrinsic value (Nafid, 2014). This phenomenon is however temporary as the laws of supply and demand will eventually drive newly issued shares towards their intrinsic value. Owing, to such reasons, studies mostly have observed that the extent IPO-underpricing gets diluted in the post-listing period. However, the difference in

[1] Research Scholar, Department of Business Administration, Vidyasagar University, Midnapore & Jt. Advisor (Finance), WBERC, Kolkata, India.
E-mail: pras.roy123@gmail.com

[2] Professor of Commerce, Vidyasagar University, Midnapore, India.
E-mail: arindamgupta69@gmail.com

views also exists. (Aggarwal & Rivoli, 1990; Ritter, 1991; Lee *et al.*, 1996; Kiymaz, 2000; Chan *et al.*, 2004; Kumar, 2007; Kenourgios *et al.*, 2007; Pande & Vaidyanathan, 2009; Sahoo & Rajib, 2010; Marisetty & Subrahmanyam, 2010; Singh & Kumar, 2012; Sharma *et al.*, 2013; Agathee *et al.*, 2014; Berk & Peterle, 2015; Dell'Acqua *et al.*, 2015; Yong *et al.*, 2015; Reddy, 2015; Pandya, 2016; Wong *et al.*, 2017; Hedau, 2018; Hawaldar *et al.*, 2018; Mehta & Patel, 2018; Killins, 2019; Pandey *et al.*, 2021) proclaim that IPOs underperform in the post-listing period whereas (Loughran *et al.*, 1994; Madhusoodanan & Thiripalraju, 1997; Madan, 2003; Das *et al.*, 2016; Manu & Saini, 2020; Manjunath *et al.*, 2020) infer oppositely.

The Indian IPO market offers an interesting setting to analyse IPO-underpricing and the post-listing performance in view of partial limitation imposed on underwriter power over allocations. In India, regulators first granted underwriters control over allocations of book-built IPOs. However, in November, 2005, the regulations changed and underwriters no longer controlled allocations. Before November, 2005, book-built IPOs in India followed a process that was similar in some respect to that in the U.S. or Europe (Bubna & Prabala, 2011). The November, 2005 allocation policy was revised by the Securities Exchange Board of India (SEBI) in July, 2009. The revised policy partially reinstated the underwriters' discretionary allocation power by allowing the underwriter to commit 30% (60% from September, 2014) of the SEBI enforced pre-determined qualified institutional buyer (QIB) quota to anchor investors at the underwriter's discretion at either the anchor price or the offer price, whichever is higher. The policy continues to enforce non-discretionary allocation to the retail investors, non-institutional investors and to the non-anchor institutional investors (Samdani, 2019). An anchor investor in a public issue refers to a QIB making an application for a value of INR 100 million or more through the book-building process and a lock-in period of 30 days is stipulated for anchor investors from the date of allotment while QIBs can sell on listing day. Anchor investors being mandated to invest in the IPO one day before the book opens to the public, a larger participation in the form of subscription from anchors is likely to convey an early signal to the market as regards the issue quality. The aspect of anchor investor is unique to India and though fundamentally similar to cornerstone investors prevalent in some other countries. Unlike anchor investors, cornerstone investors need not necessarily be institutional investors.

In the backdrop of unique setting of the Indian IPO market, the study intends to carry out post-listing performance of IPOs participated by the anchor investors. The following objectives are therefore dealt with in this study:

- To ascertain the post-listing performances of IPOs.
- To ascertain the post-listing performance of the anchor investor-participated IPOs.

- To analyse dilution in earning of IPOs participated by anchor investors after lock-in period is over.

Existing studies in the context of post-listing performance of IPOs have dwelt upon comparisons of raw returns after three months, six months and one year of listing with the listing day returns in respect of anchor investor-participated IPOs for ascertaining post-listing outperformance. The present study emphasises on post-listing performance on a day-by-day analysis up to sixty days of the anchor investor-participated IPOs and also ascertains whether anchor investors flip or remain in the market after the conclusion of 30-day lock-in period. The study, as such, add new dimension to the extant literature and thereby augment the literature with a unique setting applicable for IPOs in India only.

The rest of the article is structured as follows: Section 2 dwells on literature review and hypothesis development. Section 3 deals with data and methodology. Section 4 discusses the empirical results and analysis. Section 5 concludes the article setting out conclusions, managerial implications, limitations and future study.

Review of Literature and Hypothesis Development

The review of literature is in three parts. The first dwells upon findings at abroad, the second in India and the third deals with the performance of anchor investor-participated IPOs.

Post-listing Performance (Abroad)

Aggarwal & Rivoli (1990) with a sample comprising of 1598 U.S. IPOs pertaining to the period 1977–1987 find that post-listing abnormal returns (CAAR) is to the extent of 10.67%, 11.17%, 10.83%, 11.17% on Day1, Day 2, Day 20 and Day 100 from listing day respectively. The abnormal returns of the sample after one year corresponding to 250 days arrive to -5.45%. Ritter (1991) using a sample of 1,526 US IPOs listed in the 1975–84 period finds post-listing returns (CAAR) get negative after the fifth month from listing and the downward trend continues thereafter. Lee *et al.* (1996) find post-listing one-year return (CAAR) arrives at –18.77% employing a sample of 266 industrial IPOs getting listed in the Australian Stock Exchange Limited (ASX) from January 1976 to December 1989. Kiymaz (2000) using a sample of 163 IPOs listed on the Istanbul Stock Exchange during 1990–1996 finds that the post-listing returns (CAAR) drop down to 3% after 3 months of listing. Chan *et al.* (2004) with a sample of 570 IPOs listed on the Shenzhen stock exchange and Shanghai securities exchange by applying BHAR, observe underperformance of the IPOs in the post-listing phase. Kenourgios *et al.* (2007) employing 169 IPOs getting listed on the Athens Stock Exchange (ASE) during 1997–2002, find the market-adjusted returns on day 1, day 5 and day 21 plummets to 54.28%, 45.32% and 43.83% thereby deciphering underperformance in the post-listing phase. Agathee *et al.* (2014) with a sample comprising of 44 IPOs getting listed at the stock exchange market of Mauritius from 1989 to 2010 observe post-listing performance employing cumulative average return (CAR) turns negative after four months of listing and continues to be negative thereafter. The extent of the post-listing returns in the study undertaken by Berk & Peterle (2015) employing 172 IPOs listed during 2000–09 at the stock exchanges of Austria, Bulgaria, the Czech Republic, Poland, Romania and Slovenia by applying BHAR after 1 week, 2 weeks and 1 year comes out to 0.8%, 0.5% and 3.60% respectively thereby displaying underperformance during post-listing phase. Dell'Acqua *et al.* (2015) exploring a sample of 129 IPOs listed in the Italian stock exchange during 2011–2012 observe the post-listing extent of IPO-underpricing after 30 days drops to 5.27% from 6.75% as on listing day. Yong *et al.* (2015) with a sample of 322 IPOs getting listed in Bursa Stock exchange during 2002–2008 find post-listing one-year CAAR of -2.24% connoting the stocks underperforming in the post listing phase. Wong *et al.* (2017) find post-listing IPO-underpricing after 12 months in comparison to listing day IPO-underpricing bear a negative relationship with coefficient of –0.022 employing a sample of 313 IPOs listed in Bursa Malaysia from 2008 to 2016. Killins (2019) using a sample of 73 IPOs getting listed in the Canadian stock market from 2010 to 2017 observes post-listing results to be loss suffering to the investors displaying 12-month period BHAR and CAR of –5.73% and –5.44% respectively. Oppositely, Loughran *et al.* (1994) find IPOs to be overperforming in the post-listing phase.

Post-listing Performance (India)

Kumar (2007) finds in the post-listing phase that 156 IPOs getting listed in the NSE from January 1999 to May 2007 to underperform after 24 months of listing. Pande & Vaidyanathan (2009) using a sample of 55 book-built IPOs listed in the NSE during 2004–2006 observe the gains of investors on the listing day dispel within the next 30 days of the listing by way of arriving to the adjusted return of –1.13%. Marisetty & Subrahmanyam (2010) using a sample of 2,713 IPOs listed at BSE during 1990–2004 find 12-month post-listing CAAR and BHAR to be –0.105 and –0.366, thereby displaying underperformance. Singh & Kumar (2012) observe the level of IPO-underpricing to be 18% and the same turns to –1.96% post 120 days of the listing with a sample of 116 IPOs getting listed in BSE and NSE from January 2006 to October 2007. Sharma *et al.* (2013) using 319 IPOs getting listed on NSE during 1999–2011 find the extent of IPO-underpricing after 1 year from listing reduces to 20.75% from 25.13%. Reddy (2015) employing 133 IPOs getting listed at NSE during 2007–2009 finds the mean return after one year from listing arrives at –21.13% connoting deterioration of post-listing performance. Pandya (2016) using 183 IPOs getting listed on BSE during 2004–2013 observes that both CAAR and BHAR turn negative post 180 days of listing. Hawaldar et. al. (2018) observe post-listing performance of 464 IPOs listed at BSE during 2001–2011 (CAAR) turning negative and significant after 4 days of listing. Mehta & Patel (2018) find average post-listing returns (MAER) of 172 IPOs getting listed on NSE during 2007–2014 arriving at –4.44% demonstrating the extent of IPO-underpricing on the listing day eliminates with the passage of time. Pandey *et al.* (2021) demonstrate that BHAR as a measure to ascertain post-listing performance of the 232 IPOs getting listed at BSE and NSE from 2008 to 2017 gives negative returns of –5.40% thereby connoting that IPOs underperform in the post-listing phase. Contrarily, (Madhusoodanan & Thiripalraju, 1997; Madan, 2003; Das *et al.*, 2016; Manu & Saini, 2020; Manjunath *et al.*, 2020) report outperformance of IPOs in the post-listing period.

From the review of aforesaid literature on post-listing performance of IPOs, following alternative hypothesis is formulated

Alternative hypothesis, H1: IPOs underperform in the post-listing period.

Performance of Anchor Investor-participated IPOs

Agarwal (2021) contends institutional bidders in anchor investor-participated IPOs subscribe highly for creating opportunities to flip the shares of the hyped issue in the initial trading days and make profit. Gupta *et al.* (2019) find the 3-month, 6-month and one-year mean post-listing return of IPOs backed by the anchor investors to be 3.12%, 11.78% and 8.68% respectively being higher than the IPOs without anchor investors. Subba & Mahapatra (2021) observe that in six months and in one year after listing day, market-adjusted returns from anchor-participated IPOs are significantly higher than non-anchor-participated IPOs. Contrary to such findings portraying encouraging performance of anchor investor-participated IPOs in the post-listing period, Bhattacharya *et al.* (2020) find no evidence of anchor investor-participated IPOs outperforming non-anchor IPOs in the post-listing period whereas Gupta & Jindal (2016) find that post-listing market adjusted return turns positive to negative for both the anchor-backed and non-anchor backed IPOs after 30 days of listing. This leads to the formulation of the second alternative hypothesis.

Alternative hypothesis, H2: Anchor investor-participated IPOs outperform the non-anchor- participated IPOs in the post-listing period.

The phase after lock-in period of 30 days is expected to create a possibility for anchor investors to flip and withdraw from investment, which leads to framing the third alternative hypothesis.

Alternative hypothesis, H3: Anchor investor-participated IPOs underperform after the lock-in period in the post-listing phase.

Data and Methodology

Sample and Data

The sample comprises of 247 IPOs listed from July 2009 to March 2020 listed at the National Stock exchange (NSE). The sample is also categorised into two parts. Anchor investor-participated IPOs and non-anchor investor-participated IPOs. 156 IPOs pertain to anchor investor-participated IPOs and the remaining 91 IPOs relate to non-anchor investor-participated IPOs. Nifty 50 index data are used in the present study as the market index. The said data have been also collected from the website of NSE for the listing day and 250 days of trading from the listing day for all the 247 IPOs.

Statistical Technique Used in the Study

Market-adjusted abnormal return (MAAR), average abnormal return (AAR) and cumulative average abnormal return (CAAR) are employed to evaluate the post-listing performance of the IPOs.

Market-Adjusted Abnormal Return

The methodology of computing market-adjusted abnormal return on the listing day appears as follows which is in line with the methodology applied by Miller & Reilly (1987), Sahoo & Rajib (2010) and Pandya (2016):

$$\text{MAAR} = \left[\frac{(1+IR)}{(1+MR)} - 1\right] \times 100$$

where IR or initial return represents excess of closing price over the offer price expressed in percentage on the listing day of an IPO and

$$\text{MR or Market Return} = \left[\frac{M_C - M_O}{M_O}\right] \times 100$$

MR represents the listing day equivalent market return. Mc is the Nifty 50 index value at close of the listing day, Mo is the opening Nifty 50 index value on the listing day.

Post-listing Performance Measurement

Measurement of post-listing performance under event study approach is done by way of applying either CAAR or BHAR. Fama (1998) in this context, contends that BHAR have a positive slope and widen on long horizon returns distribution. Ritter (1991) also use CAAR. Mitchell & Stafford (2000) accentuate to apply

CAAR to evaluate post-listing performance and lay down that BHAR method overlooks problems which arise from industrial grouping or the use of time series. Manikam *et al.* (2020) advocate for CAAR stating that it is the best method to measure the post-listing performance of IPOs. This study thereby employs CAAR to evaluate the post-listing performance of IPOs.

The evaluation process in this study takes a similar approach as that of Hawaldar *et al.* (2018).

The daily raw return for security *i*, is computed as under:

$$R_{it} = \frac{P_{it} - P_{it-1}}{P_{it-1}}$$

where, R_{it} is the raw return on security i for day t, P_{it} is the closing price of security i on day t and P_{it-1} is the closing price of security i on day t−1.

The market return for the same period is computed as under:

$$R_{mt} = \frac{I_t - I_{t-1}}{I_{t-1}}$$

where, R_{mt} is the market returns on day *t*, I_t is the closing Nifty 50 index level on day t and I_{t-1} is the closing Nifty 50 level on day t−1.

Using return on Nifty 50 as the market return, the market-adjusted return (abnormal return) for stock *i* on day *t* is computed as:

$$AR_{it} = R_{it} - R_{mt}$$

where, AR_{it} is the market-adjusted return for stock i on day t. The average market-adjusted return (average abnormal return) on a portfolio of n stocks for day t is the equally weighted arithmetic average of the market-adjusted returns:

$$AAR_t = \frac{1}{n}\sum_{t=1}^{n} AR_{it}$$

where, AAR_t is the average abnormal return (market-adjusted) on a portfolio of *n* stocks for day *t*, *n* is the number of stocks in the portfolio on day *t*.

The cumulative market-adjusted post-listing performance (cumulative average abnormal return) from day *u* to day *v* is the summation of the average market-adjusted returns or AARs:

$$CAAR_{u,v} = \sum_{t=u}^{v} AAR_t$$

where $CAAR_{u,v}$ is the cumulative average abnormal return or the cumulative market-adjusted post-listing performance from day u to day v.

When a company in portfolio gets delisted from the NSE, the portfolio returns for the next day is an equally weighted average of the remaining listed companies in the portfolio. The cumulative market-adjusted return for various days, thereby, involves daily rebalancing of the portfolio.

Test of Significance (t-test)

Parametric "t-test" is employed to ascertain significance of AARs and CAARs. The conclusions are based on the results of t-stat and p-values on AARs and CAARs for the post-listing period. The t-test statistics (t-stat) for AAR for each day during the post-listing period is calculated as under:

$$t(AAR_t) = \frac{AAR_t}{SE(AAR_t)}$$

where AAR_t is the average abnormal return on day t and $SE(AAR_t)$ is the standard error of average abnormal return on day t which is computed as under:

$$SE(AAR_t) = \frac{SD(AAR_t)}{\sqrt{n}}$$

where, $SD(AAR_t)$ is the standard deviation of average abnormal return on day t and n is the number of stocks in portfolio p on day t.

The t-test statistics for CAAR for each day during the post-listing period is calculated as under:

$$t(CAAR_t) = \frac{CAAR_t}{SE(CAAR_t)}$$

where, $SE(CAAR_t)$ is the standard error of CAAR on day t which is computed as under:

$$SE(CAAR_t) = \frac{SD(CAAR_t)}{\sqrt{n}}$$

$SD(CAAR_t)$ is the standard deviation of CAAR on day *t* which is computed as under:

$$SD(CAAR_t) = SD(AAR_t) \times \sqrt{N}$$

where, *N* is the total number of days for which AAR is cumulated.

The p-value is determined representing two-tailed t-test with degrees of freedom equivalent to sample minus one corresponding to the t-statistic.

Period of Study

The extant literature provides that one-year period of post-listing study corresponds to 250 trading days from the listing day. Hence, the present study also evaluates post-listing performance for 250 days from listing day but reports the first sixty days post-listing results day by day. Thereafter results are reported after six months (125 trading days) and after one year (250 trading days). The day-by-day analysis of the first sixty trading days is of prime importance as anchor investors have 30-day lock-in period from the date of allotment. The anchor investors are allotted the shares a day before the subscription opens for the other category of investors. (Seth, Vishwanatha, & Prasad, 2018) states, the lock-in period will not expire on a specific day, but over a range of days spanning two to three weeks after listing. Two weeks corresponds to 10 trading days and three weeks corresponds to 15 trading days. Hence, 30-day lock-in period actually falls on any day between 10th to 15th trading days from the listing day. The evaluation during this phase is of high relevance.

Empirical Results and Analysis

Table 1 presents MAARs of all 247 IPOs, 91 non-anchor investor-participated IPOs and 156 anchor investor-participated IPOs. The results portray MAAR of anchor investor-participated IPOs (12.80%) is higher than that of non-anchor investor-participated IPOs (9.74%). The MAARs of both anchor and non-anchor investor-participated IPOs are also significant.

Table 1: MAARs of the IPOs

Sample	*MAAR*	*MAAR (%)*	*t-stat*	*p-value*
ALL IPOS	0.1170	11.70%	6.1300	< .001***
Non-Anchor Investor—Participated IPOs	0.0974	9.74%	6.8200	< .001***
Anchor Investor—Participated IPOs	0.1280	12.80%	2.4000	0.018*

Note: * p < .05, ** p < .01, *** p < .001.
Source: The Authors

Table 2 lists out AARs, CAARs, t-test statistics and p-values for the first sixty trading days corresponding to three months from listing for the entire sample of 247 IPOs. The results depict that AARs have been positive only on days 1, 9, 24, 26, 28, 33, 36, 37, 38, 39, 40, 43, 44, 45, 48, 51, 52, 56, 58, 59 and on remaining thirty days, AARs are negative. The p-values are significant on day 3, 5, 6, 12 and 19 with negative coefficients. CAARs are negative all along the 60 days excepting day 1 with p-values being significant from day 6 to day 60. CAARs on day 125 and 250 are –0.0619 and –0.2063 respectively and significant on day 250 (Table 5). The net market adjusted loss, as such to the investor of the IPOs holding the security up to day 250 from the date of listing arrives at –8.93%. The results, therefore, connote that IPOs underperform significantly in the post-listing period to such an extent that after one-year period from listing, the gains of an investor transform into losses significantly. The results thereby align with the findings of the extant literature. The results also align with the alternative hypothesis that IPOs underperform in the post-listing period.

Table 2: Post Listing Performance of All IPOs

Day	*AARt*	*t-stat*	*p-value*		*CAARt*	*t-stat*	*p-value*	
1	0.0019	0.4569	0.6482		0.0019	0.4569	0.6482	
2	–0.0022	–0.6093	0.5429		–0.0003	–0.0543	0.9568	
3	–0.0067	–2.2240	0.0271	*	–0.0070	–1.0134	0.3119	
4	–0.0012	–0.4783	0.6328		–0.0082	–1.0497	0.2949	
5	–0.0066	–2.0850	0.0381	*	–0.0148	–1.6749	0.0952	
6	–0.0092	–3.2823	0.0012	**	–0.0240	–2.4331	0.0157	*
7	–0.0016	–0.5290	0.5973		–0.0255	–2.4047	0.0169	*
8	–0.0014	–0.5281	0.5979		–0.0269	–2.4221	0.0162	*
9	0.0018	0.8371	0.4033		–0.0252	–2.1340	0.0338	*
10	–0.0024	–0.9126	0.3624		–0.0276	–2.2777	0.0236	*
11	–0.0035	–1.7879	0.0750		–0.0311	–2.4788	0.0139	*
12	–0.0048	–1.9846	0.0483	*	–0.0359	–2.7813	0.0058	**
13	–0.0011	–0.5447	0.5864		–0.0370	–2.7745	0.0060	**
14	–0.0007	–0.3389	0.7349		–0.0378	–2.7932	0.0056	**
15	–0.0013	–0.5836	0.5600		–0.0391	–2.8635	0.0046	**
16	–0.0035	–1.6870	0.0929		–0.0426	–3.0499	0.0025	**
17	–0.0030	–1.5135	0.1314		–0.0456	–3.1393	0.0019	**
18	–0.0004	–0.1906	0.8490		–0.0459	–3.0131	0.0029	**
19	–0.0049	–2.6435	0.0087	**	–0.0509	–3.3304	0.0010	**
20	–0.0033	–1.7016	0.0901		–0.0542	–3.4177	0.0007	***
21	–0.0023	–1.2896	0.1984		–0.0565	–3.4989	0.0006	***
22	–0.0008	–0.4134	0.6797		–0.0573	–3.3987	0.0008	***
23	–0.0015	–0.8982	0.3699		–0.0587	–3.4094	0.0008	***
24	0.0035	1.7200	0.0867		–0.0553	–3.1553	0.0018	**
25	–0.0023	–1.5479	0.1229		–0.0576	–3.2813	0.0012	**
26	0.0018	0.9849	0.3256		–0.0557	–3.1451	0.0019	**
27	–0.0013	–0.6625	0.5083		–0.0570	–3.1856	0.0016	**
28	0.0001	0.0586	0.9533		–0.0569	–3.1084	0.0021	**
29	–0.0004	–0.2342	0.8151		–0.0573	–3.0878	0.0022	**
30	–0.0008	–0.4464	0.6557		–0.0582	–3.0848	0.0023	**
31	–0.0007	–0.3817	0.7030		–0.0589	–3.0990	0.0022	**
32	–0.0027	–1.2454	0.2142		–0.0616	–3.1982	0.0016	**

Day	*AARt*	*t-stat*	*p-value*		*CAARt*	*t-stat*	*p-value*	
33	0.0006	0.3307	0.7412		−0.0610	−3.1755	0.0017	**
34	−0.0022	−1.2726	0.2044		−0.0632	−3.2476	0.0013	**
35	−0.0017	−1.0389	0.2999		−0.0649	−3.2629	0.0013	**
36	0.0025	1.5163	0.1307		−0.0624	−3.0994	0.0022	**
37	0.0002	0.1173	0.9067		−0.0622	−3.0548	0.0025	**
38	0.0026	1.2684	0.2058		−0.0596	−2.8734	0.0044	**
39	0.0000	0.0100	0.9921		−0.0596	−2.8543	0.0047	**
40	0.0013	0.7607	0.4476		−0.0583	−2.7368	0.0067	**
41	−0.0033	−1.9014	0.0584		−0.0616	−2.8867	0.0042	**
42	−0.0016	−1.0635	0.2886		−0.0632	−2.9172	0.0039	**
43	0.0001	0.0378	0.9699		−0.0631	−2.8925	0.0042	**
44	0.0018	1.0919	0.2759		−0.0613	−2.7941	0.0056	**
45	0.0023	1.2291	0.2202		−0.0590	−2.6885	0.0077	**
46	−0.0019	−1.1362	0.2570		−0.0610	−2.7729	0.0060	**
47	−0.0012	−0.7585	0.4489		−0.0622	−2.7849	0.0058	**
48	0.0009	0.5884	0.5568		−0.0613	−2.6934	0.0076	**
49	−0.0035	−0.8223	0.4117		−0.0648	−2.8209	0.0052	**
50	−0.0022	−1.2505	0.2123		−0.0670	−2.8833	0.0043	**
51	0.0037	1.7510	0.0812		−0.0633	−2.6991	0.0074	**
52	0.0019	1.0167	0.3103		−0.0614	−2.5769	0.0106	**
53	−0.0057	−1.3095	0.1916		−0.0670	−2.7420	0.0066	**
54	−0.0028	−1.7441	0.0824		−0.0699	−2.8291	0.0051	**
55	−0.0003	−0.2633	0.7925		−0.0702	−2.8108	0.0053	**
56	0.0011	0.6732	0.5015		−0.0691	−2.7685	0.0061	**
57	−0.0004	−0.2021	0.8400		−0.0695	−2.7645	0.0061	**
58	0.0004	0.1979	0.8433		−0.0691	−2.7264	0.0069	**
59	0.0026	1.5914	0.1128		−0.0665	−2.5972	0.0100	*
60	−0.0007	−0.3994	0.6900		−0.0671	−2.6070	0.0097	**

Note: * $p < .05$, ** $p < .01$, *** $p < .001$.
Source: The Authors

To exclude the effects of the anchor investors on the post-listing performance of IPOs, AARs, CAARs, t-test statistics and p-values for the first sixty trading days equivalent to three months from listing for the 91 non-anchor investor-participated IPOs are computed and the same appears in Table 3. The results postulate that AARs have been positive only on day 26, 28, 31, 36, 38, 40, 43, 44, 45, 48, 51, 52, 56, 57, 58, 59 and on remaining forty-four days, AARs are negative. P-values are significant on days 5, 6 and 12. CAARs are negative all along the sixty days with p-values being significant from day 5 to day 60. CAARs on day 125 and 250 are –0.2304 and –0.4323 respectively with p-values significant on both the days (Table 5). The net market adjusted loss to the investor subscribing to the non-anchor-participated IPOs and holding the security up to day 250 from the of listing comes to 33.49 %. The results, as such, reflect that IPOs without anchor investor participation, start underperforming from day 1 with greater magnitude. The extent of holding period loss is extremely high and significant as well. The outcome also postulates that dilution of listing gains of the IPOs in the post-listing phase is profound and intensive without the participation of anchor investor.

Table 3: Post Listing Performance of Non-anchor Investor Participated IPOs

Day	*AARt*	*t-stat*	*p-value*		*CAAR$_t$*	*t-stat*	*p-value*	
1	–0.0041	–0.4569	0.6488		–0.0041	–0.4569	0.6488	
2	–0.0031	–0.3640	0.7167		–0.0073	–0.6245	0.5339	
3	–0.0146	–2.1760	0.0322		–0.0219	–1.4317	0.1557	
4	–0.0079	–1.5836	0.1168		–0.0298	–1.7196	0.0889	
5	–0.0168	–2.2677	0.0257	*	–0.0466	–2.3350	0.0218	*
6	–0.0211	–3.2030	0.0019	**	–0.0677	–3.0366	0.0031	**
7	–0.0093	–1.4861	0.1408		–0.0770	–3.1933	0.0019	**
8	–0.0088	–1.5758	0.1186		–0.0858	–3.4479	0.0009	***
9	–0.0024	–0.5832	0.5612		–0.0882	–3.3988	0.0010	**
10	–0.0051	–0.9010	0.3700		–0.0933	–3.4445	0.0009	***
11	–0.0122	–3.2833	0.0015		–0.1055	–3.7672	0.0003	**
12	–0.0116	–2.2544	0.0266	*	–0.1171	–4.0494	0.0001	***
13	–0.0024	–0.5314	0.5965		–0.1195	–3.9025	0.0002	***
14	–0.0027	–0.6517	0.5163		–0.1222	–3.9662	0.0001	***
15	–0.0015	–0.2765	0.7828		–0.1236	–3.9918	0.0001	***
16	–0.0084	–1.8650	0.0654		–0.1321	–4.1819	0.0001	***
17	–0.0042	–1.1116	0.2693		–0.1363	–4.1455	0.0001	***
18	0.0022	0.5586	0.5778		–0.1340	–3.8326	0.0002	***
19	–0.0048	–1.5805	0.1175		–0.1388	–3.9676	0.0001	***
20	–0.0027	–0.7107	0.4791		–0.1415	–3.8817	0.0002	***

Day	AARt	t-stat	p-value		CAAR$_t$	t-stat	p-value	
21	–0.0058	–1.7897	0.0769		–0.1474	–3.9643	0.0001	***
22	–0.0023	–0.6194	0.5372		–0.1497	–3.8217	0.0002	***
23	–0.0046	–1.4633	0.1469		–0.1542	–3.8585	0.0002	***
24	0.0036	0.9869	0.3263		–0.1506	–3.7580	0.0003	***
25	–0.0025	–0.8484	0.3985		–0.1530	–3.8175	0.0002	***
26	0.0032	1.0199	0.3105		–0.1499	–3.6844	0.0004	***
27	–0.0051	–1.3855	0.1693		–0.1550	–3.7888	0.0003	***
28	0.0021	0.5623	0.5753		–0.1529	–3.6606	0.0004	***
29	–0.0032	–0.9452	0.3471		–0.1561	–3.7059	0.0004	***
30	–0.0015	–0.4558	0.6496		–0.1576	–3.7145	0.0004	***
31	0.0015	0.4410	0.6603		–0.1561	–3.6543	0.0004	***
32	–0.0016	–0.4320	0.6668		–0.1578	–3.6611	0.0004	***
33	–0.0040	–1.6002	0.1131		–0.1618	–3.7703	0.0003	***
34	–0.0051	–1.6384	0.1048		–0.1668	–3.8301	0.0002	***
35	–0.0017	–0.5586	0.5778		–0.1686	–3.7961	0.0003	***
36	0.0007	0.2533	0.8006		–0.1678	–3.7705	0.0003	***
37	–0.0016	–0.4590	0.6473		–0.1694	–3.7448	0.0003	***
38	0.0002	0.0640	0.9491		–0.1692	–3.6558	0.0004	***
39	–0.0007	–0.2334	0.8160		–0.1699	–3.6444	0.0004	***
40	0.0010	0.3326	0.7402		–0.1689	–3.5231	0.0007	**
41	–0.0042	–1.0951	0.2764		–0.1731	–3.5991	0.0005	**
42	–0.0028	–0.8859	0.3780		–0.1759	–3.5776	0.0006	**
43	0.0004	0.1398	0.8891		–0.1755	–3.5338	0.0006	***
44	0.0008	0.3099	0.7574		–0.1747	–3.5198	0.0007	***
45	0.0032	0.8286	0.4095		–0.1715	–3.4489	0.0009	**
46	–0.0017	–0.4758	0.6353		–0.1732	–3.4778	0.0008	**
47	–0.0024	–0.7650	0.4463		–0.1755	–3.4790	0.0008	**
48	0.0006	0.2361	0.8139		–0.1749	–3.4066	0.0010	**
49	–0.0121	–1.0808	0.2827		–0.1871	–3.6253	0.0005	***
50	–0.0010	–0.3438	0.7318		–0.1881	–3.5907	0.0005	***
51	0.0075	1.6728	0.0978		–0.1806	–3.3752	0.0011	**
52	0.0002	0.0437	0.9653		–0.1804	–3.3122	0.0013	**
53	–0.0034	–1.5724	0.1194		–0.1838	–3.3700	0.0011	**

Day	*AARt*	*t-stat*	*p-value*		*$CAAR_t$*	*t-stat*	*p-value*	
54	–0.0033	–1.1011	0.2738		–0.1871	–3.3987	0.0010	**
55	–0.0033	–1.3308	0.1866		–0.1904	–3.4282	0.0009	**
56	0.0033	1.0292	0.3061		–0.1871	–3.3849	0.0011	**
57	0.0027	0.7473	0.4568		–0.1844	–3.3207	0.0013	**
58	0.0031	0.8240	0.4121		–0.1813	–3.2405	0.0017	**
59	0.0022	0.8496	0.3978		–0.1791	–3.1695	0.0021	**
60	–0.0022	–0.8074	0.4216		–0.1813	–3.2078	0.0019	**

Note: * p < .05, ** p < .01, *** p < .001.
Source: The Authors

To ascertain the impact of anchor investors on post-listing performance of IPOs, AARs, CAARs, t-test statistics and p-values for the first sixty trading days equivalent to three months from listing for the 156-anchor investor–participated IPOs are computed and the same appears in Table 4. The results postulate that AARs have been positive on day 1, 4, 7, 8, 9, 11, 14, 22, 23, 24, 26, 27, 29, 33, 38, 39, 40, 44, 45, 48, 49, 51, 52, 55, 59, 60 and on remaining thirty–four days, AARs are negative. The p-value is significant only on day 19. Hence, there is no such traceable underperfomance on the expiry of the lock-in period except on day 19. Unlike the negative CAARs throughout sixty days in respect of non–anchor IPOs, the CAARs of anchor–participated IPOs, is not negative from initial days but turns negative at a stretch from day 54 to 60. CAARs on day 125 and 250 are 0.0364 and –0.0745 respectively with p-values significant on both the days (Table 5). However, the p-values are not significant on any day. The net market adjusted gains to the investor subscribing to the anchor-participated IPOs and holding the security from inception comes to 5.35 % implying that the gains from listing are not completely diluted for such investors.

Table 4: Post Listing Performance of Anchor Investor–Participated IPOs

Day	*AARt*	*t-stat*	*p-value*		*$CAAR_t$*	*t-stat*	*p-value*
1	0.0054	1.3655	0.1741		0.0054	1.3655	0.1741
2	–0.0016	–0.6052	0.5459		0.0038	0.7723	0.4411
3	–0.0021	–0.7795	0.4369		0.0017	0.2721	0.7859
4	0.0028	1.1248	0.2624		0.0045	0.6492	0.5172
5	–0.0007	–0.2781	0.7813		0.0038	0.5089	0.6116
6	–0.0022	–1.1001	0.2730		0.0015	0.1907	0.8490
7	0.0029	0.9919	0.3228		0.0044	0.5272	0.5988
8	0.0029	1.1398	0.2561		0.0074	0.8208	0.4130

Day	*AARt*	*t-stat*	*p-value*		*CAAR$_t$*	*t-stat*	*p-value*
9	0.0042	1.8163	0.0713		0.0116	1.1727	0.2427
10	–0.0008	–0.3235	0.7467		0.0108	1.1123	0.2678
11	0.0016	0.7257	0.4691		0.0123	1.2555	0.2112
12	–0.0009	–0.3685	0.7130		0.0115	1.1666	0.2452
13	–0.0004	–0.1965	0.8445		0.0111	1.1703	0.2437
14	0.0004	0.1714	0.8641		0.0115	1.1764	0.2412
15	–0.0012	–0.6739	0.5014		0.0102	1.0225	0.3081
16	–0.0006	–0.3284	0.7430		0.0096	0.9395	0.3489
17	–0.0022	–1.0246	0.3072		0.0074	0.6892	0.4918
18	–0.0019	–0.8916	0.3740		0.0054	0.4896	0.6251
19	–0.0050	–2.1124	0.0363	***	0.0004	0.0386	0.9692
20	–0.0037	–1.7213	0.0872		–0.0032	–0.2765	0.7825
21	–0.0002	–0.1197	0.9049		–0.0035	–0.2959	0.7677
22	0.0001	0.0288	0.9770		–0.0034	–0.2842	0.7766
23	0.0003	0.1912	0.8486		–0.0031	–0.2493	0.8035
24	0.0034	1.4217	0.1571		0.0003	0.0236	0.9812
25	–0.0022	–1.3424	0.1814		–0.0019	–0.1432	0.8863
26	0.0011	0.4538	0.6506		–0.0008	–0.0631	0.9498
27	0.0010	0.4841	0.6290		0.0002	0.0124	0.9901
28	–0.0010	–0.6133	0.5406		–0.0009	–0.0628	0.9500
29	0.0012	0.5664	0.5719		0.0003	0.0212	0.9831
30	–0.0005	–0.2005	0.8414		–0.0002	–0.0107	0.9915
31	–0.0020	–0.8571	0.3927		–0.0022	–0.1446	0.8852
32	–0.0033	–1.2644	0.2080		–0.0055	–0.3476	0.7286
33	0.0032	1.4048	0.1621		–0.0022	–0.1423	0.8871
34	–0.0005	–0.2531	0.8005		–0.0027	–0.1749	0.8614
35	–0.0017	–0.9001	0.3695		–0.0044	–0.2736	0.7847
36	0.0036	1.7490	0.0823		–0.0008	–0.0494	0.9607
37	0.0012	0.7364	0.4626		0.0004	0.0246	0.9804
38	0.0039	1.5894	0.1140		0.0044	0.2586	0.7963
39	0.0004	0.2351	0.8144		0.0048	0.2838	0.7770
40	0.0014	0.7223	0.4712		0.0062	0.3640	0.7163
41	–0.0027	–1.7416	0.0836		0.0035	0.2052	0.8377

Day	*AARt*	*t-stat*	*p-value*		*CAAR$_t$*	*t-stat*	*p-value*
42	−0.0009	−0.5965	0.5517		0.0025	0.1504	0.8807
43	−0.0001	−0.0560	0.9554		0.0024	0.1427	0.8867
44	0.0024	1.1156	0.2663		0.0048	0.2778	0.7816
45	0.0017	0.9240	0.3569		0.0065	0.3775	0.7063
46	−0.0020	−1.2398	0.2169		0.0045	0.2603	0.7950
47	−0.0006	−0.3090	0.7577		0.0039	0.2224	0.8243
48	0.0011	0.5568	0.5784		0.0051	0.2789	0.7807
49	0.0015	0.9372	0.3501		0.0066	0.3606	0.7189
50	−0.0029	−1.3185	0.1893		0.0037	0.1982	0.8431
51	0.0014	0.7050	0.4819		0.0051	0.2800	0.7799
52	0.0030	1.5644	0.1198		0.0081	0.4402	0.6604
53	−0.0070	−1.0366	0.3016		0.0011	0.0540	0.9570
54	−0.0026	−1.3517	0.1784		−0.0015	−0.0715	0.9431
55	0.0014	0.9795	0.3288		−0.0001	−0.0035	0.9972
56	−0.0002	−0.0825	0.9344		−0.0002	−0.0106	0.9916
57	−0.0023	−0.9012	0.3689		−0.0025	−0.1152	0.9085
58	−0.0012	−0.5325	0.5951		−0.0037	−0.1685	0.8664
59	0.0029	1.3435	0.1811		−0.0008	−0.0351	0.9721
60	0.0002	0.1013	0.9194		−0.0006	−0.0248	0.9802

Note: * $p < .05$, ** $p < .01$, *** $p < .001$.
Source: The Authors

The results portray that in the post-listing period, the anchor-participated IPOs start underperforming but at a later stage compared to non-anchor-participated IPOs. The results also convey that anchor-participated IPOs underperform in the post-listing period by a lesser magnitude compared to the extent of under-performance of non-anchor-participated IPOs implying anchor-participated IPOs outperform non-anchor-participated IPOs in the post-listing period. The outcome as such corresponds to the findings of Subba & Mahapatra (2021) contending that anchor-participated IPOs outperform non-anchor-participated IPOs. The results thereby conform to the alternative hypothesis stating anchor investor-participated IPOs outperform the non-anchor- participated IPOs in the post-listing period.

Though on day 10, 12, 13 and 15 which corresponds to the expiry of lock-in period, AARs are negative, the same cannot be attributed to flipping by the anchor investors as negative AARs is evident in non-anchor investor participated IPOs from day 1 to 17 at a stretch. Instead, such negative AARs in respect of anchor investor-participated IPOs can be possibly associated with the normal propensity of flipping by the other category of investors and flipping by some institutional investors trying to make profits as contended by Agarwal (2021). Hence, it can be construed that anchor investors by not resorting to flipping after the conclusion of the lock-in period have instilled much required trust and confidence among the investing community. The outcome also conveys that investing community considers IPOs participated by anchor investor as more credible in terms of holding the investment for a longer period of time after listing.

Table 5: Post Listing Performance of IPOs after 125 and 250 Days of Listing

Day	*AAR_t*	*t-stat*	*p-value*		*$CAAR_t$*	*t-stat*	*p-value*	
				All IPOS				
125	0.0024	1.2892	0.1985		−0.0619	−1.9485	0.0525	
250	−0.0057	−1.2660	0.2067		−0.2063	−4.0525	0.0001	***
				Non-Anchor Investor-Participated IPOs				
125	0.0046	1.2412	0.2177		−0.2304	−3.5141	0.0007	***
250	−0.0121	−1.0173	0.3117		−0.4323	−4.4148	0.0001	***
				Anchor Investor-Participated IPOs				
125	0.0011	0.5573	0.5781		0.0364	1.2054	0.2299	
250	−0.0020	−1.1126	0.2676		−0.0745	−1.3687	0.1731	

Note: * $p < .05$, ** $p < .01$, *** $p < .001$.
Source: The Authors

Conclusions, Managerial Implications, Limitations and Future Study

The present study in consonance with the existing study finds that IPOs underperform in the post-listing phase. The present study in a bid to analyse whether anchor investor-participated IPOs perform differently from that of non-anchor investor-participated IPOs, finds that the anchor investor participated IPOs outperform non-anchor investor-participated IPOs in the post-listing period. The outcome of the study demonstrates that underperformance of anchor investor-participated IPOs is witnessed at later stages in the post-listing phase compared to the non-anchor investor-participated IPOs. The extent and magnitude of underperformance of anchor investor-participated IPOs is less severe compared to non-anchor-participated IPOs. The findings of the study do not indicate that anchor investors resort to flipping on the conclusion of the lock-in period. The market regulator SEBI introduced anchor investors in the Indian IPO market in the year 2009 with an aim to improve investment opportunities for retail investors and to boost the credibility of the issuing firm thereby enabling other investors to gain confidence. The outcome reveals that as envisaged by the market regulator, the anchor investors have been successful in providing credibility to all the market participants and in boosting the confidence of the investors to invest in Indian IPOs over a longer time frame. The change in investor's behaviour as evident during the post-listing period in anchor investor-participated IPOs is likely to bring momentum and stability to the Indian security market. The market regulator therefore, needs to work in tandem with the stakeholders and contemplate in bringing out norms and policies that intensify the trust and confidence of the Indian investors so that the market participants look to invest over a longer horizon. This will further enable the Indian securities market to prosper and flourish with acceleration in the upcoming days.

The present study has been able to bring new insights into the post-listing performance of anchor investor-participated IPOs by way of analysing the performance around the lock-in period which comes as an addition to the extant literature. However, the present study is not free from limitations. Researchers in this field may eye to carry out the performance of anchor investor-participated IPOs segregating into two regimes, one before September 2014 and the other from September 2014.

References

[1] Agarwal, S. (2021). Certification role of transparency and anchor investors in Indian IPOs. *Afro-Asian J. of Finance and Accounting, 11*(1), 35. https://doi.org/10.1504/aajfa.2021.111801

[2] Agathee, U.S., Sannassee, R.V. and Brooks, C. (2014). The long-run performance of IPOs: the case of the Stock Exchange of Mauritius. *Applied Financial Economics,* 24(17), 1123–1145. https://doi.org/10.1080/09603107.2014.924294

[3] Aggarwal, R. and Rivoli, P. (1990). Fads in the Initial Public Offering Market? *Financial Management,* 19(4), 45. https://doi.org/10.2307/3665609

[4] Berk, A.S. and Peterle, P. (2015). Initial and Long-Run IPO Returns in Central and Eastern Europe. *Emerging Markets Finance and Trade*, 51(sup6), S42–S60. https://doi.org/10.1080/1540496x.2015.1080555

[5] Bhattacharya, A., Chakrabarti, B.B., Ghosh, C. and Petrova, M. (2020). Innovations in financing: The impact of anchor investors in Indian IPOs. *European Financial Management,* 26(4), 1059–1106. https://doi.org/10.1111/eufm.12257

[6] Bubna, A. and Prabhala, N.R. (2011). IPOs with and without allocation discretion: Empirical evidence. *Journal of Financial Intermediation,* 20(4), 530–561. https://doi.org/10.1016/j.jfi.2010.12.004

[7] Chan, K., Wang, J. and Wei, K. (2004). Underpricing and long-term performance of IPOs in China. *Journal of Corporate Finance*, 10(3), 409–430. https://doi.org/10.1016/s0929-1199(03)00023-3

[8] Das, G., Saha, M. and Kundu, A. (2016). Analyzing Long-run Performance of Select Initial Public Offerings Using Monthly Returns: Evidence from India. *Vision:*

The Journal of Business Perspective, 20(3), 237–248. https://doi.org/10.1177/0972262916652809

[9] Dell'Acqua, A., Etro, L., Tetia, E. and Murria, M. (2015). IPO Underpricing and Aftermarket Performance in Italy, 3(03). https://doi.org/10.18533/JEFS.V3I03.160

[10] Fama, E.F. (1998). Market efficiency, long-term returns, and behavioral finance. *Journal of financial economics*, 49(3), 283–306.

[11] Gupta, C. and Suri, S. (2017). Valuation and Pricing of Indian IPOs. *Vision: The Journal of Business Perspective*, 21(4), 375–384. https://doi.org/10.1177/0972262917734706

[12] Gupta, P. and Jindal, D. (2016). Impact of Anchor Investors on Returns on IPOs in India. *TIJ's Research Journal of Social Science & Management-RJSSM*, 6(01).

[13] Gupta, V., Singh, S. and Yadav, S.S. (2019). Impact of anchor investors on IPO returns during pre-market and aftermarket: evidence from India. *Journal of Advances in Management Research*, 17(3), 351–368. https://doi.org/10.1108/jamr-07-2019-0131

[14] Hawaldar, I.T., Naveen Kumar, K. and Mallikarjunappa, T. (2018). Pricing and performance of IPOs: Evidence from Indian stock market. *Cogent Economics & Finance*, 6(1), 1420350. https://doi.org/10.1080/23322039.2017.1420350

[15] Hedau, A. (2018). Long Run Performance of IPO-Empirical Evidence from Indian Capital Market. *Asian Journal of Management*, 9(1), 723. https://doi.org/10.5958/2321-5763.2018.00112.9

[16] Kenourgios, D.F., Papathanasiou, S. and Rafail Melas, E. (2007). Initial performance of Greek IPOs, underwriter's reputation and oversubscription. *Managerial Finance*, 33(5), 332–343. https://doi.org/10.1108/03074350710739614

[17] Killins, R.N. (2019). An investigation of the short-term performance of the Canadian IPO market. 47. https://doi.org/10.1016/J.RIBAF.2018.07.004

[18] Kiymaz, H. (2000). The initial and aftermarket performance of IPOs in an emerging market: evidence from Istanbul stock exchange. *Journal of Multinational Financial Management*, 10(2), 213–227. https://doi.org/10.1016/s1042-444x(99)00027-4

[19] Kumar, S.S.S. (2007). Short and long-run performance of bookbuilt IPOs in India.

[20] Lee, P.J., Taylor, S.L. and Walter, T.S. (1996). Australian IPO pricing in the short and long run. *Journal of Banking & Finance*, 20(7), 1189–1210. https://doi.org/10.1016/0378-4266(95)00053-4

[21] Loughran, T., Ritter, J.R. and Rydqvist, K. (1994). Initial public offerings: International insights. *Pacific-Basin Finance Journal*, 2(2–3), 165–199.

[22] Madan, A.A. (2003). Investments in IPOs in the Indian capital market. Bimaquest, 3(1), 24–34.

[23] Madhusoodanan, T.P. and Thiripalraju, M. (1997). Underpricing in initial public offerings: The Indian evidence. Vikalpa, 22(4), 17–30.

[24] Manikam, A.P., Gumanti, T.A. and Fadah, I. (2020). Short term and long term performance of IPOs: Comparison between CARs and BHARs. Jurnal Manajemen dan Usahawan Indonesia, 42(3), 19.

[25] Manjunath, B.R., Raju, J.K. and Rehaman, M. (2020). Short-run performance evaluation of under-priced Indian IPOs. *Law and Financial Markets Review*, 14(3), 170–175. https://doi.org/10.1080/17521440.2020.1759239

[26] Manu, K.S. and Saini, C. (2020). Valuation Analysis of Initial Public Offer (IPO): The Case of India. Paradigm, 24(1), 7–21. https://doi.org/10.1177/0971890720914100

[27] Marisetty, V.B. and Subrahmanyam, M.G. (2010). Group affiliation and the performance of IPOs in the Indian stock market. *Journal of Financial Markets*, 13(1), 196–223. https://doi.org/10.1016/j.finmar.2009.09.001

[28] Mehta, D. and Patel, A. (2018). Price Performance of Initial Public Offerings (IPOs): Evidence from Indian Capital Market from 2007-2014. *Apeejay Journal of Management & Technology*, 11(2), 62. https://doi.org/10.29385/apeejay.11.2.2016.74-85

[29] Miller, R.E. and Reilly, F.K. (1987). An Examination of Mispricing, Returns, and Uncertainty for Initial Public Offerings. *Financial Management*, 16(2), 33. https://doi.org/10.2307/3666001

[30] Mitchell, M.L. and Stafford, E. (2000). Managerial Decisions and Long-Term Stock Price Performance. *The Journal of Business*, 73(3), 287–329. https://doi.org/10.1086/209645

[31] Nafid, S. (2014). An historical analysis of IPO underpricing in India. *Erasmus University Rotterdam*, pp. 1–54.

[32] Pande, A. and Vaidyanathan, R. (2009). Determinants of IPO Underpricing in the National Stock Exchange of India. *IUP Journal of Applied Finance*, 15(1), 14.

[33] Pandey, S.N., Tiwari, A. and Tripathi, A.R. (2021). Performance Determinants of Initial Public Offers (IPOs) in India: Testing Window of Opportunity, Winner's Curse and Divergence of Opinion Hypotheses. *Turkish Online Journal of Qualitative Inquiry*, 12(3).

[34] Pandya, F.H. (2016). After Market Pricing Performance of Initial Public Offerings (IPOs). *Jindal Journal of Business Research*, 5(1), 1–16. https://doi.org/10.1177/2278682116670077

[35] Ritter, J.R. (1991). The Long-Run Performance of initial Public Offerings. *The Journal of Finance*, 46(1), 3–27. https://doi.org/10.1111/j.1540-6261.1991.tb03743.x

[36] Sahoo, S. and Rajib, P. (2010). After Market Pricing Performance of Initial Public Offerings (IPOs): Indian IPO Market 2002–2006. *Vikalpa: The Journal for Decision Makers*, 35(4), 27–44. https://doi.org/10.1177/0256090920100403

[37] Samdani, T. (2019). Anchor-backed IPOs, reported earnings, and heterogeneous investors' beliefs. Journal of Corporate Finance, 59, 72–87. https://doi.org/10.1016/j.jcorpfin.2017.05.002

[38] Seth, R., Vishwanatha, S.R. and Prasad, D. (2018). Allocation to Anchor Investors, Underpricing, and the After-Market Performance of IPOs. *Financial Management*, *48*(1), 159–186. https://doi.org/10.1111/fima.12210

[39] Sharma, S.K., Mittal, S. and Gupta, N.K. (2013). Post-issue Performance of IPOs in India. *GIS Business*, 8(4), 19–30. https://doi.org/10.26643/gis.v8i4.3778

[40] Singh, P. and Kumar, B. (2012). Short Run and Long Run Dynamics of Initial Public Offerings: Evidence from India. *Jindal Journal of Business Research*, 1(1), 87–113. https://doi.org/10.1177/227868211200100107

[41] Srinivasa Reddy, K. (2015). The aftermarket pricing performance of initial public offers: insights from India. *International Journal of Commerce and Management*, 25(1), 84–107. https://doi.org/10.1108/ijcoma-03-2013-0032

[42] Subba, S.K. and Mahapatra, S.S. (2021). Pre and Post Anchor Investment Impact on IPO Returns. *Turkish Online Journal of Qualitative Inquiry*, 12(3).

[43] Wong, E.S.K., Wong Wb, R. and Ting, L.S. (2017). Initial public offering (IPO) underpricing in Malaysian settings, 5(02). https://doi.org/10.18533/JEFS.V5I02.276

[44] Yong Tong, L. and I Ahmad, R. (2015). The Signaling Power of the Investment Banks' Reputation on the Performance of IPOs on Bursa Malaysia. *Jurnal Pengurusan*, 45, 27–37. https://doi.org/10.17576/pengurusan-2015-45-03

Website

1. https://www.nseindia.com

Exploring Recent Trends: A Comprehensive Investigation of Environmental Sustainability Using Corporate Social Responsibility Expenditures by Indian Private Banks

Tanbir Islam[1] and Samadrita Ghosh[2]

ABSTRACT: The Indian corporate environment has seen a significant paradigm shift in recent years, with a stronger emphasis on Corporate Social Responsibility (CSR) initiatives. The present study specifically examines CSR expenditure among Domestic Private Banks, utilizing secondary data sourced from the credible website www.csr.gov.in. The study spans from 2014–15 to 2020–2021, analysing fifteen Domestic Private Banks with adequate data availability. Results indicate that HDFC Bank allocates a substantial amount towards CSR compared to its counterparts. However, the findings also highlight a lack of significant investment in CSR initiatives promoting environmental sustainability across these banks. Overall, there appears to be a lack of sufficient CSR spending and engagement among Domestic Private Banks compared to other corporate entities. Consequently, these banks exhibit limited involvement in the government's mission for inclusive growth due to insufficient participation in CSR expenditure.

Keywords: Corporate Social Responsibility, Different Heads, Environmental Sustainability, Inclusive Growth, Indian Private Banks.

JEL Classification: G34, Q56, G21, O44.

Introduction

Sustainable development activities have become the focus of Indian private banks' CSR spending in recent decades. These banks provide funding for initiatives ranging from financial inclusion to environmental protection, with an emphasis on environmental, social, and governance (ESG) issues. This shows that they are more conscious of their contribution to the welfare of society, and their actions are more in line with international sustainability norms. This pattern is a constructive step in the direction of an ecologically and socially responsible

[1] Research Scholar, Department of Commerce, Vidyasagar University, India.
E-mail: tanbir_islam@rediffmail.com

[2] Research Scholar, Department of Commerce, Vidyasagar University, India.
E-mail: samadritaghosh002@gmail.com

banking industry in India. A company's commitment to appropriately managing the societal, ecological, and economic repercussions of its activities is known as corporate social responsibility or CSR. Conversely, environmental sustainability prioritizes resolving current demands without jeopardizing the capacity of subsequent generations to satisfy their own (Million, 2015). For socially and ecologically conscientious companies, corporate social responsibility (CSR) is a strategic instrument that facilitates sustainable development, enhances the value of the firm, and addresses environmental and social issues through charity endeavors. Corporate Social Responsibility (CSR) has become an essential component in evaluating a business's environmental effect and social responsibility in the twenty-first century. A key component of corporate social responsibility (CSR) is environmental sustainability, which entails adopting sustainable practices, cutting carbon footprints, and boosting environmental causes. These actions help businesses strengthen their reputation and cultivate stakeholder loyalty and satisfaction (Hegyes & Fekete-Farkas, 2019).

An increasing number of studies are investigating the connection between environmental sustainability and corporate social responsibility. The influence of corporate social responsibility (CSR) on a firm's sustainable performance was investigated by Li *et al.* (2022) at several plant sizes. The outcomes showed that in order to understand the connection between consumer-facing CSR and sustainable business performance, environmental sustainable development is extremely important. It was also shown that there is a strong correlation between CSR and employees' long-term success in the business. Strategic CSR, which is defined as voluntary CSR activities that improve a firm's competitiveness and reputation, was examined in three theoretical frameworks by Orlitzky *et al.* (2011). However theories of effective leadership should also be included in this perspective, the authors found that economic theories of strategic corporate social responsibility had the most potential to develop this field of study. Thus, research on the interaction between environmental sustainability and corporate social responsibility is a dynamic and expanding field. The results imply that the concept of corporate social responsibility might enhance a business's capacity to operate ethically, particularly when taking into account economic and environmental notions of strategic corporate social responsibility.

A notable shift in paradigms has occurred in the business landscape of India in recent years, with a greater focus on Corporate Social Responsibility (CSR) efforts, especially in the private banking sector. Growing resoluteness on the part of Indian private banks to match CSR spending to sustainable development objectives is indicative of this shift. Thus, this study explores at how Indian private banks have been allocating their money to corporate social responsibility recently, highlighting their strategic choices and contributions to sustainable development. Since financial institutions exert a significant influence on economic environments, it is crucial to comprehend the changing nature of corporate social responsibility (CSR) activities in the banking industry in order to evaluate the wider implications for the welfare of society and the environment.

The article is structured as follows: The subsequent section presents the foundational framework, while an extensive review of related literature, and hypothesis development have been presented in Section 3. The specifics of the research methods, including an evaluation of the research model, are presented in Section 4, while the results of the model's assessment are described in Section 5. The last section offers discussions and conclusions.

Objectives of the study

1. To investigate the CSR expenditure of Indian Private Banks.
2. To evaluate the trends of expenditure in different heads of expenditure.
3. To examine the CSR expenditure relating to Environmental Sustainability.

Review of Related Literature

Numerous studies conducted across different years and regions have extensively explored the intersections of corporate sustainability and CSR with governance, stakeholders, and societal impact. These studies collectively provide valuable insights. Research by Hahn *et al.* (2010) highlighted prevalent trade-offs between economic, environmental, and social aspects in corporate sustainability, categorized across various decision-making levels within companies. Gupta (2011) compared CSR awareness and responses among Indian and U.S. customers, revealing the need for targeted approaches by multinational corporations to enhance the impact of CSR initiatives in specific customer segments. Alena *et al.'s* (2011) study emphasized the integration of corporate governance and sustainability, underlining the role of governance in economic, social, and environmental performance, along with the significance of Global Reporting Indicators (GRI) and evolving ESG factors in decision-making. Asif's research (2012) on sustainability reporting practices in Dutch companies identified variations in reporting depth, highlighting areas like stakeholder engagement and integrated financial and non-financial reporting for improvement. Rishi & Moghe (2013) explored the interaction between organizational culture and CSR in an Indian electrical appliance manufacturing business, emphasizing the preference for employee engagement in decision-making for a satisfying work environment. Dhanesh's (2014) investigation into CSR drivers and sociocultural factors in India highlighted the balance between moral imperatives and strategic concerns in driving CSR initiatives, emphasizing employee social affinity for responsible CSR approaches. Jankalova (2015) discussed diverse CSR evaluation approaches, emphasizing the role of internal environment, labor relations, and pollution prevention in shaping CSR, while raising concerns about transparency in rating agency evaluations. Kansal *et al.* (2016) analyzed CSR disclosures in Indian Public Sector Enterprises (CPSEs), emphasizing the need for enhanced reporting initiatives, particularly regarding greenhouse gas emissions. Singh & Sarkar (2018) observed the escalating CSR spending by Indian businesses and recommended collaborative efforts to maximize societal benefits, recognizing strategic CSR investment as a vital tool for both corporate competitiveness and societal gains. Almagtome *et al.'s* (2020) study on corporate governance, stakeholders, and sustainability in Turkish companies highlighted the positive association between sustainable development and corporate governance, influenced by internal and external factors like stakeholder pressures.

Collectively, these studies underscore the complex nature of sustainability efforts, governance, and CSR practices within diverse organizational and cultural contexts, advocating for concerted action across various levels to achieve meaningful and impactful corporate social responsibility.

Research Design and Methodology

In our study, the purposive sampling method was employed to carefully select fifteen private sector banks within the Indian banking industry. Table 1 illustrates the sample chosen specifically based on data availability.

Table 1: Sample Banks for the Study

Sl. No.	*Name of the Private Sector Bank*	*Sl. no.*	*Name of the Private Sector Bank*
1.	Axis Bank Ltd.	9.	IDBI Bank Ltd.
2.	Bandhan Bank Ltd.	10.	IDFC First Bank Ltd.
3.	City Union Bank Ltd.	11.	IndusInd Bank Ltd.
4.	CSB Bank Ltd.	12.	Jammu Kashmir Bank Ltd.
5.	DCB Bank Ltd.	13.	Kotak Mahindra Bank Ltd.
6.	Dhanlaxmi Bank Ltd.	14.	RBL Bank Ltd.
7.	HDFC Bank Ltd.	15.	Yes Bank Ltd.
8.	ICICI Bank Ltd.		

Source: Authors' compilation

For this research endeavor, secondary data has been gathered from various sources including the annual reports of banks and reputable websites such as www.csr.gov.in. The investigation period spans from 2014–15 to 2020–21. The research primarily revolves around utilizing descriptive statistics and various Excel formulas to analyse data and draw insights from the data set.

Analysis and Findings

In this section, an examination of the findings pertaining to Corporate Social Responsibility (CSR) expenditure is detailed and analyzed. The subsequent presentation encapsulates the outcomes derived from the allocation and utilization of funds towards CSR initiatives.

Table 2: Actual Amount of CSR Expenditure Incurred by Indian Private Banks (₹ in crore)

Bank Names	*2014–15*	*2015–16*	*2016–17*	*2017–18*	*2018–19*	*2019–20*	*2020–21*
Axis Bank Ltd.	123.22	147.78	135.41	133.77	137.6	100.96	90.94
Bandhan Bank Ltd.	0	0	0	0	30	67.09	50.55
City Union Bank Ltd.	8.06	8.06	8.16	10.69	9.34	13.84	10.96
CSB Bank Ltd.	0.02	0.08	0.09	0.09	0.09	0	0
DCB Bank Ltd.	8.06	8.06	8.16	10.69	9.34	13.84	10.96
Dhanlaxmi Bank Ltd.	0	0	0	0	0	0	0.02
HDFC Bank Ltd.	117.56	127.28	305.42	374.55	443.78	535.31	634.42
ICICI Bank Ltd.	155.54	171.51	182.37	170.37	134.35	134.35	200.5
IDBI Bank Ltd.	9.44	9.44	2.47	1.29	0.25	0	0
IDFC First Bank Ltd.	0	1.22	1.22	14.22	25.64	7.23	19.42
IndusInd Bank Ltd.	17.54	0.08	33.81	20.47	55.46	108.14	94.72
Jammu Kashmir Bank Ltd.	13.75	28.47	21.86	31.68	12.46	2.41	0
Kotak Mahindra Bank Ltd.	8.1	11.1	11.7	12.62	25.65	74.62	79.39
RBL Bank Ltd.	1.61	1.61	3.69	0	0	0	0
Yes Bank Ltd.	29.52	41.67	37.22	45.22	51.28	38.61	0

Source: Authors' compilation

The table (Table 2) exhibits the Corporate Social Responsibility (CSR) expenditure of various Indian private banks across multiple financial years. Axis Bank Ltd. witnessed a gradual decrease in CSR spending from 2014–15 to 2020–21. Conversely, Bandhan Bank Ltd. initiated CSR spending in 2018–19, demonstrating subsequent notable increases. City Union Bank Ltd. maintained consistent but relatively low CSR expenses. CSB Bank Ltd. recorded minimal to no CSR expenditure in recent years, similar to Dhanlaxmi Bank Ltd. and RBL Bank Ltd.

HDFC Bank Ltd. displayed consistent and significant growth in CSR spending, indicating a strong commitment to social responsibility. ICICI Bank Ltd. experienced fluctuations but generally maintained substantial CSR expenses. However, IDBI Bank Ltd. decreased its CSR spending, showing minimal to no expenditure in recent years. IDFC First Bank Ltd. increased CSR spending with noticeable fluctuations. IndusInd Bank Ltd. observed fluctuations yet maintained an overall increasing trend in CSR spending. Yes Bank Ltd. depicted fluctuations, notably decreasing in recent years. Jammu & Kashmir Bank Ltd.'s CSR spending varied significantly, notably reducing in recent years.

Table 3: Descriptive Statistic of the Actual Amount of CSR Expenditure Incurred by Indian Private Banks (₹ in crore)

Year	*2014–15*	*2015–16*	*2016–17*	*2017–18*	*2018–19*	*2019–20*	*2020–21*
Mean	32.83	37.09	50.11	55.04	62.35	73.09	79.46
SD	52.57	59.59	88.85	102.06	114.60	135.85	163.60
Max	155.54	171.51	305.42	374.55	443.78	535.31	634.42
Min	0	0	0	0	0	0	0

Source: Authors' computation

The descriptive statistics (Table 3) outline the Actual CSR (Corporate Social Responsibility) expenditure by Indian Private Banks across the provided years. The average CSR expenditure showed a gradual increase from 32.83 in 2014–15 to 79.46 in 2020–21, signifying a rising trend in spending on CSR initiatives among these banks.

The standard deviation suggests wider variations in CSR spending across banks in later years compared to earlier ones, indicating greater diversity in the amounts spent on CSR over time.

The maximum CSR expenditure by a bank peaked at 634.42 in 2020–21, reflecting the highest amount spent on CSR initiatives during the specified period. Conversely, the consistent minimum CSR expenditure of 0 across all banks each year indicates that some banks did not report any CSR spending during these periods.

Table 4: Headwise Projected and Actual CSR Expenditure Incurred by Indian Private Banks (₹ in crore)

Heads of Expenditure	*Health Care*		*Education*		*Rural Development*		*Sanitation*		*Environmental Sustainability*		*Vocational Skills*		*Training To Promote Sports*		*Technology Incubators*		*Others*	
Year	*Projt Amt*	*Act Amt*	*Projt Amt*	*Act Amt*	*Projt Amt*	*Act Amt*	*Projt Amt*	*Act Amt*	*Projt Amt*	*Act Amt*	*Projt Amt*	*Act Amt*	*Projt Amt*	*Act Amt*	*Projt Amt*	*Act Amt*	*Projt Amt*	*Act Amt*
2015	24.82	22.86	38.19	36.1	229.53	201.8	0.06	0.06	16.43	14.32	14.19	14.06	0.01	0.01	0	0	173.41	155
2016	54.17	51.8	107.68	84.17	192.8	161.1	1.36	1.73	50.87	43.49	23.81	44.55	7.16	3.14	0	0	207.01	273.1
2017	35.22	32.35	70.54	62.71	362.55	353.2	1.37	0.22	51.5	43.49	1.14	0.5	8.14	8.14	0	0	181.12	243.4
2018	28.06	21.97	85.84	73.3	425.54	411.7	0.23	0.23	67.21	40.03	4.71	4.71	5.85	3.35	0	0	250.89	257.5
2019	58.14	54.11	142.5	133.9	349.59	351.3	0.19	0.19	104.15	62.91	21.51	17.19	5.92	5.81	2.2	2.2	254.72	251.5
2020	62.76	60.86	181.49	169.2	415.56	439.3	1.38	1.38	50.69	33.93	33.54	33.54	19.95	19.67	2	2	336.31	311.1
2021	5841	232.7	3763.6	104.8	11989.7	469.3	4.45	5.58	1638.2	12.86	3309	81.1	466.9	27.28	0	0	1459.7	230

Source: Authors' compilation

Table 5: Descriptive Statistics of Headwise Projected and Actual CSR Expenditure Incurred by Indian Private Banks (₹ in crore)

Heads of Expenditure	*Health Care*		*Education*		*Rural Development*		*Sanitation*		*Environmental Sustainability*		*Vocational Skills*		*Training To Promote Sports*		*Technology Incubators*		*Others*	
	Projt Amt	*Act Amt*	*Projt Amt*	*Act Amt*	*Projt Amt*	*Act Amt*	*Projt Amt*	*Act Amt*	*Projt Amt*	*Act Amt*	*Projt Amt*	*Act Amt*	*Projt Amt*	*Act Amt*	*Projt Amt*	*Act Amt*	*Projt Amt*	*Act Amt*
Mean	872.03	68.10	627.12	94.89	1995.04	341.09	1.29	1.34	282.72	35.86	486.85	27.95	73.42	9.63	0.60	0.60	409.03	245.94
SD	2191.18	74.24	1383.86	45.12	4408.12	117.69	1.52	1.98	598.27	17.62	1244.51	28.09	173.62	10.03	1.03	1.03	466.61	47.73
Max	5841.04	232.73	3763.60	169.18	11989.72	469.29	4.45	5.58	1638.17	62.91	3309.02	81.10	466.91	27.28	2.20	2.20	1459.73	311.08
Min	24.82	21.97	38.19	36.10	192.80	161.12	0.06	0.06	16.43	12.86	1.14	0.50	0.01	0.01			173.41	155.04

Source: Authors' computation

In analysing CSR expenditure trends (Table 4), the education sector revealed a disparity as projected amounts exceeded actual spending. Rural development consistently saw substantial projected allocations, sometimes surpassed in actual spending. Sanitation initiatives generally aligned with projections over the years. Environmental sustainability projects attracted significant funding, yet 2021 witnessed a shortfall in actual expenditure. Vocational skills training consistently saw lower actual spending than projected, indicating a gap in planned versus realized allocations. Sports-related CSR spending fluctuated significantly across years. Technology incubators received no allocated or spent funds throughout the study period. Diverse CSR activities under the "Others" category showed discrepancies between projected and actual spending across different years. Anomalies emerged in several categories in 2021, where projected amounts significantly exceeded actual spending in 'Healthcare', 'Rural Development', 'Environmental Sustainability', and 'Vocational Skills Training'.

The descriptive statistics in table 5, provide insights into the projected and actual Corporate Social Responsibility (CSR) expenditures by Indian Private Banks across diverse expenditure categories from 2015 to 2021. Notably, there are significant differences between the projected and actual spending in various sectors. For instance, while Healthcare had a substantially higher projected expenditure averaging at 872.03, the actual spending was notably lower at 68.10. Similarly, in Education, Rural Development, Sanitation, Environmental Sustainability, Vocational Skills Training, Sports Promotion, and Technology Incubators, there were considerable differences between the projected and actual expenditures. These statistics underscore substantial variations and disparities between the expected and realized expenditures across different CSR categories.

Table 6: Actual Amount of CSR Expenditure Incurred in the Head Environmental Sustainability by Indian Private Banks (₹ in crore)

Bank names	*2014–15*	*2015–16*	*2016–17*	*2017–18*	*2018–19*	*2019–20*	*2020–21*	*Total*
Axis Bank Ltd.					24.52	3.07		27.59
Bandhan Bank Ltd.								
City Union Bank Ltd.	1.08		0.7	0.69	3.89	4.12		10.48
CSB Bank Ltd.								
DCB Bank Ltd.	1.08		0.7	0.67	3.89	4.12		10.46
Dhanlaxmi Bank Ltd.							0.01	0.01

Bank names	*2014–15*	*2015–16*	*2016–17*	*2017–18*	*2018–19*	*2019–20*	*2020–21*	*Total*
HDFC Bank Ltd.	0.95	0.72	1.01	0.73	0.71	0.25	7.73	12.1
ICICI Bank Ltd.	2.89					2.89	0.28	6.06
IDBI Bank Ltd.	1.88	0.11	0.48	0.05				2.52
IDFC First Bank Ltd.					6.06	0.2	1.14	7.4
IndusInd Bank Ltd.	1.72	22.47	21.53	20.47	3.03	15.39	2.5	87.11
Jammu Kashmir Bank Ltd.		17.11	16.62		8.49	2		44.22
Kotak Mahindra Bank Ltd.	1	0.13			2.43		1.56	5.12
RBL Bank Ltd.								
Yes Bank Ltd.	3.72	2.67	2.45	37.91	9.89	1.89		58.53
Total	14.32	43.21	43.49	60.52	62.91	33.93	13.22	

Source: Authors' compilation

Table 6 showcases the actual Corporate Social Responsibility (CSR) expenditure by Indian Private Banks directed towards Environmental Sustainability across different years.

- Axis Bank Ltd: Recorded a CSR expenditure of 27.59 million in 2018–19.
- City Union Bank Ltd and DCB Bank Ltd: Showed expenditures totaling 10.48 million and 10.46 million respectively across various years.
- Dhanlaxmi Bank Ltd: Reported minimal CSR expenditure of 0.01 units in 2020–21.
- HDFC Bank Ltd: Demonstrated progressive spending, totaling 12.1 units in the last reported year.
- ICICI Bank Ltd: Allocated 6.06 units for Environmental Sustainability in 2020–21.
- IDBI Bank Ltd: Recorded a total of 2.52 units spent over different years.
- IDFC First Bank Ltd: Reported cumulative spending of 7.4 units across specified years.

- IndusInd Bank Ltd: Showed varying expenditures, with the highest spending of 87.11 units across specified years.
- Jammu & Kashmir Bank Ltd: Reported 44.22 units of CSR expenditure for Environmental Sustainability.
- Kotak Mahindra Bank Ltd: Recorded a total expenditure of 5.12 million across different years.
- Yes Bank Ltd: Demonstrated significant expenditure, totaling 58.53 units, notably allocating 37.91 units in 2017–18.

Table 7: Descriptive Statistic of Actual Amount of CSR Expenditure Incurred in the Head Environmental Sustainability by Indian Private Banks (₹ in crore)

Year	*2014–15*	*2015–16*	*2016–17*	*2017–18*	*2018–19*	*2019–20*	*2020–21*
Mean	1.7900	7.2017	6.2129	10.0867	6.9900	3.7700	2.2033
SD	1.0202	9.9413	8.9238	15.7937	7.1934	4.5872	2.8526
Max	3.72	22.47	21.53	37.91	24.52	15.39	7.73
Min	0.95	0.11	0.48	0.05	0.71	0.2	0.01

Source: Authors' computation

The provided table (Table 7) i.e. descriptive statistics offer insights into the Actual Amount of CSR Expenditure related to Environmental Sustainability by Indian Private Banks across different year. The average expenditure in each year indicates the typical amount spent on Environmental Sustainability by Indian Private Banks during these periods. For instance, in the year 2017–18, the mean expenditure was 10.0867 crores, suggesting relatively higher spending compared to other years.

Standard deviations indicate greater variability in expenditures across different banks and years. For example, in 2017–18, the SD was 15.7937, indicating a wider range of expenditure amounts among banks in that year.

The maximum expenditure was 37.91 crores in 2017–18, while the minimum was 0.01 crores in 2020–21, showing the range of spending from the highest to the lowest recorded amounts.

Table 8: Correlation between the Actual amount of CSR expenditure incurred in the head Environmental Sustainability with total CSR expenditure incurred by Indian Private Banks each year during the study period

Year	*2014–15*	*2015–16*	*2016–17*	*2017–18*	*2018–19*	*2019–20*	*2020–21*
Correlation	0.26663	−0.3751	−0.186	−0.1943	−0.0776	−0.1471	0.9083
N	15	15	15	15	15	15	15

Source: Authors' computation

The correlation values demonstrated in table 8 show the relationship between the Actual Amount of CSR Expenditure for Environmental Sustainability and Total CSR Expenditure by Indian Private Banks across different years.

Positive Correlation indicates a tendency for both variables to move in the same direction. For example, in 2020–21, a strong positive correlation of 0.9083 suggests that as Environmental Sustainability CSR Expenditure increased, Total CSR Expenditure by Indian Private Banks also notably increased. In years like 2015–16 to 2019–20, negative correlations ranging from –0.3751 to –0.0776 indicate a tendency for Environmental Sustainability CSR Expenditure to decrease as Total CSR Expenditure by Indian Private Banks increases, or vice versa.

Table 9: Year wise Total CSR Expenditure Incurred by Private Banks in India
(₹ in crore)

Year	*2014–15*	*2015–16*	*2016–17*	*2017–18*	*2018–19*	*2019–20*	*2020–21*	*Total*
Total CSR Exp.	492.42	556.36	751.58	825.66	935.24	1096.4	1191.88	5849.54

Source: Authors' computation

The table 9 illustrates the total Corporate Social Responsibility (CSR) expenditure by private banks in India from 2014–15 to 2020–21.
A progressive commitment shows a consistent progress towards social responsibility initiatives, with a notable increase from 492.42 in 2014–15 to 1191.88 in 2020–21.

Each year demonstrates a continuous rise in overall CSR expenditure, highlighting an ongoing effort to expand contributions toward societal welfare and sustainable development.

The escalating CSR spending underscores the dedication of private banks in India towards fulfilling their social responsibilities and making meaningful impacts in various sectors beyond financial obligations.

Table 10: Yearwise Total CSR Expenditure Incurred by India Companies
(₹ in crore)

Year	*2014–15*	*2015–16*	*2016–17*	*2017–18*	*2018–19*	*2019–20*	*2020–21*	*Total*
Total CSR exp.	10065.93	14517.21	14542.51	17098.57	20217.65	24965.82	26210.95	127618.6

Source: Authors' computation

Table 10 depicts the escalating Corporate Social Responsibility (CSR) expenditure of Indian companies from 2014–15 to 2020–21, showing a consistent and significant increase. The CSR spending surged notably from 10,065.93 in 2014–15 to 26,210.95 in 2020–21, underlining substantial overall growth. Each subsequent year witnessed an upswing in CSR expenditure, signifying the ongoing commitment of Indian companies toward social welfare and sustainable development. The cumulative CSR expenditure for 2014–15 to 2020–21 reached 127,618.6, highlighting the substantial financial commitment of Indian companies to social causes and community development. This sustained and substantial increase in CSR spending reflects their strong dedication to supporting diverse social initiatives and fostering a positive impact on society.

Table 11: Yearwise Percentage of Total CSR Expenditure Incurred by Indian Private Banks

Year	*2014–15*	*2015–16*	*2016–17*	*2017–18*	*2018–19*	*2019–20*	*2020–21*
Percentage	4.89%	3.83%	5.17%	4.83%	4.63%	4.39%	4.55%

Source: Authors' computation

Table 11 illustrates the yearly percentage of Corporate Social Responsibility (CSR) expenditure by Indian private banks compared to the total CSR spending by all Indian companies from 2014–15 to 2020–21. The percentages range between 3.83% and 5.17%, consistently hovering around 4% to 5% over the specified period. This stability signifies a steady contribution by private banks towards CSR initiatives, highlighting their significant involvement in social

Table 12: Bank-wise Percentage of Total CSR Expenditure Incurred by Indian Private Banks over Total Expenditure Incurred by Private Banks of India Altogether

Bank name	*Percentage*	*Bank Name*	*Percentage*
Axis Bank Ltd.	14.87%	IDFC First Bank Ltd.	1.18%
Bandhan Bank Ltd.	2.52%	Indusind Bank Ltd.	5.65%
City Union Bank Ltd.	1.18%	Jammu Kashmir Bank Ltd.	1.89%
CSB Bnak Ltd.	0.01%	Kotak Mahindra Bank Ltd.	3.82%
DCB Bank Ltd.	1.18%	RBL Bank Ltd.	0.12%
Dhanlaxmi Bank Ltd.	0.00%	Yes Bank Ltd.	4.16%
HDFC Bank Ltd.	43.39%	IDFC First Bank Ltd.	1.18%
ICICI Bank Ltd.	19.64%	Indusind Bank Ltd.	5.65%
IDBI Bank Ltd.	0.39%		

Source: Authors' computation

responsibility efforts compared to other sectors. Despite minor fluctuations, the consistent 4–5% contribution emphasizes their ongoing commitment to CSR activities and active engagement in societal welfare programs.

The percentages shown in Table 12 represent the proportion of Corporate Social Responsibility (CSR) expenditure contributed by various Indian private banks relative to the total CSR spending by all private banks in India. HDFC Bank Ltd. leads with 43.39%, followed by ICICI Bank Ltd. at 19.64%, and Axis Bank Ltd. at 14.87%. Other banks contribute varying percentages, highlighting their individual shares in the total CSR expenditure among private banks in India.

Findings

The findings from the analysis reveal diverse patterns in Corporate Social Responsibility (CSR) expenditure among banks, showcasing varying trends such as consistent growth, fluctuations, or minimal spending. Notably, banks like HDFC, ICICI, and Kotak Mahindra have demonstrated a consistent commitment to escalating their CSR spending over the analyzed period. The following findings are:

1. The CSR expenditure reflects diverse patterns among banks, with some showing consistent growth, fluctuations, or minimal spending. Banks like HDFC, ICICI, and Kotak Mahindra have shown a commitment to increasing CSR spending over the years, while others have varied patterns or limited expenditures.
2. The descriptive statistics illustrate an increasing trend in average CSR expenditure among Indian private banks over the years, with a widening range of amounts spent among banks, but with some banks consistently reporting no CSR expenditure.
3. The CSR expenditure showcases varied spending patterns across different CSR categories with discrepancies between the projected and actual expenditures in certain areas, suggesting a need for alignment between planned allocations and realized spending in some sectors.
4. There are substantial variations between the planned (projected) allocations and the actual realized spending for CSR initiatives across Indian Private Banks, highlighting inconsistencies or discrepancies in spending patterns across different categories.
5. The cumulative CSR expenditure on Environmental Sustainability by all mentioned banks for each studied year ranged from 13.22 units to 62.91 units over the reported years.
6. Table 6 provides a comprehensive overview of the average expenditure, its variability, and the range of values across different years. This table

highlights fluctuations in spending patterns, identifying years of higher and lower expenditures and the diversity in spending among Indian Private Banks in the domain of Environmental Sustainability.

7. The correlation values suggest varying relationships between the Environmental Sustainability CSR Expenditure and the Total CSR Expenditure. A strong positive correlation in a particular year implies that when there's an increase (or decrease) in the Environmental Sustainability CSR Expenditure, there's a corresponding notable increase (or decrease) in the Total CSR Expenditure by Indian Private Banks. Conversely, negative correlations indicate an inverse relationship between these two variables in those respective years.
8. In essence, the information relating to CSR expenditure signifies a positive trend in CSR spending by private banks in India, showcasing a growing commitment to supporting social causes and contributing to the betterment of communities and society as a whole.
9. The percentages depict the consistent but varying contribution of Indian private banks to the total CSR expenditure by all Indian companies, highlighting their sustained involvement in social responsibility efforts throughout the specified years.
10. Table 10 highlights HDFC Bank's significant contribution, accounting for more than 43% of the overall CSR expenditure among all private banks in India. This remarkable achievement stands as a testament to the bank's robust commitment to Corporate Social Responsibility initiatives. Notably, this outcome aligns with the findings of Mallick *et al.*, 2021.

Conclusion and Recommendation

The findings present several crucial observations regarding the Corporate Social Responsibility (CSR) expenditure by Indian private banks, especially concerning specific areas like Environmental Sustainability, Technology Incubators, Vocational Skill Training, and Sports Promotion. Here's a reframed version of the conclusions drawn from the findings:

1. Insufficient Spending and Participation: Indian private banks ought to augment their actual expenditure compared to the projected amounts, showcasing relatively low participation in CSR expenditure compared to other corporate entities operating within India.
2. Need for Emphasising Environmental Sustainability: There's a conspicuous lack of investment by Indian private banks in Environmental Sustainability through CSR activities. Banks should prioritize and exhibit more interest in contributing towards Environmental Sustainability to bolster the nation's green banking initiatives.

3. Negligible Spending in Technology Incubators: The absence or minimal CSR expenditure by private banks in Technology Incubators implies a lack of support for IT students' research and technological innovation, potentially hindering India's advancements in technology.
4. Disparity in Vocational Skill Training Expenditure: A substantial contrast exists between projected and actual expenditure in Vocational Skill Training by Indian private banks. Enhancing spending in this area can empower the country's youth with diverse skills, aligning with the government's "Skill India Mission" and potentially curbing unemployment.
5. Lack of CSR Allocation for Sports Promotion: Notably, there's a dearth of CSR spending by banks to support government initiatives like "Khelega India Tabhi To Badega India" aimed at promoting sports. Banks should consider contributing to these initiatives to foster sporting talent and national growth.
6. Encouraging Participation and Sustainable Spending: Many banks exhibit minimal involvement in CSR expenditure, necessitating increased participation and sustained investment in areas that align with sustainable goals. This proactive approach can bolster the government's initiatives and contribute significantly to India's sustainable development objectives.

Recommendation

The findings underscore the need for Indian private banks to enhance their CSR spending, especially in critical areas like Environmental Sustainability, Technology Incubators, Vocational Skill Training, and Sports Promotion. Balancing expenditure across CSR activities is crucial for a more effective and comprehensive CSR strategy, ensuring resources are utilized optimally. Moreover, adhering to legal guidelines such as the Companies Act 2013 is recommended to manage unutilized CSR funds by allocating them to designated accounts within the specified timeframe, and subsequently, transferring such funds to the PMCARES account if unspent for three years. This ensures compliance with regulations and contributes to societal welfare through government initiatives.

References

[1] Almagtome, A., Khaghaany, M. and Saime, O. (2020), Corporate Governance Quality, Stakeholders' Pressure, and Sustainable Development: An Integrated Approach, *International Journal of Mathematical, Engineering and Management Sciences*, 5(6), 1077–1090.

[2] Asif, M. Searcy, C. Santos, P and Kensah, D. (2012), A Review of Dutch Corporate Sustainable Development Reports, *Corporate Social Responsibility and Environmental Management*, 20, 321–339.

[3] Dhanesh, G.S. (2014). Why Corporate Social Responsibility? An Analysis of Drivers of CSR in India. *Management Communication Quarterly*, 1–16.

[4] Gupta, S. (2011). Consumer stakeholder view of corporate social responsibility: a comparative analysis from USA and India. *Social Responsibility Journal*, 363–380.

[5] Hahn, T. Figge, F. Pinkse, J and Preuss, L. (2010). Trade-offs in corporate Sustainability: You Can't Have Your Cake and Eat It, Business Strategy and the Environment, 19, 217–229.

[6] Hegyes, E.G. and Fekete-Farkas, M. (2019). Internal CSR as A Strategic Management Tool in Reduction of Labour Shortages. *Polish Journal of Management Studies*, 19(2), 167–181.Li, H., Kuo, Y., Mir, M.M., and Omar, M. (2022). Corporate Social Responsibility And Environmental Sustainability: Achieving Firms Sustainable Performance Supported By Plant Capability. *Economic Research-Ekonomska Istraživanja, 35*, 4580 – 4602.

[7] Jankalova, M. (2015). Approaches to the evaluation of Corporate Social Responsibility, *Procedia Economics and Finance*, 39, 580–587.

[8] Kansal, M., Joshi, M., Babu, S. and Sharma, S. (2016). Reporting of Corporate Social Responsibility in Central Public Sector Enterprises: A Study of Post Mandatory Regime in India. *Springer Science+Business Media Dordrecht*, 1–16.

[9] Kocmanová, A. Hřebíček, J and Dočekalová, M. (2011). Corporate Governance and Sustainability, *Economics and Management*, 16, 543–550.

[10] Millon, D. (2015). Corporate Social Responsibility and Environmental Sustainability. In B. Sjåfjell and B.J. Richardson (Eds.), *Company law and sustainability: Legal barriers and opportunities* (pp. 35–78). Cambridge University Press.

[11] Orlitzky, M., Siegel, D.S. and Waldman, D.A. (2011). Strategic Corporate Social Responsibility and Environmental Sustainability. *Business & Society, 50*, 27 – 6.

[12] Rishi, P. and Moghe, S. (2013). Integrating Corporate Social Responsibility and Culture as a Strategy for Holistic Corporate Success in India. Greenleaf Publishing, 17–37.

[13] Singh, P. and Sarkar, S. (2018). Revolutionising Corporate Social Responsibility in India: Is It Truly Revolutionised? *Asia-Pacific Journal of Management Research and Innovation*, 1–18.

The Future of Transactions: Understanding the Digital Payment Trends in India

Priya Gupta[1] and Samir Ghosh[2]

ABSTRACT: Digital banking is the automation of traditional banking services through a digital platform. Digitally-enabled banks allow users to access all banking services 24×7 without the need to personally visit the bank branch – all you need is a mobile phone or a computer. In total payments share Digital Payments is more than 95% both in account and amount. Among digital payments share of RTGS for large transaction is highest (more than 70%). The growth rate of RTGS transaction is 11.27%. In retail payments for credit transfer share of NEFT transaction is highest followed by UPI, IMPS etc. respectively. The compounded annual growth rate of UPI is highest (234.41%), followed by IMPS growth (60.86%) and NEFT growth (21.33%). In Debit transfer, Card transaction is highest followed by NACH debit.As digital banking becomes more popular, fraudsters are becoming more sophisticated in their tactics, making it increasingly difficult for banks and their customers to identify and prevent fraudulent activities.

Keywords: Debit Card, Digital Payment, Mobile Banking, NEFT, NEFT, RTGS, UPI.

Introduction

The banking sector has been the backbone of every economy whether developed or emerging. It plans and implements the economic reforms. Any change in this sector through the adoption of technology will have an extensive impact on an economy's growth. In 1988, the Reserve Bank of India (RBI) set up a committee to evaluate the possibility of digitizing the banking sector. With the advent of personal computers, information technology was adopted by Indian banks, and they migrated to local area network (LAN) connectivity. Core banking solutions allowed banks to provide 'Anywhere and Anytime Banking' for enhanced customer convenience.

The Unified Payments Interface (UPI) system launched in 2016 enabled banks to easily transfer funds. Customers were also encouraged to link their bank accounts with their Aadhar number for higher security. Presently, banks in India

[1] UGC-Senior Research Fellow, Department of Commerce, Vidyasagar University, India. E-mail: rscf_priyagupta@mail.vidyasagar.ac.in

[2] Professor, Department of Commerce, Vidyasagar University, India.
E-mail: samirghoshvu@gmail.com

are seeking ways to offer a quick, accurate, and quality customer experience, and digitalization is one of their biggest priorities. Digital banking is the automation of traditional banking services through a digital platform. There are many advantages to digitally-enabled banking, not just for the user, but also for banks. Financial institutions offering their services online with digital banking do away with tedious paperwork like cheques, demand drafts, and pay slips.

Digitally-enabled banks allow users to access all banking services 24×7 without the need to personally visit the bank branch. Nowadays, banks are seeking unconventional ways to provide and differentiate amongst their diverse services. Both corporate as well as retail customers are no longer willing to queue in banks, or wait on the phone, for the basic banking services. They require and expect a facility to conduct their banking activities at any time and place. Plastic money (Credit Cards, Debit Cards and Smart Cards); internet banking including electronic payment services, online investments, online trading accounts, electronic fund transfer and clearing services, branch networking; telephone banking; mobile applications and wallet are some of the recent products and services acting as the drivers to the growth of banking sector. The Reserve Bank's endeavour to build a less-cash society continued with the largescale adoption of digital modes of payments in the country. Digital banking started taking shape in India during the late 1990s. With increased transparency and cost-efficiency, digital banking has paved the way for safer and faster financial transactions.

Review of Literature

Rajat Deb (2020) investigated the relationship between household saving and spending behaviour and the adoption of pre- and post-mobile apps. According to this study, decisions about saving and spending have increased by over 50% after using mobile apps compared to before. In their research, Ravikumar *et al.* (2019) examined how digital payments affected real GDP (gross domestic product) growth. According to the authors, only retail electronic payments have a short-term, positive influence on the real GDP among the several digital payment types; but, over an extended period of time, retail electronic payments have no effect on the real GDP. Furthermore, over time, neither retail electronic payments nor digital payments in general directly support India's economic expansion. Pricing is the biggest obstacle facing consumer-facing digital media businesses, according to Richard Reisman (2019). Fairpay, or fair pricing, is a game that buyers and sellers play repeatedly, according to the author. Furthermore, Fairpay is a novel approach to problem-solving since it improves upon developments in the contemporary Business to Consumer (B2C) industry. According to David *et al.* (2018), distributed ledger technology (DLT) is important for payment and settlement systems. It also presents potential and problems for long-term acceptance and implementation. This study found that DLT can be used for identity management, payments, clearing, and settlement, including cross-border payments. It can also be used to transfer and record ownership of digital assets, store information immutably and securely, andother evolvingoperations through peer-to-peer networking.

Objectives of the Study

The study aims:

- To study the growth of digital payments in India.
- To analyse the difference in growth across the categories of digital payments.

Research Methodology

The study analyses the growth of digital payment in India and focuses on the growth of each category or mode of digital payment system from 2014–15 to 2022–23. To analyse the growth during the study period, both the value and volume of transactions have been considered. The study revolves around seven different modes of digital payment and one paper based offline payment system. Mean, compounded annual growth rate,

Analysis and Discussion

Mode of Payment System	*Volume (₹ Lakh)*		*Value (₹ lakh crore)*	
	Mean	*CAGR (%)*	*Mean*	*CAGR (%)*
Unified Payments Interface (UPI)	244063.43	234.41%	82.32	196.54%
Immediate Payment Service (IMPS)	21935.44	60.86%	68.37	66.05%
National Electronic Funds Transfer	25811.67	21.33%	826.12	21.19%
Real Time Gross Settlement	1466.89	11.27%	4973.14	7.94%
Prepaid Payment Instruments (PPI)	39339.89	42.18%	7.36	33.51%
Credit cards	16390.56	18.87%	24.14	25.17%
Debit cards	31817.22	17.39%	23.67	21.88%
Paper-based Instruments	9905.78	–5.65%	318.79	–1.94%

Source: Computed by authors

From the above table, it is found that in Total payments share Digital Payments is more than 95% both in account and amount. Traditional Banking or paper-based instruments are used by a certain percentage of Indian; they do not participate in online transaction at all. This happens mainly because traditional banking is what many people are used to protect from different frauds of digital transactions and it will take time for them to break habits. So, online banking marketers should focus on ways to convince traditional banking users to start using online banking services. These marketing efforts should specifically highlight the numerous benefits of online transactions. Among digital payments share of RTGS for large transaction is highest (more than 70%). The growth rate of RTGS transaction is. In retail payments for credit transfer share of NEFT transaction is highest followed by UPI, IMPS etc. respectively. The average growth rate of UPI is highest (234.41%), followed by IMPS growth (60.86%) and NEFT growth (21.33%). In Debit transfer Card transaction is highest followed by NACH debit.

Benefits of Digital Banking for Businesses

Digital banking has benefited every part of the financial ecosystem – users, financial institutions, banks, governments, and businesses.

Efficiency and Convenience

Businesses are no longer tied to the bank's working hours – they can access all the services they need 24×7. This feature is beneficial especially when transactional activities occur at a high rate.

Improved Usability

The integrated features of KYC and AML enable customers to open accounts from their own homes. In addition, online ID verification systems and risk assessment procedures enable banks to serve customers easily and quickly.

Cost Saving

Digital software for banking reduces the number of steps and people involved in daily transactions, which in turn reduces the risk of costly financial errors.

More Collaboration with Banks

More businesses are becoming open to collaborating with banks, which is seen as an opportunity to connect and strengthen financial relationships.

Personalized Services

Digital banks offer users informational and engaging content – financial options, educational resources, and interactive tools.

Variety of Features

Digital banks offer features that an established bank cannot provide to its customers – investing in cryptocurrencies, gold, or stock markets directly through the online banking app.

Digital Banking vs Online Banking

Digital Banking	*Online Banking*
An umbrella term for everything to do with banking that is done digitally	A part of digital banking where users can take all their banking processes online
Includes actions like payroll, accounting, vendor management, and more	Includes daily transactions like payments, balance checking and bill payments

Digital Banking Risks

While digitally-enabled banking is undoubtedly a blessing to the financial industry, there are certain risks that we have to keep in mind:

- Information and Cyber-security Risk
- Operational Risk
- Personal Conduct Risk
- Technology Stability and Resilience Risk
- Regulatory Risk
- Third-party Risk
- Money Laundering Risk

Future of Digital Banking in India

Digital banks, neobanks, and challenger banks have brought a fresh, new perspective to the dusty, obsolete banking industry. As per reports, digital banking is at an inflection point with the market, projecting to grow at a compound rate of 23.1% from 2022 to 2030. It is evident that the future of finance involves online banking services. However, this is only possible with the acceptance of digital banks as a substitute for traditional banks. The global pandemic that saw the entire world under a lockdown has forced even reluctant users to switch to a digital savings account and other online banking services. The shift is not temporary as an increasing number of customers are using this type of banking for its convenient and streamlined procedure. Moreover, artificial intelligence (AI) and business analytics (BA) potentially can further boost a huge shift in the Indian banking industry. Robotics-enabled AI is expected to be a significant game-changer in the future of the financial services industry. Several large private sector banks are considering using robots for several things including customer servicing.

Conclusion

It is expected that digital banking in India will become the most preferred way of using banking services in the country. Presently, a complete replacement of branch banking with digitalization seems difficult. Digital services are beneficial for recurring and regular banking transactions. However, customers still prefer some level of human interaction for more important and irregular transactions, such as applying for a loan or negotiating the terms and conditions. Nonetheless, digitalization is important for the banking industry. Online banking is becoming a part of the culture and seeing increased adoption by customers.

Servicing customers in more efficient ways via digital solutions is the way forward for the banks and this growth will be driven by advanced technology. Digital banking fraud is a type of fraud that targets online or mobile banking systems. It involves a range of fraudulent practices, such as stealing personal information, gaining unauthorised access to accounts, and making fraudulent transactions. Hackers and cybercriminals use different methods to commit digital banking fraud, including phishing, malware, and social engineering tactics. As digital banking becomes more popular, fraudsters are becoming more sophisticated in their tactics, making it increasingly difficult for banks and their customers to identify and prevent fraudulent activities. Therefore, it is important for both individuals and financial institutions to be aware of the causes of banking fraud and take appropriate measures to protect themselves from such threats. As digital banking continues to evolve, it is crucial to remain vigilant and take necessary precautions to safeguard sensitive personal and financial information.

References

[1] Aladwani, A.M. (2001). Online Banking: A Field Study of Drivers, Development Challenges, and Expectations. *International Journal of Information Management*, 21, 213–225.

[2] Harris, L. and Spence, L.J. (2002). The ethics of Banking. *Journal of Electronic Commerce Research*, 3(2), 59–66.

[3] Chavan, J. (2013). Internet Banking - Benefits and Challenges in an Emerging Economy. *International Journal of Research in Business Management*, 1(1), 19–26.

[4] Dheenadhayalan, V. (2010). Automation of Banking Sector in India. Yojana, 32–40.

[5] Ingle, A. and Pardeshi, R. Internet Banking in India: Challenges and Opportunities. *IBMRD's Journal of Management and Research*, 1, 13–18.

[6] Surulivel, S.T. (2010). A Study on the Impact of Technology on the Performance of Indian Banking Industry (Doctoral Thesis). Viewed on November 30, 2017 http:// hdl.handle.net/10603/5600

[8] Gupta, N. (2017). The Effect of Electronic Payment on Customer Satisfaction, *IJARIIE*, 3(3)

[9] Khurana, Sunayna (2010). Service Quality Gap and Customers' Satisfaction of Private Sector Banks: an Empirical Study. *International Journal of Electronic Customer Relationship Management*, 4(1).

[10] Mukherjee, A. and Nath, P. (2003). A Model of trust in online relationship banking. *International Journal of Bank Marketing*, 21(1).

Relationship between Financial Leverage and Financial Performance: Evidence from Non-Banking Financial Companies of India

Jaba Rani Patta[1] **and Ram Ranjan Routh**[2]

ABSTRACT: Non-banking finance companies (NBFCs) form an important part of the Indian financial system. They play a significant role by complementing the banking sector in reaching out credit to the unbanked sections of society, especially to the micro, small and medium enterprises (MSMEs), which form the base of entrepreneurship and innovation. An optimal capital structure can influence the value of a firm and wealth of shareholders through reduced cost of capital. Hence, determination of optimal debt level and its effect on the firm's overall capital structure is regarded as an integral part of a firm's financial decision. So, the present study is an attempt to investigate the relationship between financial leverage and financial performance of selected Non-bank financial companies (NBFCs) in India. 16 NBFCs companies have been selected from those listed in Bombay Stock Exchange (BSE) 500 for a period of 10 years from 2014 to 2023. Return on Assets, Return on Equity and Market value to Book value are taken as indicators of firm's financial performance. The technique of panel data regression has been used on STATA. The study shows leverage is a significant and foremost element in determining the financial performance of NBFCs in India.

Keywords: Financial Leverage Firm Performance, Non-bank Financial Companies.

Introduction

An optimal capital structure can influence the value of firm and wealth of shareholders through reduced cost of capital. Hence, determination of optimal debt level and its effect on the firms over all capital structure is regarded as an integral part of a firm's financial decision. A company finances its assets through some combination of equity, debt and hybrid securities. Leverage is employed to avoid using too much equity to fund operations. The financial leverage is a pre requisite for achieving optimal capital structure. Financial leverage is the use of debt in the capital structure of the company. As debt

[1] Assistant Professor, Department of Commerce, AKPC Mahavidyalaya, Bengai, Hooghly, India. E-mail: jabarani.routh@gmail.com

[2] Assistant Professor, Department of Commerce, Kharagpur College, Kharagpur, Paschim Medinipur, India. E-mail: ramranjan.routh@gmail.com

increases, financial leverage increases. The companies that are run by aggressive leaders tend to use more financial leverage. In this respect, their purpose for using financial leverage is not only to increase the performance of the company, but to also help ensure their control of the company. An excessive amount of financial leverage increases the risk of failure, since it becomes more difficult to repay debt. The use of financial leverage varies greatly by industry and by business sector. Financial leverage may be an acceptable alternative when a company is located in an industry with steady revenue levels, large cash reserves, and high barriers to entry, since operating conditions are sufficiently steady to support a large amount of leverage with little downside. Amongst the research issues in the field of corporate finance, financing decision is one of the most significant research problems. Sometimes, organizations face the problem of insolvency or bankruptcy due to improper capital mix. So, it is required for all companies to maintain an optimal capital structure. The present study focuses on non-banking financial companies. Non-banking finance companies (NBFCs) form an integral part of the Indian financial system. They play an important role by complementing the banking sector in reaching out credit to the unbanked segments of society, especially to the micro, small and medium enterprises (MSMEs), which form the base of entrepreneurship and innovation. The role of NBFCs becomes even more important now, especially when the government has a strong focus on promoting entrepreneurship so that India can emerge as a country of job creators instead of being one of job seekers. The NBFC sector in India has undergone a significant transformation over the past few years. The success of NBFCs can be clearly attributed to their better product lines, lower cost, wider and effective reach, strong risk management capabilities to check and control bad debts, and better understanding of their customer segments. NBFCs are certainly emerging as better alternatives to the conventional banks for meeting the financial needs of various sectors. However, to survive and to constantly grow, NBFCs have to focus on their core strengths while improving on weaknesses. They will have to be very dynamic and constantly endeavour to search for new products and services in order to survive in this ever-competitive financial market. In this context, the present study is an attempt to investigate the relationship between financial leverage and financial performance of selected Non-bank financial companies (NBFCs) in India.

Review of Literature

The results from the notable studies that have been carried out are briefly mentioned below. Franklin & Muthusamy (2011), in their article "Determinants of Financial Leverage in Indian Pharmaceutical Industry" revealed that variables like interest, asset structure, retained earnings and intrinsic value of share are positively associated with leverage while cash flow and interest coverage bear negative association with leverage. The study also showed that Indian pharmaceutical Companies employ substantial amounts of debt. Akinlo & Asaolu (2012), in their study "Profitability and Leverage: Evidence from Nigerian Firms" found that firm size has a significant positive effect on profitability, while leverage has negative effect. The paper suggests that expansion, increased sales and low debt ratios enhance firm profitability. Rehman (2013), in his article "Relationship between Financial Leverage and Financial Performance: Empirical Evidence of Listed Sugar Companies of Pakistan" showed the positive relationship of debt equity ratio with return on assets and sales growth and negative relationship with debt equity ratio with earning per share, net profit margin and return on equity.Granath & Thorsell (2014), in their study "Leverage and how it affects shareholder value" found that factors that affect a firm's capital structure are profitability, firm size and firm risk and the firm's leverage has a positive effect on shareholders' value. Rajkumar (2014), in his study "Impact of Financial Leverage on Financial Performance: Special Reference to John Keells Holdings plc in Sri Lanka" showed that a negative relationship between the financial leverage and the financial performance of the John Keells Holdings plc. But the financial leverage has a significant impact on the financial performance of the John Keells Holdings plc in Sri Lanka. Gweyi & Karanja (2014), in their articles "Effect of Financial Leverage on Financial Performance of Deposit Taking Savings and Credit Co-operative in Kenya" showed a perfect positive correlation between debt equity ratio with return on equity and profit after tax and a weak positive correlation between debt equity ratio with return on assets income growth. Al-Shamaileh & Khanfar (2014), in their study "The Effect of the Financial Leverage on the Profitability in the Tourism Companies (Analytical Study-Tourism Sector-Jordan)" indicated the presence of a statistically significant impact for the financial leverage on the profitability of the Tourism Companies listed in the Amman Exchange. Innocent, Ikechukwu & Nnagbogu (2014), in their study "The Effect of Financial Leverage on Financial Performance: Evidence of Quoted Pharmaceutical Companies in Nigeria" showed that debt ratio and debt-equity ratio have negative insignificance relationship with Return on Assets while interest coverage ratio has a positive insignificant relationship with Return on Assets. Moghadam & Jafar (2015), in their article "The Role of Financial Leverage in the Performance of Companies Listed in the Stock Exchange" indicated that financial leverage has a significant positive relationship with the performance of sample companies. Mule & Mukras (2015), in their article "Financial Leverage and Performance of Listed Firms in a Frontier Market: Panel Evidence from Kenya" showed that the financial leverage has significant negative impact on Return on Assets and Tobin's Q and ownership concentration significantly negatively associated with Tobin's Q. The study also revealed that the asset tangibility has significant positive impact on Return on Equity and Tobin's Q. Adetunji, Akinyemi & Rasheed (2016), in their study "Financial Leverage and Firms' Value: A Study of Selected Firms in Nigeria" the study recommended that financial leverage be optimized by firms to aid maximization of firm's value. Chavali, K., & Rosario, S. (2018), in their study "Relationship between capital structure and profitability: A study of nonbanking Finance Companies in India" investigates the relationship between NBFCs' capital structure and their net profit, return on capital employed, return on equity, return on assets, and interest coverage ratio. The study found Non-Banking Finance Companies are vital to the financial system. Dutta, P., Jain, A., & Gupta, A. (2020)), in their study "Performance analysis of non-banking finance companies using two-stage data envelopment analysis" performed a data envelopment analysis on Indian NBFC performance (DEA). The study found that a positive correlation was estimated between financial efficiency and profitability. There was no correlation between social effectiveness and voluntary disclosure rate. This article contributed to the academic literature by identifying new factors that influence voluntary disclosure. On the basis of the above literature, it is found that A large number of studies in various countries and industries have been conducted to assess the effect of financial leverage on firm's performance. But there is no general consensus for any country or for any specific industry. In this context, the present study is an attempt to investigate the relationship between financial leverage and financial performance of selected Non-bank financial companies (NBFCs) in India.

Objective of the Study

To assess empirically the relationship between financial leverage and financial performance of selected Non-bank financial companies (NBFCs) in India.

Hypotheses

The following hypotheses have been formulated to find out the relationship between the attitudes towards

(a) **H0**: There is no significant relationship between the financial leverage and ROA.

H1: There is significant a relation between the financial leverage and ROA.

(b) **H0**: There is no significant relationship between the financial leverage and ROE

H1: There is significant relationship between the financial leverage and ROE

(c) **H0**: There is no significant relationship between the financial leverage and Market value to Book value

H1: There is significant relationship between the financial leverage and Market value to Book value.

Database and Methodology

The study is mainly based on secondary data. Data are collected from the published annual reports of the selected companies and Ace Equity database. Here we have selected 16 NBFCs companies from the top 500 listed companies in Bombay Stock Exchange (BSE). The study covered a period of ten years starting from the financial year 2014 to 2023. In this study balanced panel data consist of 160 observations for 16 companies for ten years. In order to assess the relationship between financial leverage and financial performance of selected Non-bank financial companies (NBFCs) in India, panel data regression has been applied. Firm's financial performance has been analyzed with the help of Return on Assets (ROA), Return on Equity (ROE) and Market value to Book value (M/B). We have calculated mean, Min, Max and standard deviation of different variables. To check the presence of multicollinearity, construct a correlation matrix.

Estimation Techniques

Multiple regression analysis has been carried out to assess the effect of financial leverage on firm's financial performance of some selective NBFC companies India. In order to capture the effects of firm and time specific heterogeneities panel data models (Pooled OLS regression model, Fixed effects model and Random effect model) have been used. The choice amongst the three models, three statistical tests, viz, the Restricted F Test, Breusch-Pagan Lagrange Multiplier Test and Hausman Test have been carried out. The Restricted F Test is applied to make a choice between Pooled OLS regression model and FEM. On the other hand, Breusch-Pagan Lagrange Multiplier Test is applied to make a choice between Pooled OLS regression model and REM. The Hausman Test (1978) is applied to make a choice between the FEM and REM. Moreover, the specification tests like, Levin-Lin-Chu unit-root test, Pearson correlation coefficients, Variance Inflation Factor and Robust standard error are applied for unbiased and efficient regression results. To judge the stationarity of the selected variables we have carried out the Levin-Lin-Chu unit-root test. To check the presence of multi-collinearity, a correlation matrix (Pearson correlation coefficients) has been constructed. VIF is used to measure the degree of multicollinearity of an independent variable with the other independent variables in a regression model. Robust standard error (Huber/White or sandwich estimators) is used to remove the problem of heteroskedasticity in the models. In order to assess the relationship between financial leverage and financial performance of selected Non-bank financial companies (NBFCs) in India, we have fitted three regression models.

Model Specification

The effect of financial leverage on firm's financial performance is investigated using balanced panel data and run on STATA. The models are as follows.

Model 1: Return on Assets (ROA) has been used as a performance indicator with debt-equity ratio, tangibility and firm's size as the independent variables. ROA measures the efficiency of the firm in utilizing the assets for the firm's growth.

$$ROA_{it} = \beta_0 + \beta_1 (D/E)_{it} + \beta_2 (Tangibility)_{it} + \beta_3 (Size)_{it} + u_{it} \quad \text{... [model 1]}$$

Model 2: Return on Equity (ROE) has been used as a performance indicator with debt-equity ratio, tangibility and firm's size as the independent variables.

$$ROE_{it} = \beta_0 + \beta_1 (D/E)_{it} + \beta_2 (Tangibility)_{it} + \beta_3 (Size)_{it} + u_{it} \quad \text{... [model 2]}$$

Model 3: Market value to Book value (M/B) has been used as a performance indicator with debt-equity ratio, tangibility and firm's size as the independent variables.

$$M/B_{it} = \beta_0 + \beta_1 (D/E)_{it} + \beta_2 (Tangibility)_{it} + \beta_3 (Size)_{it} + u_{it} \quad \text{... [model 3]}$$

Return on Assets (ROA), Return on Equity (ROE) and Market value to Book value (M/B) has been used as a measure of firm's performance. Debt-equity ratio (D/E) is measured financial leverage of selected companies. Tangibility refers to assets tangibility defined as the ratio of the fixed tangible assets divided by the total assets of selected companies. Natural logarithm of sales is representing size and u is the error term.

Findings

In order to study the relationship between financial leverage and financial performance of selected Non-bank financial companies (NBFCs) in India, we have calculated the profitability ratio, leverage ratio and other related ratios which are depicted in the following table 1.

Table 1: Descriptive Statistics of Variables

Statistics	*Dependent Variables*			*Independent Variables*		
	Return on Assets (ROA)	*Return on Equity (ROE)*	*Market Value to Book Value (M/B)*	*Debt-Equity Ratio (D/E)*	*Tangibility*	*Size*
Mean	3.926	12.478	2.262	2.556	.013	3.189
Min	–5.05	–26.07	0	0	0	0.54
Max	37.26	59.57	13.97	8.21	.063	4.55
Std. Dev.	4.622	10.365	2.264	2.251	.016	.812
N	160	160	160	160	160	160

Source: Computed by authors

From Table 1 it is found that the average Return on Assets (ROA) of the NBFC Company is 3.926 with a standard deviation 4.622 during the study period. It ranges between -5.05 and 37.26.

The average Return on equity (ROE) of the NBFC Company is 12.478 with a standard deviation 10.365 during the study period. It ranges between –26.07 and 59.57.

The average Market value to Book value (M/B) of the NBFC Company is 2.262 with a standard deviation 2.264 during the study period. It ranges between 0.0 and 13.97.

Return on assets and return on equity range is negative to moderate positive, this is due to sum NBFC companies are running at a loss, whereas sum NBFC companies are earning moderate profit.

The average Debt-Equity Ratio (D/E) of the NBFC Company is 2.556 with a standard deviation 2.251 during the study period. It ranges between 0.0 and 8.21. Its minimum value is zero because debt's funds of some companies are mostly zero.

The average tangibility of the NBFC Company is 0.013 with a standard deviation 0.016 during the study period. It ranges between 0.0 and 0.063.

The Market Size is measured by Natural logarithm of sale. A greater volume is more favorable. The average size is 3.198 with a standard deviation .812 during the study period. It ranges between 0.54 and 4.55.

Correlation Analysis

Pearson correlation coefficients for the independent variables are used to assess the problem of multicollinearity.

Table 2: Pearson Correlation Coefficient among Independent Variables

Independent Variables	*Debt-Equity Ratio*	*Tangibility*	*Size*
Debt-Equity Ratio	1		
Tangibility	0.1416	1	
Size	0.6382	0.2745	1

Source: Computed by authors

From the Table 2 it is found that there are low correlation coefficients for all the independent variables. It implies that the problem of multicollinearity does not exist.

Regression Analysis

In order to assess the effect of financial leverage on firm's financial performance, three regression equations have been developed and panel data regression has been run. STATA has been given the following empirical findings for the regression equations.

Here Levin-Lin-Chu unit-root test is applied for all variables used in the analysis in order to avoid spurious regression results. It is found that all the variables are stationary, some of them are stationary at level, and some are stationary at lag 1. This implies that the results obtained are not spurious.

The regression results show the relationship between financial leverage and financial performance of some selected NBFC Companies in India for Pooled OLS model, Fixed effect model (FEM) and Random effect model (REM). The F statistics of the pooled regression model and fixed effect model are statistically significant and also the Wald-statistics of the random-effect model is statistically significant. Therefore, they are well fitted.

It is difficult to identify the severity of the collinearity problem from only relying on the correlation results. The variance inflation factor (VIF) is a widely used measure of the degree of multicollinearity of an independent variable with the other independent variables in a regression model. It measures the variance of an estimated regression coefficient is increased, as a result of collinearity. As a rule of thumb, VIF $\geq$ 10 indicates multicollinearity. So VIF is undertaken. From Appendix III, it is found that in all cases, all the VIFs are less than 2. Hence, collinearity does not seem to be a problem in the regression models.

In order to select the appropriate model Pooled OLS regression model, fixed effects model (FEM) and Random effect model (REM) are carried out. It is found that test statistics in Restricted F Test, Breusch-Pagan Lagrange Multiplier Test are statistically significant. The Hausman Test is not statistically significant in Model 2 but Hausman Test is statistically significant in Model 1 & 3. Hence the regression results of the REM in Model 2 and FEM in Model 1 & 3 are used for statistical inference and further analysis of the individual coefficients.

Finally, we have made a robust estimation of the coefficients of the regression models under study. These models take care of the autocorrelation as well as heteroskedasticity in the observation and the estimates are unbiased and efficient. The regression results are presented below:

The effect of the financial leverage on return on assets

Table 3: Model 1: ROA as a measure of firm's financial performance

Independent Variables	*Coefficient*	*Robust Standard Error*	*t Stat*	*p-value*
Debt-Equity Ratio	–.148453	.3085686	–0.48	0.637
Tangibility	–157.902*	55.56745	–2.84	0.012
Size	3.393543*	.9648517	3.52	0.003
Intercept	–4.524153	2.833134	–1.60	0.131
Total Panel (Balanced) Observations	160			
Adjusted R2-Within	0.2104			
Adjusted R2-Between	0.0013			
Adjusted R2-Overall	0.0570			
F statistics	4.62*			
Prob. (F)	0.0176			

Notes: '*' implies significant at 1% probability level; '**' implies significant at 5% probability level.
Source: Computed by authors

Since Wald χ^2 test is significant at 1% probability level, therefore model 1 is well fitted. From Table 3 it is observed that leverage has an insignificant negative effect on return on assets (ROA). The firm's tangibility has a negative highly significant effect on ROA. It implies that a high level of investment in fixed assets indicates low financial health of the company. The variable, Market size has positively and statistically significant on return on assets. Market Size is positively highly significant with profitability, which implies that larger Market Sizes seem to favor profitability, therefore larger firms are more profitable.

The effect of the financial leverage on return on equity:

Table 4: Model 2: ROE as a measure of firm's financial performance

Independent Variables	*Coefficient*	*Robust Standard Error*	*z Stat*	*p-value*
Debt-Equity Ratio	1.347789*	.4538762	2.97	0.003
Tangibility	–233.82968*	78.10003	–2.99	0.003
Size	4.730192*	1.692006	2.80	0.005
Intercept	–3.100975	5.08225	-0.61	0.542
Total Panel(Balanced) observations	160			

Independent Variables	*Coefficient*	*Robust Standard Error*	*z Stat*	*p-value*
Adjusted R2-Within		0.1858		
Adjusted R2-Between		0.3145		
Adjusted R2-Overall		0.2472		
Wald χ^2 statistics		26.21*		
Prob. (Wald chi2)		0.0000		

Notes: '*' implies significant at 1% probability level; '**' implies significant at 5% probability level.
Source: Computed by authors

Since Wald χ^2 test is significant at 1% probability level, therefore model 2 is well fitted. From Table 4 it is observed that leverage has a positive highly significant effect on return on equity (ROE). It implies that a high level of debt ratio indicates high return for equity shareholders. The firm's tangibility has a negative highly significant effect on ROE. It implies that a high level of investment in fixed assets indicates low financial health of the company. The variable, Market size has positively and statistically significant on return on assets. Market Size is positive highly significant with profitability, which implies that larger Market Sizes seem to favor profitability therefore larger firms are more profitable.

The effect of financial leverage on market value to book value (M/B):

Table 5: Model 3: M/B as a measure of firm's financial performance

Independent Variables	*Coefficient*	*Robust Standard Error*	*t Stat*	*p-value*
Debt-Equity Ratio	–.7573308***	.4015439	–1.89	0.079
Tangibility	19.97442	16.08986	1.24	0.234
Size	1.498012*	.4625931	3.24	0.006
Intercept	–.8325868	.9101206	–0.91	0.375
Total Panel Observations		160		
Adjusted R2-Within		0.2517		
Adjusted R2-Between		0.0066		
Adjusted R2-Overall		0.0408		
F statistics		4.13**		
Prob. (F)		0.0254		

Notes: '*' implies significant at 1% probability level; '**' implies significant at 5% probability level.

Source: Computed by authors

Since *F* test is significant at 5% probability level, therefore model 1 is well fitted. From Table 5 it is observed that leverage has a negative significant effect on

M/B. It implies that a high level of debt ratio indicates low financial health of the company. The firm's tangibility has an insignificant positive effect on M/B. The variable, Market size is positively and statistically significant on M/B. Market Size is positive highly significant with profitability, which implies that larger Market Sizes seem to favor profitability, therefore larger firms are more profitable.

Conclusion

The present study is an attempt to investigate empirically the relationship between financial leverage and financial performance of selected Non-bank financial companies (NBFCs) in India. Here we have selected 16 NBFCs companies from the top 500 listed companies in Bombay Stock Exchange (BSE) for a period of 10 years from 2014 to 2023. Return on Assets, Return on Equity and Market value to Book value (M/B) are taken as indicators of firm's performance. The technique of panel data regression has been used on STATA. The results showed that financial leverage has a negative highly significant effect on return on equity (ROE) and Market value to Book value (M/B). It implies that a high level of debt ratio indicates low financial health of the company. The firm's tangibility has a negative highly significant effect on ROA and ROE. It implies that a high level of investment in fixed assets indicates low financial health of the company. The variable, Market size is positively and statistically significant on ROA, ROE and M/B. It implies that larger Market Sizes seem to favour profitability, therefore larger firms are more profitable. From the above findings, it is recommended for financial managers to consider decreasing the level of financial leverage as sources of funds while forming the capital structure of the Indian NBFC sector. In other words, it implies that it would be better for NBFC firms if they finance the total assets by shareholders' fund rather than debt fund, which can enhance their performance. This study and its result are helpful to the policy makers when they decide on their regulatory framework in which these companies operate.

References

[1] Adetunji, A.A., Akinyemi, I.A. and Rasheed, K.O. (2016). Financial Leverage and Firms' Value: A Study of Selected Firms in Nigeria. *European Journal of Research and Reflection in Management Sciences,* 4(1), 14–32, 2056–5992.

[2] Akhtar, S., Javed, B., Maryam, A. and Sadia, H. (2012). Relationship between Financial Leverage and Financial Performance: Evidence from Fuel & Energy Sector of Pakistan. *European Journal of Business and Management,* 4(11), 2222–1905.

[3] Akinlo, O. and Asaolu, T. (2012). Profitability and Leverage: Evidence from Nigerian Firms. *Global Journal of Business Research,* 6(1), 17–25.

[4] Al-Shamaileh, M.O. and Khanfar, S.M. (2014). Effect of the Financial Leverage on the Profitability in the Tourism Companies (Analytical Study- Tourism Sector-Jordan). *Business and Economic Research,* 4(2), 251–264. 2162–4860.

[5] Cheng, M.C. and Tzeng, Z.C. (2011). The Effect of Leverage on Firm Value and How the Firm financially Qualify Influence on This Effect. *World Journal of Management,* 3(2).

[6] Chavali, K. and Rosario, S. (2018). Relationship between capital structure and profitability: A study of nonbanking Finance Companies in India. Academy of Accounting and Financial Studies Journal, 22(1), 1–8.

[7] Dutta, P., Jain, A. and Gupta, A. (2020). Performance analysis of non-banking finance companies using two-stage data envelopment analysis. Annals of Operations Research, 295, 91–116.

[8] Franklin, J.S. and Muthusamy, K. (2011). Determinants of Financial Leverage in Indian Pharmaceutical Industry. *International Journal of Applied Engineering Research.* 2(1). 273–282. 0976–4259.

[9] Granath, D. and Thorsell, P. (2014). Leverage and how it affects shareholder value. *Financial Thesis paper.* University of Gothenburg.

[10] Gweyi, M.O. and Karanja, J. (2014). Effect of Financial Leverage on Financial Performance of Deposit Taking Savings and Credit Co-operative in Kenya. *International Journal of Academic Research in Accounting, Finance and Management Sciences,* 4(2), 176–184, 2225–8329.

[11] Hasanzadeh, B., Torabynia, S., Esgandari, K. and Kordbacheh, S. (2013). Evaluating Effects of Financial Leverage on Future Stock Value at Stock Exchange. *Research Journal of Recent Sciences,* 2(2), 81–84.

[12] Innocent, E.C., Ikechukwu, A.C. and Nnagbogu, E.K. (2014). The Effect of Financial Leverage on Financial Performance: Evidence of Quoted Pharmaceutical Companies in Nigeria. *IOSR Journal of Economics and Finance,* 5(3), 17–25, 2321–5933.

[13] Jasinthan, T. and Achchuthan, S. (2012). Impact of 39 Financial, Operating Leverage on the Financial Performance: Special Reference to Lanka Orix Leasing Company Plc in Sri-Lanka. *International Journal of Engineering Sciences Paradigms and Researches,* 01(01), 2319–6564.

[14] Jensen, M.C. and Meckling, W.H. (1976). Theory of the Firm: Managerial Behavior, Agency Costs and Ownership Structure. *Journal of Financial Economics,* 3(4), 305–360.

[15] Kraus, A. and Litzenberger, R. (1973). A State-Preference Model of Optimal Financial Leverage. *The Journal of Finance,* 28(4), 911–922.

[16] Long, S. and Malitz, B. (1985). Investment Patterns and Financial Leverage. *University of Chicago Press.* http://www.nber.org/books/frie85-1.

[17] Myers, S. (1984). The Capital Structure Puzzle. *The Journal of Finance,* 39(3), 575–592.

[18] Moghadam, M.D. and Jafar, M. (2015). The Role of Financial Leverage in the Performance of Companies Listed in the Stock Exchange. *Indian Journal of Natural Sciences,* 5(30), 7402–7411.

[19] Mule, R.K. and Mukras, M.S. (2015). Financial Leverage and Performance of Listed Firms in a Frontier Market: Panel Evidence from Kenya. *European Scientific Journal.* 11(7). 534–550. 1857–7431.

[20] Myers, S. (1984). The Capital Structure Puzzle. *The Journal of Finance.* 39(3). 575–592.

[21] Ojo, S.A. (2012). The Effect of Financial Leverage on Corporate Performance of Some Selected Companies in Nigeria. *Canadian Social Science.* 8(1). 85–91.

[22] Pachori, S. and Totala, K. (2012). Influence of Financial Leverage on Shareholders Return and Market Capitalization: A Study of Automotive Cluster Companies of Pithampur, (M.P.), India. *2nd International Conference on Humanities, Geography and Economics (ICHGE'2012), Singapore.*

[23] Rajkumar, P. (2014). Impact of Financial Leverage on Financial Performance: Special Reference to John Keells Holdings plc in Sri Lanka. *Scientific Research Journal (SCIRJ),* 2(2), 15–20.

[24] Saini, R. (2012). Impact of financial leverage on shareholders returns and market capitalization: Empirical evidence of telecommunication sector companies, India. *International Journal of Research in IT, Management and Engineering,* 2(12).

[25] Singh, A.K. and Bansal, P. (2016). Impact of Financial Leverage on Firms's Performance and Valuation: A Panel Data Analysis. *Indian Journal of Accounting,* XL VII(2), 73–80, 2395–6127.

[26] Taani, K. (2012). Impact of Working Capital Management Policy and Financial Leverage on Financial Performance: Empirical evidence from Amman Stock Exchange – listed companies. *International Journal of Management Sciences and Business Research,* 1(8), 2226–8235.

[27] Ujah, U. and Brusa, O. The Effect of Financial Leverage and Cash Flow Volatility on Earnings Management. *Texas A&M International University.*

Appendices

Appendix I: List of Selected NBFC Companies

Aditya Birla Capital Ltd.	Mahindra & Mahindra Financial Services Ltd.
Bajaj Finance Ltd.	Manappuram Finance Ltd.
Bajaj Holdings & Investment Ltd.	Muthoot Finance Ltd.
Cholamandalam Investment and Finance Company Ltd.	Piramal Enterprises Ltd.
Credit Access Grameen Ltd.	Poonawalla Fincorp Ltd.
Five-Star Business Finance Ltd.	SBI Cards and Payment Services Ltd.
IDFC Ltd.	Shriram Finance Ltd.
L&T Finance Holdings Ltd.	Tata Investment Corporation Ltd.

Appendix II: Variables Definition

ROA Return on assets is EBIT/total assets

ROE Return on equity is Profit after tax/Shareholders capital

M/B Market value/Book value

D/E Debt equity ratio is Debt/Equity

Tangibility Assets tangibility is fixed tangible assets/total assets

Size Size is the natural logarithm of sales

Appendix III: Result of Variance Inflation Factor (VIF) of Selected NBFC Companies in India

Independent Variables	*ROA (Model 1)/ROE (Model 2)/ M/B (Model 3)*
Debt-Equity Ratio	1.79
Tangibility	1.69
Size	1.08

The Future of Sustainable Investing: A Look at the Performance of Ethical Funds in India

Samarpita Seth[1] and Samyabrata Das[2]

ABSTRACT: In today's financial landscape, socially responsible investing and sustainable investing are the buzzwords. Ethical funds in India are equity mutual funds which follow the rules of Shariah in picking stocks. The study takes into consideration two actively managed Ethical funds: Tata Ethical Fund and Taurus Ethical Fund and compares their performance with the selected benchmark index (NIFTY 500 Shariah TRI) from various risk-return perspectives from April 2013 to April 2023. The results revealed that the Taurus Ethical Fund underperformed the benchmark in all periods whereas the Tata Ethical Fund outperformed the benchmark index in 3 out of 5 periods. Moreover, the fund managers of Tata Ethical Fund performed better than their counterparts in selecting quality stocks. Further, both the funds remained defensive and exhibited decent diversification across the periods. Tata Ethical Fund outperformed Taurus Ethical Fund and the benchmark in terms of return from the 'Systematic Investment Plan' (SIP).

Keywords: Ethical Funds, Shariah, SIP, Sustainable Investing.

JEL Code: G11.

Background of the Study

Sustainable investing is gaining momentum in developing countries. India is also embracing it by integrating environmental, social and governance (popularly known as ESG) factors in its investment landscape. The role of the Government and the regulator (the Securities and Exchange Board of India) is praiseworthy in this direction. A section of Indian investors is committed to sustainable investing to a great extent.

Indian mutual fund industry witnessed radical transformation in the last two decades both in qualitative and quantitative terms. Ethical funds are equity mutual funds which invest in Shariah-compliant stocks. Mutual funds that rigorously adhere to Shariah principles are categorised as 'Shariah-compliant' funds and fall under the purview of Socially Responsible Investing (SRI). Due to the restrictions

---

[1] Associate Professor, Department of Economics, New Alipore College, Kolkata, India. E-mail: samarpitaseth@gmail.com

[2] Associate Professor, Department of Commerce, New Alipore College, Kolkata, India. E-mail: samyabrata1@gmail.com

put on investments by Shariah law, such funds must adhere to the same and thus represent a specific investment philosophy. Actively managed funds represent funds where fund managers select stocks on behalf of the investors. As such, the stock-picking and market-timing abilities of fund managers matter a lot in such funds. Equity funds invest a significant chunk in stocks and other related equity instruments. The distinctive characteristics of Shariah-compliant funds in India include any time entry or exit (open-ended funds), long-term capital gains (LTCG) tax benefits up to Rs. 100000, reduced LTCG tax rate (10%) and investing in Shariah-compliant stocks.

Survey of Related Literature

A brief survey of related literature is exhibited. While analysing the performance of UK ethical funds, Gregory *et al.* (1997) concluded that there was no significant difference in the returns generated by ethical and non-ethical funds and that both types of funds underperformed the FTSA benchmark index. In the opinion of Cummings (2000), while examining the performance of seven ethical equity funds in Australia during the period between 1986 and 1994, observed no significant differences in their returns when compared to both a large and a small-cap benchmark. Kreander *et al.* (2002), the performance of European ethical funds was similar to that of the Morgan Stanley Capital International (MSCI) World Index. However, when compared to a Swedish benchmark, the performance of Swedish ethical funds is remarkable, yet it is far more subdued when compared to a worldwide index. Davis (2008) opined that Shariah-compliant investment instruments raised socially responsible investing to a higher threshold, demonstrating that informed investing does not always result in lower returns. According to Natarajan & Dharani (2012), equity-based Shariah-compliant investment is a feasible and ethical investment route, particularly for retail individual ethical investors. Habib & Islam (2014) observed that the Islamic Index remained less risky than the conventional index in India but underperformed the unscreened index during the study period (2003–2013) from the perspective of risk-adjusted return. According to Tripathi & Bhandari (2015), the compromise that was made in terms of diversification by investing in ethical funds was amply rewarded by providing higher returns in the Indian context. Usha Kiran & Tadoori (2018) gave an interesting observation. According to them, investors looking at mutual fund performance may ignore investing in socially responsible funds unless they are religious-minded or have a strong belief in ethical investing. The fund studied depicted higher costs as well. Abdul-Rahim *et al.* (2019) examined the performance of 833 Shariah and conventional funds in six emerging markets from 2000 to 2015 and discovered that the former (Shariah funds) outperformed the latter in Malaysia, Pakistan, and South Africa. Fasadinisari *et al.* (2020) found no difference in risk and return between Shariah mutual funds and conventional funds. Rahahieh & Bhatti (2022) found that

Shariah-compliant mutual funds exhibited insignificant alpha implying that these funds neither performed better nor demonstrated inferior performance as against their benchmark in Saudi Arabia. Nabi *et al.* (2022) revealed that Islamic fund managers outperformed traditional fund managers in terms of liquidity and volatility timing. The abilities of mutual fund managers were negatively correlated with mutual fund performance, although not a significant one, according to Marsono *et al.* (2022). According to Aqeeq and Chamadia (2023), actively managed equity funds (AMEFs) were unable to outperform the market index in terms of stock selection or market timing. AMEFs, on the other hand, demonstrated increased performance in the post-global financial crisis period, when traditional and Islamic AMEFs achieved significant rewards for the given degree of risk. Barafwala (2023) observed that the Tata Ethical Fund was heavily tilted towards the technology sector with TCS and Infosys being the main two stocks in its portfolio. That apart, the fund exhibited lower risk, decent risk-adjusted return and the fund managers succeeded in identifying and selecting quality stocks.

Research Gap

Islamic finance has not made much strides in India. But in the mutual funds space, there exist two actively managed Shariah-compliant funds and one passively managed fund complying with the principles of Shariah. It is observed from the survey of literature that a comprehensive study is lacking in the Indian context so far as the performance of Shariah-compliant funds is concerned. There is a dearth of literature in this area in India and available literature is mostly from newspapers and periodicals. The Benchmark selection (S&P BSE 500 Shariah TRI) has also been done as per the guidelines of the regulator. Previous studies have considered the Price Return Index and not the Total Return Index or TRI. As a result, the study will provide a comprehensive picture because Price Return Indices can only represent capital appreciation and overlook dividend payments. However, the Total Return Index (TRI) considers both of them (capital appreciation and dividend). Aside from that, the study has divided the time into 1-year, 3-year, 5-year, 7-year, and 10-year intervals to assess consistency in performance. In addition, the research paper has considered a 'Direct Plan' whereas the past studies were based on a 'Regular Plan' of the chosen funds. Incorporating SIP return as a measure of performance is another area which was neglected in earlier studies.

Objectives of the Study

This study has a trio of main objectives: (a) to understand the features of the Shariah-compliant funds, (b) to assess the performance of the selected funds from multiple perspectives, and (c) to outline the future possibilities of ethical investing in India.

Research Questions

The study strives to investigate these specific research queries:

1. In terms of return, do the funds outperform the benchmark?
2. Are the funds riskier than the benchmark index?
3. Are the funds capable of outperforming the chosen benchmark in terms of risk-adjusted return?
4. How good are the fund managers' stock-picking abilities?
5. Is the nature of the funds defensive in relation to the benchmark?
6. Are the funds suitably diversified?
7. How is the performance of the chosen funds in terms of return from the "Systematic Investment Plan." (SIP)?

Methodology

The study examines the performance of actively managed Shariah-compliant funds in India and compares it to the pertinent benchmark index. The research relies on secondary data. The study runs from April 2013 to April 2023. The impact of 'Entry Load,' brokerage, and 'Exit Load' has not been considered. The benchmark index has been designated as the S&P BSE 500 Shariah TRI. Here, 8.2675% is taken as the risk-free rate of return. It is the average rate of return provided over the course of the research period by the Public Provident Fund (PPF) that the Government of India administers. The 'growth' option, rather than the 'dividend' option, has been explored. The funds' 'Direct Plans', rather than the funds' 'Regular Plans', have been selected for the research. The study collects NAV (Net Asset Value) figures for the funds (month-end) and closing values for the chosen benchmark index (month-end) for computing monthly returns for the funds and the benchmark. The formula used for calculating the monthly returns is as follows:

$$R_p = [(NAV_t - NAV_{t-1})/NAV_{t-1}] \times 100$$

$$R_b = [(Value_t - Value_{t-1})/Value_{t-1}] \times 100$$

Where, NAV_t = Closing NAV of the chosen fund for month t, NAV_{t-1} = Closing NAV of the chosen fund for the preceding month (t–1), $Value_t$ = Closing Value of the relevant Benchmark Index for month t, $Value_{t-1}$ = Closing Value of the relevant Benchmark Index for the preceding month (t–1). Standard Deviation (S.D.) has been determined using these monthly returns for measuring total risk. Furthermore, the Compounded Annual Growth Rate of the selected funds ($CAGR_p$) and the Benchmark ($CAGR_b$) have been determined. When computing SIP returns, it is presumed that Rs. 1000 is invested at the end of each month at the funds' respective closing NAVs. Likewise, SIP return calculation of the corresponding benchmark index has been done assuming that Rs. 1000 is invested at the closing values of the benchmark at the end of the month. Breaking the periods into different parts like one-year, three-year, five-year, seven-year and ten-year has been done to assess performance consistency. Measures like CAGR, Standard Deviation, Sharpe Ratio, Jensen alpha, Beta and Coefficient of Determination (R^2) and beta have also been employed. Two actively managed open-ended Shariah funds are available in the Indian mutual fund industry. This research paper considers both funds.

Analysis and Findings

The returns generated by the funds and the benchmark index are presented in Table 1.

Table 1: CAGR Generated by Shariah-Complaint Funds and the Benchmark (%)

	Year				
	1	*3*	*5*	*7*	*10*
Tata Ethical Fund	2.69	24.56	12.30	13.26	15.62
Taurus Ethical Fund	–2.30	19.10	10.43	12.47	14.68
NIFTY 500 Shariah TRI	–2.12	23.07	11.42	14.35	15.59

Source: Computations done by the Researchers

Table 1 shows that Tata Ethical Fund has generated CAGR over the Benchmark on most of the occasions viz., 1-year, 3-year, 5-year and 10-year period of study while it underperformed the benchmark in 7 years. However, the Taurus Ethical Fund underperformed the benchmark as well as the Tata Ethical Fund during the entire period of study.

Table 2 exhibits the total risk (measured by standard deviation) of the selected funds and the benchmark index. Table 2 exhibits the total risk (measured by standard deviation) of the selected funds and the benchmark index.

Table 2: Total Risk Associated with Shariah-Complaint Funds and Benchmark (Standard Deviation)

Fund	*Year*				
	1	*3*	*5*	*7*	*10*
Tata Ethical Fund	11.86	13.33	15.66	14.44	14.63
Taurus Ethical Fund	13.02	12.18	15.49	14.23	14.57
NIFTY 500 Shariah TRI	13.85	14.46	16.40	15.09	14.43

Source: Computations done by the Researchers

It is evident from Table 2 that both Tata Ethical Fund and Taurus Ethical Fund performed better than the benchmark in terms of total risk on most occasions barring the 10 years. However, Taurus Ethical Fund outperformed Tata Ethical Fund on 4 out of 5 occasions, 1 year being the exception.

Sharpe Ratio reveals the risk-adjusted return and Table 3 shows the risk-adjusted-return figures of the chosen funds and the benchmark index.

Table 3: Risk-Adjusted Return (RAR) Associated with Shariah-Complaint Funds and Benchmark (Sharpe Ratio)

Fund	*Year*				
	1	*3*	*5*	*7*	*10*
Tata Ethical Fund	–0.471	1.222	0.257	0.345	0.503
Taurus Ethical Fund	–0.811	0.889	0.140	0.295	0.440
NIFTY 500 Shariah TRI	–0.750	1.024	0.192	0.403	0.507

Source: Computations done by the Researchers

Sharpe ratio figures from Table 3 reveal that Tata Ethical Fund outperformed the benchmark during 1-year, 3-year and 5-year. It underperformed the benchmark index in 7-year (significantly) and 10-year (marginally). Taurus Ethical fund, on the other hand, underperformed the benchmark in all periods of study. Further, in the 1 year, both the funds and the benchmark delivered negative risk-adjusted returns.

Alpha values, which measure the ability and skill of the fund managers in picking quality stocks, are presented in Table 4.

Table 4: Alpha Value

Fund	*Year*				
	1	*3*	*5*	*7*	*10*
Tata Ethical Fund	0.360	0.288	0.125	0.003	0.121
Taurus Ethical Fund	–0.035	0.093	0.021	–0.007	0.053

Measuring Fund Managers' Stock-picking Ability.
Source: Computations done by the Researchers

It is evident from Table 4 that fund managers of Tata Ethical Fund demonstrated the ability to choose quality stocks in all the periods of study (Alpha > 0). However, fund managers of Taurus Ethical Fund showed the ability to pick quality stocks only in 3-year, 5-year and 10-year. In terms of alpha value, Tata Ethical Fund performed better than Taurus Ethical Fund in all periods. Table 5 depicts the aggressiveness/defensiveness of the funds with respect to the benchmark index. Beta values are associated with determining the aggressiveness or otherwise of the funds.

Table 5: Beta Values

Fund	*Year*				
	1	*3*	*5*	*7*	*10*
Tata Ethical Fund	0.81	0.89	0.93	0.92	0.90
Taurus Ethical Fund	0.88	0.78	0.89	0.88	0.91

Source: Computations done by the Researchers

It is evident from Table 5 that the beta values of both funds are less than one. Such a phenomenon indicates that both funds remained defensive throughout the period of study. The coefficient of determination (RSQ) measures the unsystematic risk management by the fund. It also signifies the extent of diversification. Table 6 shows the RSQ values of the funds.

Table 6: RSQ Values

Fund	*Year*				
	1	*3*	*5*	*7*	*10*
Tata Ethical Fund	0.899	0.935	0.955	0.934	0.903
Taurus Ethical Fund	0.874	0.866	0.898	0.878	0.860

Source: Computations done by the Researchers

It is visible from Table 6 that both the funds have RSQ values very close to one. As such, it can be inferred that the chosen funds succeeded in minimising unsystematic risk to a great extent. Further, it can be said that the funds are adequately diversified. Moreover, Tata Ethical Fund outperformed Taurus Ethical Fund in terms of RSQ values during the entire period of study. Table 7 presents the SIP returns of the funds and the benchmark index.

Table 7: SIP Returns of the Funds and the Benchmark Index

Fund	*Year*				
	1	*3*	*5*	*7*	*10*
Tata Ethical Fund	4.0021	12.9614	15.5955	14.1492	13.6626
Taurus Ethical Fund	–2.2211	7.4182	11.5405	11.6941	12.0606
NIFTY 500 Shariah TRI	–2.2670	8.8356	13.4826	13.0014	13.5431

Source: Computations done by the Researchers

A look at Table 7 reveals that Tata Ethical Fund performed better than the other two (Taurus Ethical Fund and the Benchmark Index) during the entire study period. Taurus Ethical Fund underperformed the benchmark in all periods except 1 year. Further, both Taurus Ethical Fund and NIFTY 500 Shariah TRI exhibited negative SIP returns in 1 year. That apart, it is also evident that SIP returns of the funds and the benchmark were in double digits in 5 years, 7 years and 10 years which signifies that SIP is an effective instrument of wealth creation in medium to long-term periods.

Conclusions of the Study

Based on research questions, the summary of findings is as follows:

- Tata Ethical Fund outperformed the benchmark on most occasions, including the 1-year, 3-year, 5-year, and 10-year periods of research, while underperforming the benchmark in the 7 years. Throughout the study period, however, the Taurus Ethical Fund underperformed both the benchmark and the Tata Ethical Fund.
- Except for the 10 years, Tata Ethical Fund and Taurus Ethical Fund outperformed the benchmark on other occasions from the viewpoint of total risk. However, Taurus Ethical Fund outperformed Tata Ethical Fund in four out of five instances, except for one year.
- Tata Ethical Fund surpassed the benchmark across one, three, and five years in terms of risk-adjusted return. However, the performance in the seven-year period is significantly below the benchmark whereas in ten years it marginally underperformed the benchmark index. Taurus Ethical Fund, on the contrary, underperformed the benchmark across all study periods. Furthermore, both the funds and the benchmark posted negative risk-adjusted returns in 1 year.
- Fund managers responsible for managing the portfolio of Tata Ethical Fund displayed the capacity to select quality stocks across all research periods (Alpha > 0). But managers of Taurus Ethical Fund have shown the capacity to select quality stocks only over three, five and ten years. Regarding alpha value, the Tata Ethical Fund outperformed the Taurus Ethical Fund throughout all periods.
- Over the entire study period, the two funds stayed conservative (Beta value <1).
- The selected funds were effective in reducing unsystematic risk to a large extent. Furthermore, the funds exhibited sufficient diversification. In addition, in terms of RSQ values, the Tata Ethical Fund outperformed the Taurus Ethical Fund throughout the study period.
- In terms of SIP return, the Tata Ethical Fund outperformed the other two (Taurus Ethical Fund and the Benchmark Index) over the entire research

period. Taurus Ethical Fund, on the other hand, outperformed the benchmark in all periods (except one year).

- Advancements in technology, support from the Government and the regulator, increased investor awareness and a strong global ESG trend act as positives for ethical investment in India. In the mutual fund space, more ethical funds are expected in the coming years because a sizeable section of today's investors want to link financial returns with moral and ethical values.
- Shariah-compliant equity mutual funds can deliver decent returns. In our nation, Muslims are substantial in number. Bringing them under the umbrella of Shariah-compliant mutual funds is a gradual process which needs continuous training and awareness programmes. Nevertheless, their participation in such funds, it is expected, can be increased in the future.

Scope for Further Research

In the context of the Indian financial environment, detailed studies of ethical investing are of immense importance. Through investigating these fields, scholars can offer significant perspectives that will aid in resolving current issues and driving the expansion of ethical investing in India. In addition to helping investors and financial institutions, research in the following areas will further the nation's larger objectives of sustainable development and ethical investing.

(a) The perception of Indian investors towards ethical investing in general and ethical mutual funds, in particular, may be a research area.

(b) Research on whether investors should opt for actively managed Shariah-compliant equity funds or their passive counterparts can be done by analysing the performance of the two categories.

(c) Research in the area of ethical investing scenarios in India and other nations (China, Brazil, South Africa etc.) may be conducted.

(d) How the Governments and regulatory bodies function in promoting an ethical research environment may be a research area.

References

[1] Abdul-Rahim, R., Abdul-Rahman, A. and Ling, P.S. (2019). Performance of Shariah Versus Conventional Funds: Lessons from Emerging Markets. *Journal of Nusantara Studies (JONUS)*, *4*(2), 193–218.

[2] Aqeeq, M.A. and Chamadia, S. (2023). Do Actively Managed Equity Funds Add Value in Developing Economies?–The Case Of 'Inverse Gruber Puzzle'in Pakistan. *Journal of Islamic Accounting and Business Research.*

[3] Barafwala, N.R. (2023). Performance Excellence: Analyzing the Success of Shariah-Compliant Tata Ethical Fund in India. GAP Interdisciplinarities, 6(4), 9–12.

[4] Cummings, L. (2000). The Financial Performance of Ethical Investment Trusts: An Australian Perspective. *Journal of Business Ethics*, 25, 79–92.

[5] Davis, G.S. (2008). Shariah Compliance Principles. Retrieved from http://www.investopedia.com/stockanalysis/2008/shariah_compliance_principles_gs_aig.aspx, on 25/10/2014.

[6] Fasadinisari, W., Lihan, I. and Hendrawaty, E. (2020). The Comparative Analysis of Conventional and Sharia Mutual Funds Performance From January 2017 to December 2018. SSRG International Journal of Economics and Management Studies, 7(3), 100–113. Retrieved on 13.06.2024 from http://repository.lppm.unila.ac.id/21908/1/IJEMS-V7I3P115.pdf.

[7] Gregory, A., Matatko, J. and Luther, R. (1997). Ethical Unit Trust Financial Performance: Small Company Effects and Fund Size Effects. *Journal of Business Finance and Accounting*, 24(5), 705–25.

[8] Habib, M. and Islam, K.U. (2014). Performance of Shariah Compliant Index: A Comparative Study of India and Malaysia. International Journal of Interdisciplinary and Multidisciplinary Studies (IJIMS), 1(6), 231–241.

[9] Kreander, N., Gray, R.H., Power, D.M. and Sinclair, C.D. (2002). The Financial Performance of European Ethical Funds 1996–1998. *Journal of Accounting and Finance*, 1, 3 – 22.

[10] Marsono, A.D., Salim, U., Ratnawati, K., and Aisjah, S. (2022). An Empirical Analysis of Factors Influencing Performance of Shariah Mutual Funds in Indonesia. *Jurnal Aplikasi Manajemen*, 20(4). doi: 10.21776/ub.jam.2022.020.04.11.

[11] Nabi, G., Rehman, R.U. and Ali, R. (2023). Islamic Fund Managers' Market Timing Abilities and Their Impact on Fund Performances. *Pakistan Journal of Humanities and Social Sciences*, *11*(2), 1111–1125.

[12] Natarajan, P. and Dharani, M. (2012). Shariah Compliant Stocks in India – A Viable and Ethical Investment Vehicle. *Arabian Journal of Business and Management Review*, 1(6), 50–62.

[13] Rahahleh, N.A. and Bhatti, I. (2022). Empirical Comparison of Shariah-compliant vs Conventional Mutual Fund Performance. *International Journal of Emerging Markets*. doi: 10.1108/ijoem-05-2020-0565.

[14] Tripathi, V. and Bhandari, V. (2015). Performance Evaluation of Ethical and Conventional Funds—A Study of Taurus Mutual Fund in India. Financial Markets and Economic Development. India: Bloomsbury Publishing. Available at SSRN: https://ssrn.com/abstract=2601297 or http://dx.doi.org/10.2139/ssrn.2601297.

[15] Usha Kiran, V. and Tadoori, G. (2018). Integration of ESG Investment with the Traditional Portfolio—a Study of TATA Mutual Funds. *Himalaya Publishing House*, 59–64. Available at SSRN: https://ssrn.com/abstract=3704684 or http://dx.doi.org/10.2139/ssrn.3704684.

The Impact of Demographic Characteristics on the Usage of Fintech Services in India

Brajaballav Pal[1], Jatin Basumatary[2] and Biki Digar[3]

ABSTRACT: FinTech is the use of technology in financial sectors. It has emerged as a critical factor in the financial sector, especially in the state of Assam, India, where there is a large unbanked and underbanked population. The adoption of FinTech varies depending on demographic characteristics. The study examines the impact of demographic characteristics on the use of FinTech services, particularly in the Biswanath district of Assam. The Pearson Chi-Square test revealed that income, education, and occupation have statistically significant impact on both the duration of usage FinTech usage and usage during COVID-19 pandemic, whereas area and gender do not. Moreover, it has demonstrated a moderate reliability in internal consistency among the items, where internet connectivity and digital banking are essential for the prospects of FinTech. Finally, the findings of the study may have implications for FinTech service providers, regulators, and other stakeholders.

Keywords: COVID-19, Demographic Characteristics, Financial Inclusion, Fintech.

JEL Classification: G20, G28, O31, O32, O33, R2.

I. Introduction

The word "FinTech" is a short form of Financial Technology that improves the dissemination financial services. In the 21st century[4], it was used primarily by technical employees in financial institutions like banks. However, since 2018, it has become consumer-oriented services (Kagan, 2023). Now, it avails financial services digitally, such as payments, insurance, and advances. Cryptocurrencies such as Bitcoin, and different sectors and industries like education, and retail banking are also providing digital services. In India, it started in 2015 (Paddalwar & P, 2022) but emerged as a critical issue in financial inclusion. Thus, traditional

[1] Professor, Department of Commerce, Vidyasagar University, Midnapore, West Bengal-721102, India. E-mail: pal.brajaballav@gmail.com

[2] Research Scholar, Department of Commerce, Vidyasagar University, Midnapore, West Bengal-721102, India. E-mail: jatinbasumatary1@gmail.com

[3] Assistant Professor, Department of Commerce, K.D. College of Commerce and General Studies, Midnapore, West Bengal, India. E-mail: biki21296@gmail.com

[4] https://www.investopedia.com/terms/f/fintech.asp

economic forces are still completely unavoidable. According to Maheshwari (2020), a collaborative effort between banks, regulatory authorities, and FinTech companies is required to expand financial inclusion properly. India is the fastest growing nation in adopting the FinTech ecosystem worldwide (Paddalwar & P, 2022) and has contributed to the growth of SDGs (Sustainable Development Goals) by 2030 (Surya & Naker, 2022). However, existing regulatory problems are the major concern. The adoption and usage of FinTech services may vary depending on various factors, such as demographic characteristics, awareness, trust, and preferences of the users.

New technologies, including machine learning (ML) or artificial intelligence (AI), predictive-behavioral analytics, and data-driven marketing are significantly influencing FinTech. FinTech assists customers by utilizing chatbots and AI interfaces to perform basic financial tasks including mobile payments, peer-to-peer (P2P) lending, crowdfunding, robo-advisors, digital banking, etc. (Dabbeeru & Rao, 2021). Thus, it has potentiality to enhance financial inclusion, efficiency, and convenience to consumers. Since the revolution of internet connectivity, the usage of FinTech has explosively grown. According to Surya & Naker (2022), India has achieved an average of eighty-seven percent account ownership, which is higher than the global average of seventy-six percent and ranked second position after China in worldwide (Surya & Naker, 2022).

Factors Influencing FinTech Adoption and Usage

Some of the common factors that affect FinTech adoption and usage are:

- **Perceived usefulness**: The degree to which users believe that using FinTech services will enhance their performance or outcomes.
- **Perceived ease of use**: The degree to which users believe that using FinTech services will be easy, user-friendly, or accessible.
- **Trust**: Users are more likely to adopt and use services if they trust them to be safe, trustworthy, or credible.
- **Financial literacy**: Users are more likely to adopt and use FinTech services if they have higher levels of financial literacy, awareness, or education.
- **Social influence**: FinTech service adoption is influenced by social opinions, behaviors, or expectations.
- **Regulatory environment**: The degree to which the legal, policy, and institutional frameworks support the development and adoption of FinTech services.

The study is broadly discussed in five sections. Section I includes introduction, followed by Section II and III which cover literature review and objectives, data and methodology. The penultimate section relates to the findings of the study, and finally, Section V addresses conclusion, limitation, and policy recommendations.

II. Literature Review

While adopting FinTech services, there is a significant impact of demographic characteristics in developing nations like India. It is significantly associated with income inequality (Demir *et al.*, 2022) and other demographic characteristics (Das & Das, 2020) in the state of Assam in India. The growth of financial inclusion can be achieved ensuring access to digital financial services. Tse *et al.* (2020), FinTech become a crucial aspect of economic growth by availing different financial services like savings, credit, insurance facility, etc. The people who are financially excluded (Dabbeeru & Rao, 2021) are availing banking service facilities. Currently, Singapore is leading digital financial inclusion globally and accelerated growing more than fifty percent by 2026 (Blitz, 2016). Jai Kisan (Prove, 2022), a digital platform is improving socio-economic status of marginal agricultural workers in Maharashtra (Wachira *et al.*, 2021) but the customer value addition is the key aspect in FinTech adoption (Singh *et al.*, 2020). Thus, the challenges of cost, complexity, and privacy elements are majorly affecting to users' intention (Kajol *et al.*, 2022). Whereas, in Jordan (Hu *et al.*, 2019) and in Côte d'Ivoire, users' intention towards FinTech adoption is gradually increasing since COVID-19 pandemic (Demirgüç-Kunt *et al.*, 2021; Yan *et al.*, 2023) as well as Indonesian women also adopted greatly (Setiawan *et al.*, 2023) but not by perceived by risk and trust (Kim, 2023). Thus, the irrelevant provisions have condensed confidence level and trusts (Rahi *et al.*, 2020) while accessing digital banking services (Hossain, 2019) in Pakistan. Moreover, conscientiousness, agreeableness, and openness to new experiences are also significantly influences (Agyei *et al.*, 2020; Lagarde, 2017) as per the studies in Nigeria and China (Akinwale & Kyari, 2020; Yu *et al.*, 2018). The structural equation modeling is also resulted influencing of trust to attitudes in FinTech adoption (Setiawan *et al.*, 2023). Moreover, perception and trust (Shree *et al.*, 2021), and information and communication technology (ICT) competitiveness, and demographic factors (Das & Das, 2020) greatly influences. In contrast, according to Asif *et al.* (2023) FinTech companies notably aided financial inclusion, especially people from rural areas. They are often deprived off due to lack of awareness, expensiveness and limitation of other infrastructure upgradation (Das & Das, 2020). According to Maheshwari (2020), Self-Help Groups (SHGs) has extended banking services in the remote rural areas through Electronic Benefits Transfer (EBT). The study on Central Banking and FinTech by Lagarde (2017) documented that virtual currencies provide P2P financial transactions to the clients and considered as a path for entering new companies that are user-friendly in unbanked and underserved areas (Prove, 2022). Inversely, it has proved a negative impact of demographic profile on digital financial performance of commercial banks (Wachira *et al.*, 2021) and small business entrepreneurs' (Alshari & Lokhande, 2022; Karsh & Abufara, 2020; Lv *et al.*, 2022) profitability. Therefore, a collaborative effort among FinTech industry players, governments, policymakers, and industry bodies required to formulate a healthy ecosystem. According to Singh *et al.* (2020), the barrier of internet connectivity and lack of awareness are the key factors that differs rural-urban areas to avail digital financial services in the state.

Research Gap

The several studies have explored the factors affecting the adoption and usage of FinTech services nationally and internationally. However, there is a lack of empirical evidence on how different demographic characteristics, such as age, gender, income, education, and occupation (Das & Das, 2020; Shree *et al.*, 2021) influences FinTech adoption, especially in the Biswanath district of Assam in India. Furthermore, much of the existing literature does not reflect the situations, where financial inclusion and digital literacy are still low. Therefore, more comprehensive and representative research is needed to find the impact of demographic characteristics on the usage of FinTech services, the components and users' future prospects.

Objectives of the Study

In this paper, we aim to analyze the impact of demographic characteristics on the usage of FinTech with the following objectives:

1. To analyze the impact of demographic characteristics on the usage of FinTech services for cashless transactions.
2. To analyze the impact of demographic characteristics on the usage of FinTech services during the COVID-pandemic.
3. To analyze the major components affecting the adaption of FinTech services.
4. To analyze the future prospects for using FinTech services in India.

Hypotheses framed

H_{A1}: There is no significant impact of demographic characteristics on the usage of FinTech services for cashless transactions.

H_{A2}: There is a significant impact of demographic characteristics on the usage of FinTech services for cashless transactions.

H_{B1}: There is no significant impact of demographic characteristics on the usage of FinTech services during COVID-19 pandemic.

H_{B2}: There is a significant impact of demographic characteristics on the usage of FinTech services during COVID-pandemic.

III. Data and Methodology

Sampling Method: The non-probability sampling method is applied in the present study.

Sources of Data: The required data are accessed from both primary and secondary sources. The primary data are gathered through field surveys and the secondary data are obtained from existing literature related to India and foreign countries, as well as other sources.

Tools of Survey: A structured questionnaire was developed for both online and offline surveys.

Sample Size: We conducted the survey with 105 active FinTech service users who have basic educational qualification from the Biswanath district of Assam in India.

Statistical tools: We employed frequency distributions, cross tabs, Pearson Chi-Square test, and Reliability test using MS Excel and IBM SPSS Statistics 25 for data analysis.

This study examines the influences of demographic characteristics, such as area/location, average monthly income level, education, gender, and occupation on adoption and usage of FinTech services both generally, and during COVID-19 pandemic. Moreover, the components of FinTech services and users' future prospects are discussed in the study.

IV. Findings of the study

Demographic Characteristics of Respondents

It has considered (Table 1) five demographic characteristics: area/location, average monthly income level, educational qualification, gender, and occupation. Forty one percent and 58 percent are from rural and urban areas, respectively. Forty one percent of users have an average monthly income level of Rs. 10001 to 20000, followed by 27 percent of Rs. 5001 to 10000. Only 22 percent of users' have average monthly income level of more than Rs. 20000, while 11 percent have Rs. 5000 or less. Moreover, 36 percent of users are graduates and 29 percent have secondary qualifications. Only 12 percent of users hold M.Phil./Ph.D. degree. Male users, at 67 percent, outnumber female users at 33 percent. Thirty one percent are unemployed, but looking for a job, followed by students at 30 percent. However, only 20 percent of users are employed in any sector except teaching.

Table 1: Demographic Characteristics

Demographic Characteristics	*Categories*	*Frequency*	*Percent*
Area/Location	Urban	44	42
	Rural	61	58
	Total	**105**	**100**
Average monthly income level (in Rs.)	0–5000	11	11
	5001–10000	28	27
	10001–20000	43	41
	More than 20000	23	22
	Total	**105**	**100**
Educational Qualification	Secondary	30	29
	Graduation	38	36
	Post Graduation	24	23
	M.Phil./Ph.D.	13	12
	Total	**105**	**100**
Gender	Male	70	67
	Female	35	33
	Total	**105**	**100**
Occupation	Student	31	30
	Unemployed but looking for job	32	31
	Employed in any sectors except teacher	21	20
	Teacher	21	20
	Total	**105**	**100**

Source: Primary data

Impact of demographic characteristics on the usage of FinTech services

The analysis of the impact of demographic characteristics on the usage of FinTech services for cashless transactions is based on the following hypothesis.

Null Hypothesis (H_{A1}): There is no significant impact of demographic characteristics on the usage of FinTech services for cashless transactions.

The following frequency (Table 2) demonstrates the usage of FinTech service, where 71 users use services "Sometimes" and 34 uses them on a "Daily" basis. The Pearson Chi-Square test determined the significant impact of demographic factors on usage of FinTech services over time. For the demographic characteristics of area/location (p=0.113>0.05) and gender (p=0.768>0.05), the p-values are greater than the 0.05 significance level. Therefore, we accept the null hypothesis and conclude that these two factors do not have significant impact on the usage of FinTech services. However, the p-values for the remaining demographic factors including average monthly income level (in Rs.) (p=.000<.05), education (p=.000<.05), and occupation (p=.000<.05), are significant at the 5 percent level' leading us to accept the alternative hypothesis. Hence, we conclude that these factors have significant influences on the usage of FinTech services.

Table 2: Cross tabs and Pearson Chi-Square Test

Demographic Characteristics	*Categories*	*Usage of FinTech Service*			
		Daily	*Sometimes*	*Total*	*Pearson Chi-Square Test (Σ2)*
Area/Location	Urban	18	26	44	χ^2 = 2.516, p = .113>.05
	Rural	16	45	61	
	Total	34	71	105	
Average monthly income level (in Rs.)	0 to 5000	3	8	11	χ^2 = 25.270, p = .000<.05
	5001 to 10000	1	27	28	
	10001 to 20000	14	29	43	
	More than 20000	16	7	23	
	Total	34	71	105	
Educational qualification	Secondary	5	25	30	χ^2 = 19.196, p = .000<.05
	Graduation	7	31	38	
	Post Graduation	14	10	24	
	M.Phil./Ph.D.	8	5	13	
	Total	34	71	105	
Gender	Male	22	48	70	χ^2= 0.087, p = .768>.05
	Female	12	23	35	
	Total	34	71	105	
Occupation	Student	5	26	31	χ^2=19.298, p = .000<.05
	Unemployed, but looking for job	8	24	32	
	Employed in any sectors, except teacher	15	6	21	
	Teacher	6	15	21	
	Total	34	71	105	

Source: Author's compilation

Impact of demographic characteristics on adoption of FinTech during COVID-19 pandemic

Null hypothesis (H_{C1})**:** There is no significant impact of demographic characteristics on usage of FinTech services during COVID-19 pandemic.

For this hypothesis, the Cross tabs (Table 3) has been employed where a total 34 respondents have started to use FinTech services after COVID-19 pandemic, followed by 33 respondents whose usage has increased during pandemic. However, 37 respondents were using it prior to pandemic. Out of the total respondents, 61 were from rural areas, which is more than the 44 respondents from urban areas. The least number of respondents do not use the services until now. The increase in the amount of average monthly income level is affecting the number of users of services respectively. There are only 11 users whose average monthly income level less than Rs. 5,000. Thus, the number of users with average monthly income levels of Rs. 5,001 to 10,000, Rs. 10,001 to 20,000, and more than Rs. 20,000 are 28, 43 and 23 respectively. The maximum number, i.e., 38 respondents, are graduates followed by 30 respondents with secondary educational qualifications. Twenty four respondents are post-graduates and 13 are M.Phil/Ph.D qualified. Out of the total, 70 users are male which is greater than the 35 female users. In case of occupation, 32 respondents are unemployed but looking for job, followed by 31 students, whereas 21 are employed but not as teachers and the same number employed as teachers. The p-values for areas and gender are greater at 5 percent significance level and are insignificant but the rest are significant.

Table 3: Cross Tabs and Pearson Chi-Square Test

Demographic Factors	*Categories*	*Usage of FinTech during COVID-19 Pandemic.*					*Pearson Chi-Square Test (Σ^2)*
		Yes. I Started Using After COVID-19 Pandemic	*Yes. My Usage Increased during COVID-19 Pandemic*	*No. I was Using Before COVID-19*	*No. I Don't Use Even Now*	*Total*	
Area/Location	Urban	10	19	15	0	44	$\Sigma^2 = 6.258$ p=.10>0.05
	Rural	24	14	22	1	61	
	Total	34	33	37	1	105	

Demographic Factors	*Categories*	*Usage of FinTech during COVID-19 Pandemic.*					*Pearson Chi-Square Test (Σ^2)*
		Yes. I Started Using After COVID-19 Pandemic	*Yes. My Usage Increased during COVID-19 Pandemic*	*No. I was Using Before COVID-19*	*No. I Don't Use Even Now*	*Total*	
Average monthly income level (in Rs.)	0 to 5000	9	1	1	0	11	Σ^2 = 53.330 p=.00<0.05
	5001 to 10000	9	1	17	1	28	
	10001 to 20000	6	28	9	0	43	
	More than 20000	10	3	10	0	23	
	Total	**34**	**33**	**37**	**1**	**105**	
Educational Qualification	Secondary	7	6	16	1	30	Σ^2 = 26.063 p=.00<0.05
	Graduation	17	13	8	0	38	
	Post Graduation	5	14	5	0	24	
	M.Phil./Ph.D.	5	0	8	0	13	
	Total	**34**	**33**	**37**	**1**	**105**	
Gender	Male	25	20	24	1	70	Σ^2 = 01.820 p=.61>0.05
	Female	9	13	13	0	35	
	Total	**34**	**33**	**37**	**1**	**105**	
Occupation	Student	22	6	3	0	31	Σ^2 = 87.859 p=.00<0.05
	Unemployed, but looking for job	8	10	13	1	32	
	Employed in any sectors, except teacher	4	17	0	0	21	
	Teacher	0	0	21	0	21	
	Total	34	33	37	1	105	

Source: Author's compilation

Analyzing the major components affecting in FinTech services adoption

Table 4: Major Components

Particulars	*Frequency*	*Percent*
Adaption new FinTech	11	10
Ease of usage	14	13
Speed Services	25	24
Uses-Friendly and Trust worthy services	55	52
Total	**105**	**100**

Source: Primary data

It has analysed the major components (Table 4) as the reasons for FinTech services adoption by users. Out of total 105 users, 55 adopted the services because they found them user-friendly and trustworthy followed by 25 users who adopted them for their speed. Fourteen users adopted them for ease of usage, whereas only 11 users adopted them for the new technology.

The above frequency distribution of components affecting in FinTech services adoption as shown below:

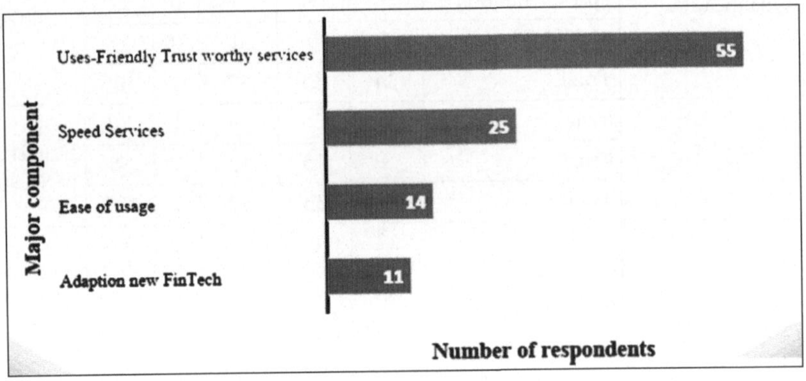

Figure 1: Major Components for FinTech Service Adoption

Analysing the Future Prospects for using FinTech Services

It has explored the future prospects for using FinTech services (Table 5). Twenty one percent of users preferred AI Powered financial assistance, followed by 19 percent who prioritized internet connectivity. The percentages for digital banking and financial inclusion are 16 percent and 15 percent, respectively. There is an equal preference for both cybersecurity and government regulation at 9 percent, while 7 percent prefer investment opportunities. Further, the ratio of users' preference for invisible forms of identification and wider adoption is also equal at 2 percent.

Table 5: Frequency Distribution (Multiple response)

Items/Particulars	*Frequency*	*Percent*
Financial Inclusion	51	15
AI Powered financial assistance	70	21
Invisible forms of Identification	05	02
Wider adoption	06	02
Investment opportunities	23	07
Cybersecurity	31	09
Digital Banking	52	16
Government Regulatory	31	09
Internet connectivity	62	19
Total	331	100

Source: Primary data

The reliability statistics (Table 6) measured the significance of internal-consistency between the items with the help of the value of Cronbach's Alpha. The Cronbach's Alpha represents the reliability coefficient which ranges from 0 to 1 (Kimberlin & Winterstein, 2008). A higher coefficient indicates a higher level of reliability among the items (George & Mallery, 2021; Kimberlin & Winterstein, 2008) and less random error (Nelson, 1980).

Table 6: Criteria of Reliability

Cronbach's Alpha Score (α)	*Level of Reliability*
>.90	Excellent
>.80	Good
>.70	Acceptable
>.60	Questionable
>.50	Poor
<.50	Unacceptable

(George & Mallery, 2021)

In the following reliability test, the initial Cronbach's Alpha value was 0.48 considering nine items, which was lower than the acceptable criteria for alpha values as shown above. Therefore, "AI Powered financial assistance" which had a higher alpha value of 0.690, was removed and we considered only eight items out of the original nine. Finally, we found the overall alpha value to be moderate and at an acceptable level of internal consistency among the items (Table 6).

Table 7: Reliability Statistics

Cronbach's Alpha	*No. of Items*
0.69	8

Source: Computed by researchers

In Table 7, the Cronbach's Alpha values for Financial Inclusion, Invisible forms of Identification, Wider adoption, Investment opportunities are slightly higher than the original value of 0.69, indicating that they do not contribute much to the scale's reliability and should be removed. However, the rest of the items have lower alpha values. Therefore, these items contribute to the reliability of the scales and should be retained to maintain internal consistency.

Table 8: Item-Total Statistics

Items/Particulars	*Scale Mean if Item Deleted*	*Scale Variance if Item Deleted*	*Cronbach's Alpha if Item Deleted*
Financial Inclusion	2.00	3.06	0.71
Invisible forms of Identification	2.44	3.56	0.71
Wider adoption	2.43	3.59	0.72
Investment opportunities	2.27	3.14	0.70
Cybersecurity	2.19	2.81	0.66
Digital Banking	1.99	2.20	0.54
Government Regulatory	2.19	2.81	0.66
Internet connectivity	1.90	2.10	0.50

Source: Author's compilation

V. Conclusion

The findings show that the majority of users are from rural areas, indicating the potential of FinTech services to reach the unbanked and under banked population. The average monthly income level also affected the highest proportion of users belonging to the middle-income group, making FinTech services more affordable and accessible. Using FinTech services requires a certain level of literacy and awareness. There are more male users than female, and many users are unemployed or student s. Further, the COVID-19 pandemic also affects the users. The crosstabs and Pearson chi-square test (Table 2) show that the demographic characteristics of area and gender did not impact on usage of FinTech services, except for income, education, and occupation. This result was similar during the COVID-19 pandemic (Table 3). User-friendly and trustworthy services as well as speedy services, are the most common components (Table 4) affecting the adoption of FinTech. Internet connectivity and digital banking are the most preferred issues (Table 7) when adopting FinTech services in the state of Assam.

Finally, these findings can help FinTech providers, policymakers and other stakeholders to understand the characteristics and behaviours of the FinTech users and design appropriate products and services including network connectivity and banking awareness to cater to their needs and expectations.

Limitation of the Study

The present study has considered adoption and usage of FinTech services in the Biswanath district of Assam. Only the active internet users having basic educational qualifications are considered as the sample size.

Policy Recommendation

The study will help to provide literature and a roadmap for potential implications of findings to policy-makers, practitioners, or future researchers. Additionally, it aids government, non-government organizations and others which eventually results in the holistic development and growth of FinTech services.

References

[1] Agyei, J., Sun, S., Abrokwah, E., Penney, E.K. and Ofori-boafo, R. (2020). Mobile Banking Adoption: Examining the Role of Personality Traits. *SAGE Open*, 1–15. https://doi.org/10.1177/2158244020932918

[2] Akinwale, Y.O. and Kyari, A.K. (2020). Factors influencing attitudes and intention to adopt financial technology services among the end-users in Lagos State, Nigeria. *African Journal of Science, Technology, Innovation and Development*, 1–8. https://doi.org/10.1080/20421338.2020.1835177

[3] Alshari, H.A. and Lokhande, M.A. (2022). The impact of demographic factors of clients' attitudes and their intentions to use FinTech services on the banking sector in the least developed countries. *Cogent Business & Management*, *9*(1). https://doi.org/10.1080/23311975.2022.2114305

[4] Asif, M., Khan, M.N., Tiwari, S., Wani, S.K. and Alam, F. (2023). The Impact of Fintech and Digital Financial Services on Financial Inclusion in India. *Journal of Risk and Financial Management*, *16*(2). https://doi.org/10.3390/jrfm16020122

[5] Blitz, D. (2016). *FinTech in India: A global growth story* (Issue June). www.KPMG.com/in

[6] Dabbeeru, R. and Rao, D.N. (2021). FinTech Applications in Banking and Financial Services Industry in India. *SSRN Electronic Journal*, 1–12. https://doi.org/10.2139/ssrn.3881967

[7] Das, A. and Das, D. (2020). Perception, Adoption, and Pattern of Usage of FinTech Services by Bank Customers: Evidences from Hojai District of Assam. *Emerging Economy Studies*, *6*(1), 7–22. https://doi.org/10.1177/2394901520907728

[8] Demir, A., Pesqué-cela, V., Altunbas, Y. and Murinde, V. (2022). FinTech, financial inclusion and income inequality: a quantile regression approach. *The European Journal of Finance*, *28*(1), 86–107. https://doi.org/10.1080/1351847X.2020.1772335

[9] Demirgüç-Kunt, A., Klapper, L., Singer, D. and Ansar, S. (2021). *Financial Inclusion, Digital Payments, and Resilience in the Age of COVID-19*. World Bank Publication. https://doi.org/10.1596/978-1-4648-1897-4

[10] George, D. and Mallery, P. (2021). *IBM SPSS Statistics 27 Step by Step: A Simple Guide and Reference* (Seventeent). Routledge. https://doi.org/10.4324/971003205333

[11] Hossain, A. (2019). Security perception in the adoption of mobile payment and the moderating effect of gender. *PSU Research Review*, *3*(3), 179–190. https://doi.org/10.1108/PRR-03-2019-0006

[12] Hu, Z., Ding, S., Li, S., Chen, L. and Yang, S. (2019). Adoption Intention of FinTech Services for Bank Users: An Empirical Examination with an Extended Technology Acceptance Model. *Symmetry*, *11*(340), 1–16. https://doi.org/10.3390/sym11030340

[13] Kagan, J. (2023). *Financial Technology (FinTech): Its Uses and Impact on Our Lives*. Amanda Bellucco-Chatham. https://www.investopedia.com/terms/f/FinTech.asp

[14] Kajol, K., Singh, R. and Paul, J. (2022). Technological Forecasting & Social Change Adoption of digital financial transactions: A review of literature and future research agenda. *Technological Forecasting & Social Change*, *184*(January), 121991. https://doi.org/10.1016/j.techfore.2022.121991

[15] Karsh, S.A. and Abufara, Y. (2020). The new era of financial technology in banking industry. *Journal of Southwest Jiaotong University*, *55*(4), 1–13. https://doi.org/10.35741/issn.0258-2724.55.4.54

[16] Kim, S. (2023). An overview of FinTech, pandemic and the financial system: challenges and opportunities. *In International Finance Review*, 3–9. https://doi.org/10.1108/s1569-376720220000022001

[17] Kimberlin, C.l. and Winterstein, almut G. (2008). Validity and reliability of measurement instruments used in research. *American Society of Health-System Pharmacy*, *65*(23), 2276–2284. https://doi.org/10.2146/ajhp070364

[18] Lagarde, C. (2017). Central Banking and FinTech: A Brave new World. *Innovations: Technology, Governance, Globalization*, *12*(1–2), 4–8. https://www-01.ibm.com/common/ssi/cgi-bin/ssialias?html- fid=WRL12345USEN.

[19] Lv, S., Du, Y. and Liu, Y. (2022). How Do FinTechs Impact Banks' Profitability? An Empirical Study Based on Banks in China. *FinTech 2022*, *1*, 155–163. https://doi.org/10.3390/FinTech102001

[20] Maheshwari, S. (2020). *The FinTech route to greater financial inclusion in India*. https://sustainabledevelopment.un.org/

[21] Nelson, A.A. (1980). Research Design: Measurement, Reliability, and Validity. *American Journal of Hospital Pharmacy*, *37*(6), 851–857. https://doi.org/10.1093/ajhp/37.6.851

[22] Paddalwar, S.S. and P, L. (2022). FinTech in India-Demographics affecting the FinTech services. *3rd International Conference on New Trends in Social Sciences*, 14–31. www.ntssconf.org

[23] Prove (2022). *Boosting Financial Inclusion in India: The FinTech Solution* (pp. 1–11).

[24] Rahi, S., Ghani, M.A. and Ngah, A.H. (2020). Factors propelling the adoption of internet banking: the role of e-customer service, website design, brand image and customer satisfaction. *Int. J. Business Information Systems, 33*(4), 549–569.

[25] Setiawan, B., Phan, T.D., Medina, J., Wieriks, M., Nathan, R.J. and Fekete-Farkas, M. (2023). Quest for financial inclusion via digital financial services (FinTech) during COVID-19 pandemic: case study of women in Indonesia. *Journal of Financial Services Marketing*, 1–15. https://doi.org/10.1057/s41264-023-00217-9

[26] Shree, S., Pratap, B., Saroy, R. and Dhal, S. (2021). Digital payments and consumer experience in India: a survey based empirical study. *Journal of Banking and Financial Technology, 5*(1), 1–20. https://doi.org/10.1007/s42786-020-00024-z

[27] Singh, S., Sahni, M.M. and Kovid, R.K. (2020). *What drives FinTech adoption? A multi-method evaluation using an adapted technology acceptance model. 2015.* https://doi.org/10.1108/MD-09-2019-1318

[28] Surya, N. and Naker, N. (2022). *Executive Summary* (II, Issue September). https://assets.ey.com/content/dam/ey-sites/ey-com/en_in/topics/consulting/2022/ey-winds-of-change-india-FinTech-report-2022.pdf?download

[29] Tse, T., Cosentino, A. and Esposito, M. (2020). 5 types of FinTech startups that can drive financial inclusion. *MIT Technology Review Insights*, 1–12. https://www.weforum.org/agenda/2020/08/financial-inclusion-FinTech-underbanked-technology

[30] Wachira, V.K., Kalui, F. and Gathii, J. (2021). Digital financial innovation services and their impact on the performance of commercial banks in Kenya. *European Journal of Economic and Financial Research, 5*(3), 19–22. https://doi.org/10.46827/ejefr.v5i3.1174

[31] Yan, C., Siddik, A.B., Akter, N. and Dong, Q. (2023). Factors influencing the adoption intention of using mobile financial service during the COVID-19 pandemic: the role of FinTech. *Environmental Science and Pollution Research, 30*(22), 61271–61289. https://doi.org/10.1007/s11356-021-17437-y

[32] Yu, L., Cao, X., Liu, Z., Gong, M. and Adeel, L. (2018). Understanding mobile payment users' continuance intention: a trust transfer perspective. *Internet Research*, 1–25. https://doi.org/10.1108/IntR-11-2016-0359

[33] https://www.investopedia.com/terms/f/fintech.asp

Climate Finance as a Way Towards Sustainability: The Indian Experience

Abhishek Dutta[1] **and Baitali Paul**[2]

ABSTRACT: The worldwide issue of climate change calls for enormous financial resources to shift global patterns of production and consumption. For poor nations, who are frequently the most susceptible to this problem, it is very expensive. Financing for climate change can help with this since it makes mitigation and adaptation possible. Climate finance refers to local, national, or international funding that is used to assist climate change adaptation and mitigation initiatives. This funding might come from public, private, or alternative sources of funding. Since major investments are needed to cut emissions, climate finance is necessary for mitigation. In this exploratory research, the authors have tried to throw light on the concept of climate finance, the trend of India's climate sector and the nature of climate equity funds during the period 2021–22.

India tries to reduce its overall emission through willing customers, climate tech business and supportive policy environment. All of these are targeting net-zero emissions by 2070. It was observed that equity funding for climate tech reduced in 2022 as compared to the previous year but the investment is diversified as debt financing picked up in renewables, FV recycling and the waste management. Post-pandemic, the need for climate finance is further enhanced which needs efforts from all concerned. Healthy climate will lead to sustainability. The road-map of the country has to be decided accordingly keeping in view the goal of sustainable development.

Keywords: Climate Equity Funds, Climate Finance, Sustainability.

Introduction

As a result of human activity, greenhouse gases (carbon dioxide and other gases) are released into the atmosphere during the production of goods and services. Global warming is ultimately caused by greenhouse gases that are released into the atmosphere by industries, transportation, food production, and fossil fuels. Emissions of greenhouse gases have an impact beyond borders and the nations that produce the pollution. Global warming is exposed as a result. Extreme weather conditions are becoming more likely due to greenhouse gas

[1] SACT-I, Department of Commerce, New Alipore College, Kolkata, India.
E-mail: abhishekdutta@newaliporecollege.ac.in

[2] SACT-I, Department of Commerce, New Alipore College, Kolkata, India.
E-mail: baitalipaul@newaliporecollege.ac.in

accumulation, according to the most recent assessment report from the International Panel on Climate Change. The average global temperatures rose near about 1°C which is quite alarming. As a result of such increment of temperature we frequently observed various natural disasters such as severe storms, drought and flood, low productivity of foodgrains which ultimately increased poverty and financial distress of an economy. To avoid such unwanted situations, leaders of major countries have taken various measures. The government of India have launched various project under these circumstances popularly known as National Action Plan for Climate Change (NAPCC) which aims to mitigate the adverse impact of climate change. In this backdrop the importance and necessity of climate finance is being realized gradually. Climate finance' is a multifaceted concept. In general, it refers to funding for initiatives meant to lessen or prepare for the effects of climate change. It is occasionally confused, nevertheless, with the closely linked and overlapping ideas of low-carbon finance, sustainable finance, and green finance.

Although there is no single definition of climate finance, the United Nations Framework Convention on Climate Change (UNFCCC) Standing Committee on Finance provides the closest thing to an official version: "Climate finance aims at reducing emissions and enhancing sinks of greenhouse gases and aims at reducing the vulnerability of, and maintaining and increasing the resilience of, human and ecological systems to negative climate change impacts." According to this definition, climate financing is the flow of money to any initiatives, programs, or projects aimed at addressing climate change, worldwide, encompassing all economic sectors and addressing both adaptation and mitigation.

The world is currently dealing with two major issues: COVID-19 and climate change. Many world leaders have praised India as a global leader for its efforts to combat COVID-19 and climate change. Donald Trump was among the many leaders who recognised India's role as a rising power in the battle against climate change. While the developed world's extremes are largely to blame for India's climate change crisis, there are also some internal factors at play, such as thermal power and agricultural policies. A poor agricultural policy exacerbates crop yield and climate change, with thermal power accounting for roughly 68% of all greenhouse gas emissions. Roughly 80% of groundwater is used for wheat and rice, and nearly 90% is used for irrigation. A study from a Japanese research institute claims that the measures to reduce poverty would cause a 50% rise in greenhouse gas emissions. However, this increase can be limited by implementing appropriate food, energy, and transportation policies.

Review of Literature

In recent years, scholars have focused a great deal of attention on the subject of climate finance and have investigated a number of research directions. Even though this research is extensive, it must be condensed in order to address the main themes, the way it developed, and the directions it should go in the future. According to Heal & Millner (2013), there are two types of sources of ambiguity: scientific (like the effect of atmospheric CO_2 concentrations on surface temperatures) and socioeconomic (like the fact that, even if we knew the model for the climate effects of CO_2, we would still be unsure about how societies react to these effects). analysing projections from multiple meta-analyses and climate studies. Brock & Hansen (2018) show how the top climate models' forecast distributions differ significantly from one another. The differences in parameter values within those models and in the temperature anomalies predicted by various models. Olijslagers & Van Wijnbergen (2019) suggest that damage uncertainty can be compared to a compound lottery. As long as relative risk aversion is greater than one, which is usually assumed in calibrations of macro and finance models, carbon mitigation gains significant value and raises the social cost of carbon in situations where the agent draws a particularly unfavourable damage parameter. In light of model uncertainty, Johannes, Lochstoer, and Mou (2016) observed that Bayesian economic agents gradually modify their assumptions about their surroundings as new data become available. Due to the martingale behaviour of Bayesian posteriors, these updates appear to the learner as constant shocks. According to Engle *et al.* (2020), agents that have recursive preferences are more vulnerable to these belief update shocks, which raises risk premia when compared to baseline models that don't have ambiguity or recursive utility. This "learning as a long-run risk" perspective informs the empirical analysis's assessment of climate risk through news arrival. Lemoine (2021) asserts that accounting for model uncertainty causes estimates of the social cost of carbon to increase above what they would otherwise be. When it comes to the economic damages brought on by rising temperatures, recursive preference models show that the social cost of carbon is ten times higher than in a model with the same preference structure but no ambiguity. The parameters governing climate-related economic damages are random variables when viewed through the lens of model uncertainty. Therefore, covariance between model parameters and agent consumption influences asset prices through a new channel that uncertainty creates. This leads to precautionary savings and risk premia effects in addition to the effects resulting from stochastic shocks in standard unambiguous models.

Research Gap

Studies conducted on climate finance are limited in number in the Indian context. Moreover, these studies were mainly published in newspapers and periodicals. As such, there is a lack of comprehensive study on climate finance in the Indian scenario.

Objective of the Study

In this exploratory research, the authors have tried to understand the concept of climate finance, the trend of India's climate sector and the nature of climate equity funds during the period 2021–22.

Data Source and Research Methodology

The nature of the study is "exploratory." The most recent research on this specific subject that is currently available in the form of books, journal articles, research projects, websites, and other materials forms the basis of the study's "exploratory" section.

Conceptual Framework on Climate Finance

The idea of 'climate finance' is a multifaceted. In general, it refers to funding for initiatives meant to lessen or prepare for the effects of climate change. Although there is no single definition of climate finance, the United Nations Framework Convention on Climate Change (UNFCCC) describes it as "Climate finance aims at reducing emissions and enhancing sinks of greenhouse gases and aims at reducing the vulnerability of, and maintaining and increasing the resilience of, human and ecological systems to negative climate change impacts." According to this definition, climate financing is the flow of money to any initiatives, programs, or projects aimed at addressing climate change, worldwide, encompassing all economic sectors and addressing both adaptation and mitigation.

Climate finance is a subset of environmental, or green finance. Green finance refers to funding for addressing all environmental issues, including climate change.

Need and Importance of Climate Finance

For countries to effectively address climate change, they must invest in both building resilience against climate change (e.g., constructing coastal defences and disaster response teams) and mitigating climate change (e.g., reforestation, land reforms, clean energy technologies, etc.). Estimates indicate that one percent of the world GDP would be needed in capital to achieve the SDG targets related to the environment. The Stern Committee's estimate is conditional on the fact that poor policies or postponed decisions would cause the amount of capital needed for remedial action to rise sharply. There is an estimated $30 billion shortfall in this yearly financing, according to recently available estimates. Achieving the planet-related SDG targets that each country set out in the Paris Agreement may be hampered by the disparity between capital requirements and availability. Reports are periodically submitted to the UNFCCC detailing the progress made towards these nation-specific targets, known as the nationally determined contribution (NDC). For developing nations with limited domestic resources, the impact of the financing gap on achieving NDCs is especially pronounced. To close the financing gap, developing nations must thus concentrate on luring capital. As a signatory to the Paris Agreement, India, for example, has acknowledged its responsibility to reduce carbon emissions. Each of the SDGs has particular goals that the nation has published, one of which is a one-third decrease in GDP's emission intensity by 2030 when compared to levels in 2005. India, a well-known emerging economy, can serve as an example for other developing nations looking to shift to cleaner production methods. For policymakers in India, raising the necessary funds to successfully shift the economy to a "greener" growth trajectory continues to be their top priority. Until 2030, there is expected to be a $565 billion annual shortfall in NDCs compared to a $960 billion requirement. This funding shortfall exceeds the $520 billion Indian government budgeted expenditure for 2022–2023.

Climate Finance – Indian Experience

India's climate finance requirements are estimated in many ways, but understanding those figures is challenging due to three main problems. First, estimates of the financing needs are probably influenced by the conceptual ambiguity surrounding the definitional aspects of climate finance, particularly the concept of additionality. For instance, The Economic Survey 2012–13, provided the first clear statement of domestic climate finance requirements when it projected that Rs. 230,000 crore (Rs. 2,300 billion) would be required to meet the NAPCC's mission objectives. The national missions prioritise sustainable development, with co-benefits including mitigation and adaptation to climate change. On the other hand, the opportunity cost to the economy of adopting a low-carbon growth pathway is quantified by the Planning Commission report, which estimates the total cost to the Indian economy of low-carbon strategies as US$ 834 billion (in constant 2011 dollars) over 20 years from 2011. Furthermore, as per preliminary estimates, India's Nationally Determined Contribution (NDC) states that, in order to meet its climate change actions between 2015 and 2030, the country will need to raise at least US$ 2.5 trillion. But it's not entirely clear from the document how this figure was determined.

Second, the methodology used to generate any of these estimates is not cited. An impartial assessment of India's NAPCC, for instance, notes that it is unclear how the figures for the financial estimates for some of the missions were determined. An additional study evaluating the State Action Plans on Climate Change (SAPCCs) found glaring disparities in the estimates provided by the various states and no objective standards for selecting the actions that should be prioritised.

Thirdly, these estimations were all made in various circumstances. As an illustration, the Economic Survey is a crucial government document that is used to prepare union budgets and, as such, represents the necessity of domestic resources for the execution of various plans and initiatives. India, on the other hand, submitted its Intended Nationally Determined Contribution (INDC) to the UNFCCC as part of a negotiation process prior to the 21st Conference of the Parties in Paris. The fact that India's NDC is conditional suggests that the availability of international climate finance will determine whether or not some of the targets are met.

These various cost estimates have different metrics, which makes it intrinsically difficult to compare them. Having some conceptually coherent formulation is part of the government's job, though, since these are all official estimates. India's current funding sources and amount for climate change initiatives have been mapped out in a number of different ways.

Three reasons why equity investments (and investors) will grow include the following:

1. **Limited Partners (LPs) like climate:** Investing in the climate is challenging, especially when compared to consumer or SaaS plays. VCs find it challenging to invest in climate startups because most of them have lengthy B2B sales cycles and are hardware plays with a lot of assets. Still, in the next two to three years, climate tech is likely to face numerous positive headwinds. Only a prompt from their limited partners (LPs) has the power to alter the VC playbook. Pension funds, sovereign investors, and family offices seeking to contribute capital to climate action have been our guests at meeting after meeting over the past year. In the beginning of 2023, a minimum of ten fund managers from India are cultivating funds with a climate focus. These new funds may be able to make longer-term, more pertinent investments for climate startups with mission-aligned limited partners.
2. **There is a significant pipeline of startups:** In the past two years, investors have frequently told us that there are simply not enough intriguing startups to invest in. That may be about to change, and quickly at that. In the past three years, 240 startups have raised a seed round. There is enough deal flow for the mid-to-late stage investors if even 30% of these go on to raise additional funding. At the same time, new businesses are starting to emerge. In India, there are 22,000 startups focused on agritech, green technologies, and renewable energy; this is a sizable pipeline for the numerous general partners (GPs) who are raising money for climate funds.
3. **Positive climate tech policies:** Long-term investors need a supportive policy environment (with climate tech investment horizons longer than the typical VC lifecycle). Positive developments occurred this year in a number of areas:

- The deadline for the ALMM (Approved List of Models and Manufacturers) has been extended, and solar policy appears to have finally stabilised following the ups and downs on net metering and open access.
- The EV industry has been granted several policy incentives.
- EPR regulations, which have been strengthened for plastics and electronic waste and will soon apply to batteries, will probably facilitate the development of a robust circular economy.

Debt Markets: in 2022, Domestic Lenders will Prosper

The previous year was among the busiest that the domestic debt markets have ever seen. In addition to expanding and diversifying into new markets like electric mobility, traditional project financiers have also been seen to develop a number of innovative solutions.

EVs in particular appear to have perfected the art of using a combination of asset leasing, lending, and other off-balance sheet strategies to turn an asset-heavy industry into something akin to a venture capital play. Due to the emergence of several venture debt players, working capital, which was previously a barrier to the growth of climate tech due to the lengthy B2B collection cycles, appears to be resolved as well. Lenders are able and willing to provide capital well in advance of profitability once you have achieved the goal of raising a successful equity round. However, debt still comes before equity.

Analysis and Findings

Climate equity funding reduced but diversified in 2022

Table 1: Sectoral Breakup of Equity Funding in Climate Tech in 2022

Sector	*Sustainable Agriculture*	*Waste & Circularity*	*Emerging Sectors*	*Energy Transition*	*Clean Mobility*	*Total Equity Funding in 2022*
Amount (in USD)	755 million	108 million	151 million	2.25 billion	1.44 billion	4.70 billion

Source: The State of Climate Finance Report in India 2023

Investments in industries other than renewables, which desperately need to expand, went up. Total equity funding in the year 2022 was around US $4.70 billion. Out of which in the energy transition the requirement of equity funding is highest as compared to other sectors. 12 billion USD in debt was attributed to renewables, most likely as a result of companies that focused on debt leverage in

2022 after large equity rounds in 2021. Renewables will continue to be the largest climate play for a while.

Table 2: Actual and Expected Installed Energy Capacity in India

Year	*Captive Energy Capacity*	*Renewable Energy Share*
2010	25.11 EJ	2.79 EJ
2020	31.48 EJ	5.12 EJ
2021	33.97 EJ	5.53 EJ
2030 (Projected from stated policies)	43.71 EJ	9.59 EJ
2050 (Projected from stated policies)	46.33 EJ	23.87 EJ

Source: IEA World Energy Outlook 2022

From the above table it is seen that the usage of renewable energy is increased day by day projected from the stated policies.

The future of climate finance: what the road to 2030 looks like

In order to meet its climate goals by 2030, India is expected to require roughly a trillion dollars, or roughly USD 120 billion in new investments annually, according to estimate from last year. According to other reports, the difference could be as high as USD 170 billion annually.

Table 3: Renewable Energy Capacity Trends in India (in GW)

Year	*Renewable Energy Capacity*	*Solar*	*Wind*
2020	73 GW	35 GW	38 GW
2021	89 GW	40 GW	49 GW
2022	105 GW	63 GW	42 GW
2030 (Targeted)	450 GW	280 GW	170 GW

Source: Ministry of New and Renewable Energy, Government of India

For a few years now, solar energy has been the top technology and investment choice. On the other hand, 2022 saw a number of investments in platforms and wind energy companies that were developing solar and wind hybrid projects. The emergence of solar/wind hybrid projects was the driving force behind this. Although India's obsession with coal is unlikely to fade anytime soon, hybrid energy projects are more reliable and economically viable than standalone solar and wind farms.

Table 4: Different Sources of Climate Finance

		Sources of Capital			
		Domestic Capital	*Concessional Climate Finance*	*Developmental Financial Institution*	*Private Capital*
Climate Finance needed, $ billions	Business as used capital	$22 bn	$1 bn	$2 bn	$7 bn
	New funds to be raised	$38 bn	$8 bn	$9 bn	$33 bn

Source: The State of Climate Finance Report in India 2023

By 2030, India will require roughly a trillion dollars, or roughly USD 120 billion in new investments annually, to meet its climate goals. When broken up into potential sources of capital, the numbers do not look as daunting. Additional domestic capital is only about 1% of India's GDP. It is entirely possible that our USD 120 billion estimate itself is understated - we do believe it captures climate mitigation adequately, but additional spends will likely be needed as adaptation becomes a priority.

Concluding Observations

(a) In 2022, the total amount of equity funding was approximately $4.70 billion.

(b) Change in energy when compared to other industries, the demand for equity funding is the highest.

(c) Renewable energy was linked to $12 billion USD in debt, most likely as a result of businesses that prioritised debt leverage in 2022 following significant equity rounds in 2021.

(d) As predicted by the policies mentioned, the use of renewable energy is growing day by day.

(e) Several investments were made in wind energy companies and platforms that were working on hybrid solar and wind projects in 2022. This was primarily caused by the rise of hybrid solar/wind projects.

(f) Compared to standalone solar and wind farms, hybrid energy projects are more dependable and financially feasible.

References

[1] Brock, W.A. and Hansen, L.P. (2018). Wrestling with uncertainty in climate economic models. *Work. Pap.* 2019–2071, Becker Friedman Inst. Econ., Univ. Chicago.

[2] Engle, R.F., Giglio, S., Kelly, B., Lee, H. and Stroebel, J. (2020). Hedging climate change news. *Rev. Finance. Stud.,* 33(3):1184–216.

[3] Heal, G. and Millner, A. (2013). Uncertainty and decision in climate change economics. NBER Working Paper, 18929.

[4] Johannes, M., Lochstoer, L.A. and Mou, Y. (2016). Learning about consumption dynamics. *J. Finance,* 71(2). 551–600.

[5] Lemoine, D. (2021). The climate risk premium: how uncertainty affects the social cost of carbon. *J. Assoc. Environ. Res. Econ.,* 8(1). 27–57.

[6] Olijslagers, S. and van Wijnbergen, S. (2019). Discounting the future: on climate change, ambiguity aversion and Epstein Zin preferences. Discussion Paper. 19-030/VI, Tinbergen Inst., Amsterdam.

[7] Raptis, E., Oberschelp, C. and Pfister, S. (2020). The greenhouse gas emissions, water consumption, and heat emissions of global steam-electric power production: A generating unit level analysis and database. *Environmental Research Letters,* 15(10), 104029, 2020.

Insurance Penetration and Insurance Density in India: An Analysis

Iqbal Abdul Latif[1] and Abhishek Dutta[2]

ABSTRACT: The insurance sector is an important segment of the economy. Applying the mechanism of individuals as well as business houses mitigates their financial risk. In addition to serving as a financial mediator and mobilizer of funds, the insurance industry also encourages investment activity. It can have an important contribution to a nation's economic development, and economic progress in and of itself can encourage the insurance industry's expansion. The degree of development of the insurance sector in a nation is indicated by the penetration rate. The ratio of the premium underwritten in a given year to GDP is used to calculate the penetration rate. On the other hand, insurance density refers to the ratio of premiums collected by insurance companies to the country's population. It is observed that Insurance penetration in India during 2021–22 was 4.2 per cent remained the same as in 2020–21. On the other hand, Insurance density in India increased from USD 78 in 2020–21 to USD 91 in 2021–22. The level of insurance density has reported a consistent increase from USD 11.5 in 2001–02 to USD 64.4 in the year 2010–11. After some ups and downs, insurance density recorded a steady increase from the year 2016–17. Life insurance density has increased from USD 9.1 in 2001–02 to USD 69 in 2021–22. Whereas a rise in non-life insurance density from USD 2.4 to USD 22 has occurred throughout the same period, In this exploratory research, the researchers tried to describe the national and international scenario of the insurance sector in terms of insurance penetration and density for the period 2021–22.

Keywords: Financial Risk, Insurance Density, Insurance Penetration, Insurance Sector.

Introduction

With current prices, India's GDP is predicted to reach 272.41 lakh crore in 2022–2023 compared to 234.71 lakh crore in 2021–2022, representing a 16.1% growth rate. The rate of gross domestic saving as percent to gross national disposable income (GNDI) surged to 30 per cent in 2021–22 from 28.4 percent in the preceding year, led by lower dissaving of the general

[1] Assistant Professor, Department of Chemistry, New Alipore College, Kolkata, India. E-mail: iqbal.a.latif@gmail.com

[2] SACT – Category I, Department of Commerce, New Alipore College, Kolkata, India. E-mail: dabhishek108@gmail.com

government sector, which offset the drop in household savings. The global economy continues to slowdown and inflation remains a primary global macroeconomic concern. Despite such challenges, the insurance industry is expected to remain resilient. Over the years, India's life insurance market has consistently seen an increase in premiums. With premium income of 7.83 lakh crore in 2022–2023, the life insurance sector saw growth of 12.98 percent.

The private sector life insurers have clocked a growth of 16.34 per cent in premium, while the public sector life insurer recorded 10.90 per cent growth in premium. The goal of the IRDAI is to improve penetration and restructure the nation's insurance market.

The primary objective of these efforts is to enhance availability, accessibility, and affordability of insurance for all citizens and businesses. Towards this objectified has taken various steps to promote healthy growth of the insurance industry.

- **Easy access for new entrants into the insurance industry:** To make the integration easier, the Single Window NOC Portal (www.noc.irdai.gov.in) was introduced.
- **Quick launch of Insurance Products:** Insurers can now launch all Health & General Insurance products, as well as the majority of Life Insurance products, without seeking prior approval from IRDAI.
- **Ease of doing business:** IRDAI has taken several actions to lessen the burden of compliance.
- **Addressing dynamic needs of the industry:** IRDAI has facilitated various measures as per the evolving needs of the sector, such as Tech-based add-ons IRDAI has brought in following key changes in the regulatory framework to promote ease of doing business.
  - The IRDAI (Registration of Indian Insurance Companies) Regulations, 2022 introduced flexibility for insurers by making Special Purpose Vehicle (SPV) investments optional for Private Equity (PE).
  - IRDAI (Assets, Liabilities and Solvency Margin of General Insurance Business) Regulations, 2022- With a view to increase crop insurance penetration and efficient use of capital by general insurers.

In order to pay claims, cover administrative expenses, and turn a profit, the insurance company sets the policy pricing, or premiums, accordingly. Utilizing mortality data produced by actuaries, the cost of insurance is determined. Statistics-based tables that display the anticipated yearly death rates of individuals at various ages are called mortality tables. Insurance firms use the mortality tables to measure risk and adjust premiums based on age, since people are more likely to die as they age. In order to the control of taxes, such estimations may be important.

In the 1980s and 1990s, the SOA 1975–80 Basic Select & Ultimate tables were the typical reference points, while the 2001 VBT and 2001 CSO tables were published more recently. The updated data include distinct mortality tables for smokers and non-smokers in addition to the standard demographics of age and gender. The CSO figures also provide separate tables for favoured classes.

The applicant's health and family history are also considered when determining the cost of insurance, while the mortality figures serve as a starting point (except in the case of Group policies). We refer to this inquiry and the assessment that comes from it as underwriting. Questions about lifestyle and health are posed, and some answers may call for more research.

Literature Review

Kshetrimayum (2011) examined the effects of privatization and the function that private enterprises performed in the Indian insurance sector. Additionally, the author examined the insurance penetration between 1999 and 2009 and concluded that there is a direct relationship between insurance density and GDP performance.

Raja (2012) observed significant changes made to the Indian insurance industry between 2001 and 2010. He believed that the growth of the insurance industry depends on the country's general economic development and that the Indian government must act to create jobs across a range of industries to support the sector.

Insurance Times Magazine (2012) reported that in 2010, India's life insurance penetration above the global average. It went on to say that the total average is higher than that of Brazil, Russia, and the majority of other Asian nations, such as Bangladesh, Pakistan, China, and Sri Lanka.

Insurance Times Magazine (2013) expressed the opinion that there is a correlation between the GDP of the nation and the penetration of insurance. The penetration of insurance rises proportionately with each unit increase in GDP.

Insurance Times Magazine (2018) compared insurance penetration worldwide and stated that one of the main causes of this low level of insurance is that insurance prices rise in tandem with the frequency of natural disasters like flooding. Consequently, insurance deters less-at-risk individuals, governments, and corporations from getting it.

Objectives of the Study

In this exploratory research, the researchers tried to describe the national and international scenario of the insurance sector in terms of insurance penetration and density for the period 2002–22.

Data Source and Research Methodology

The secondary data used in the study was gathered from IRDA journal, articles and annual reports. Additionally, a few websites have also been considered. The paper's dataset spans the years 2002 through 2022.

Conceptual Framework of Insurance Penetration and Density

Among other measures, insurance penetration and density are often used to evaluate the degree of development of an insurance sector in a nation. Insurance density is computed as the ratio of premium to population (per capita premium), whereas insurance penetration is defined as the percentage of insurance premiums to GDP.

Discussion

Table 1: International Comparison of Insurance Penetration

(In Percentage)

S. No.	*Country*	*2021*			*2022*		
		Life	*Non-Life*	*Total*	*Life*	*Non-Life*	*Total*
America							
1.	USA	2.6	9.1	11.7	2.6	9.0	11.6
2.	Canada	3.3	4.8	8.1	3.3	4.6	8.0
3.	Brazil	2.1	1.7	3.9	2.1	1.9	4.0
4.	Mexico	1.2	1.3	2.5	1.1	1.3	2.4
5.	Argentina	0.3	1.9	2.2	0.2	1.8	2.0
Europe-Middle East-Africa							
6.	South Africa	10.0	2.2	12.2	9.1	2.2	11.3
7.	UK	8.9	2.2	11.1	8.1	2.4	10.5
8.	Sweden	5.8	1.9	7.6	7.5	1.8	9.3
9.	France	6.1	3.4	9.5	5.5	3.3	8.7
10.	Netherlands	1.4	7.7	9.1	1.2	7.3	8.5
11.	Italy	6.9	2.2	9.1	5.8	2.2	8.0
12.	Switzerland	3.1	4.0	7.1	3.0	4.0	6.9
13.	Germany	2.6	3.9	6.5	2.4	3.5	5.9
14.	Spain	2.0	3.2	5.1	2.0	2.8	4.9
15.	Turkey	0.2	1.1	1.3	0.2	1.3	1.5
16.	Saudi Arabia	0.1	1.3	1.3	0.0	1.2	1.3

S. No.	Country	2021			2022		
		Life	*Non-Life*	*Total*	*Life*	*Non-Life*	*Total*
17.	Russia	0.4	0.9	1.3	0.3	0.6	0.9
Asia Pacific							
18.	Taiwan	11.6	3.2	14.8	8.2	3.1	11.4
19.	South Korea	5.8	5.2	10.9	5.4	5.8	11.1
20.	Singapore	7.5	1.8	9.3	7.4	1.8	9.2
21.	Japan	6.1	2.2	8.4	5.9	2.3	8.2
22.	Thailand	3.4	1.9	5.4	3.4	1.9	5.3
23.	Malaysia	3.9	1.4	5.3	3.7	1.3	5.0
24.	Australia	1.0	3.5	4.4	0.9	3.3	4.2
25.	India	3.2	1.0	4.2	3.0	1.0	4.0
26.	China	2.1	1.9	3.9	2.0	1.9	3.9
27.	New Zealand	0.8	4.0	4.8	0.8	3.0	3.8
28.	Indonesia	1.1	0.5	1.6	0.9	0.5	1.4
29.	Pakistan	0.5	0.2	0.7	0.6	0.3	0.8
	World	3.0	3.9	7.0	2.8	4.0	6.8

Source: Swiss Re, Sigma Reports on World Insurance 4/2022 and 3/2023
Note: Insurance penetration is measured as ratio of premium (in US Dollars) to GDP (in USD).

In the American Zone, most of the countries preferred non-life insurance than life insurance for the year 2021 and 2022 out of which USA is the best-performing country for both 2021 and 2022 in terms of insurance penetration. Most of the countries in Europe-Middle East-African zone and Asia Pacific zone preferred life insurance than non-life insurance for the year 2021 and 2022. South Africa and Taiwan have the highest insurance penetration among other country in the respective groups for both 2021 and 2022.

Table 2: International Comparison of Insurance Density

(In USD)

S. No.	Country	2021			2022		
		Life	*Non-Life*	*Total*	*Life*	*Non-Life*	*Total*
America							
1.	USA	1,837	6,356	8,193	2,017	6,868	8,885
2.	Canada	1,697	2,520	4217	1,840	2,552	4,392
3.	Brazil	160	130	290	184	168	352
4.	Argentina	31	207	238	29	252	281

S. No.	Country	2021			2022		
		Life	Non-Life	Total	Life	Non-Life	Total
5.	Mexico	115	131	247	118	146	265
Europe-Middle East-Africa							
6.	Switzerland	2,866	3,744	6,610	2,730	3,634	6,364
7.	Sweden	3,478	1,119	4,597	4,203	976	5,180
8.	UK	4,234	1,039	5,273	3,669	1,111	4,781
9.	Netherlands	805	4,497	5,301	657	4,074	4,731
10.	France	2,654	1,486	4,140	2,239	1,339	3,578
11.	Germany	1,321	1,992	3,313	1,182	1,699	2,881
12.	Italy	2,467	785	3,253	1,966	750	2,716
13.	Spain	591	960	1,551	601	832	1,433
14.	South Africa	698	154	852	614	149	764
15.	Saudi Arabia	13	299	312	14	393	407
16.	Turkey	22	102	124	21	133	154
17.	Russia	49	111	160	47	87	134
Asia Pacific							
18.	Singapore	5,414	1,327	6,742	6,074	1,489	7,563
19.	Taiwan	3,772	1,032	4,804	2,656	1,006	3,662
20.	South Korea	1,971	1,764	3,735	1,705	1,836	3,541
21.	Australia	623	2,195	2,817	609	2,149	2,758
22.	Japan	2,347	855	3,202	1,942	748	2,690
23.	New Zealand	403	1,936	2,339	373	1,395	1,768
24.	Malaysia	444	157	600	432	159	592
25.	China	253	229	482	255	234	489
26.	Thailand	246	141	387	235	134	469
27.	India	69	22	91	70	22	92
28.	Indonesia	48	22	70	43	26	68
29.	Pakistan	7	4	11	8	4	12
	World	382	492	874	354	499	853

Source: Swiss Re, Sigma Reports on World Insurance 4/2022 and 3/2023
Note: Insurance penetration is measured as ratio of premium (in US Dollars) to Total Population.

In respect of per capita premiums, in American Zone and Europe-Middle East-African zone most of the countries preferred non-life insurance over life insurance for the year 2021 and 2022 out of which the USA is the best-performing country for both 2021 and 2022 in terms of insurance density. In the Asia Pacific zone most of the countries preferred life insurance than non-life insurance for the year 2021 and 2022. In the Europe-Middle East-African zone countries like Switzerland, Netherlands, Germany, Spain, Saudi Arabia, Turkey and Russia the greater density in nonlife insurance than life insurance.

Table 3: Penetration of Life and Non-Life Insurance in India

(in percentage)

Year	*Life*	*Non-Life*	*Total*
2002	2.15%	0.56%	2.71%
2003	2.59%	0.67%	3.26%
2004	2.26%	0.62%	2.88%
2005	2.53%	0.64%	3.17%
2006	2.53%	0.61%	3.14%
2007	4.10%	0.60%	4.70%
2008	4.00%	0.60%	4.60%
2009	4.00%	0.60%	4.60%
2010	4.60%	0.60%	5.20%
2011	4.40%	0.71%	5.11%
2012	3.40%	0.70%	4.10%
2013	3.17%	0.78%	3.95%
2014	3.10%	0.80%	3.90%
2015	2.60%	0.70%	3.30%
2016	2.72%	0.72%	3.44%
2017	2.72%	0.77%	3.49%
2018	2.76%	0.93%	3.69%
2019	2.74%	0.97%	3.71%
2020	2.82%	0.94%	3.76%
2021	3.20%	1.00%	4.20%
2022	3.20%	1.00%	4.20%

Source: www.statista.com

From the above table, it can be observed that, most of the Indian citizen preferred life insurance than non-life insurance over years. In case of life insurance from the year 2002 to 2010 the penetration has been increased there after a downfall noticed upto the year 2020. In the year 2021 and 2022 a steady increase has been noticed. In case non-life insurance, a steady growth has been observed from the year 2015.

Table 4: Density of Life and Non-life Insurance in India

(Premium per capita in U.S dollars)

Year	*Life*	*Non-Life*	*Total*
2002	9.1	2.4	11.5
2003	11.7	3.0	14.7
2004	12.9	3.5	16.4
2005	15.7	4.0	19.7
2006	18.3	4.4	22.7
2007	33.2	5.2	38.4
2008	40.4	6.2	46.6
2009	41.2	6.2	47.4
2010	44.7	6.7	51.4
2011	55.7	8.7	64.4
2012	49.0	10.5	59.5
2013	42.7	10.5	53.2
2014	41.0	11.0	52.0
2015	44.0	11.0	55.0
2016	43.2	11.5	54.7
2017	46.5	13.2	59.7
2018	55.0	18.0	73.0
2019	55.0	19.0	74.0
2020	58.0	19.0	77.0
2021	59.0	19.0	78.0
2022	69.0	22.0	91.0

Source: www.statista.com

In respect of per capita premiums, there is near about a steady growth observed over years for both in life insurance and non-life insurance sector.

Suggestions for improvement of Insurance Penetration and Insurance Density in Indian Insurance Sector

- Every government should prioritise boosting insurance activity while also ensuring insurance penetration and density via a study on the factors that contribute to its growth.
- Nowadays people are required to have serious concerns about issues like health conditions, the environment, social life support and financial protection. Therefore, it is important to keep in mind to avoid the misconception that young and healthy people do not require financial protection when it comes to their health.
- The life insurance premium is recommended to be equipped with a saving package.
- The life insurance provider should effectively explain the package with accurate information which is delivered in a language and in a context that is easily understood by all walks of life, will have a better impact on increasing understanding and knowledge of life insurance products. In addition, the package coverage may also increase the health care access such as include to outpatient care.

Concluding Observations

- In the American Zone, most of the countries preferred non-life insurance than life insurance for the year 2021 and 2022.
- USA is the best-performing country in American zone for both 2021 and 2022 in terms of insurance penetration.
- Most of the countries in Europe-Middle East-African zone and Asia Pacific zone preferred life insurance than non-life insurance for the year 2021 and 2022.
- South Africa and Taiwan have the highest insurance penetration among other country in the respective groups for both 2021 and 2022.
- In respect of per capita premiums, we can say that in American Zone and Europe-Middle East-African zone, most of the countries preferred non-life insurance over life insurance for the year 2021 and 2022.
- Out of countries in American zone, the USA is the best-performing country for both 2021 and 2022 in terms of insurance density.
- In the Asia Pacific zone most of the countries preferred life insurance than non-life insurance for the year 2021 and 2022.
- In the Europe-Middle East-African zone countries like Switzerland, Netherlands, Germany, Spain, Saudi Arabia, Turkey and Russia the greater density in nonlife insurance than life insurance.
- Most of the Indian citizen preferred life insurance than non-life insurance over years.

- In respect to insurance penetration and per capita premiums, there is near about a steady growth observed over years for both in life insurance and non-life insurance sectors in India.

References

[1] Asaduzzaman, M., Hamid, M.K. and Afrin, S. (2014). Corporate Environmental Reporting (CER) practices: empirical evidence from selected non-financial companies in Bangladesh. *International Journal of Business and general Management*, *3*(1), 1–8.

[2] IRDA Annual Report 2021–22.

[3] IRDA Annual Report 2022–23.

[4] Insurance Times Magazine (2012).

[5] Insurance Times Magazine (2013).

[6] Insurance Times Magazine (2018).

[7] Sastry, D.V.S. (2011). Life insurance penetration in India, *Journal of Social and Economic Policy, 8*(2), 207–215.

Illuminating the Dark Corners of Fintech Through Review of Literature

Sampriti Dey[1], Sourav Misra[2] and Dipa Banerjee[3]

ABSTRACT: The world of finance has changed due to the quick development of fintech, which offers previously uncommon ease of use and effectiveness. But there are dark sides to this rapidly changing technology as well. Like the dual nature of fintech, this study is on the darker side of fintech which means the challenging part of financial technology. This work is based on a study of literature review. In the banking industry, the rise of technology brought a huge positive change on the other hand it also has some possible hazards as well as unfavourable consequences due to advancement of technology. The dark side of fintech also means how people are exclusive to using fintech. This study will look into identifying many problems that the shadowy side of fintech presents, significant structural hazards, or risks involved in the rise of fintech through a review of literature.

Keywords: Challenges, Dark Corners, Financial Technology, Fintech.

Introduction

Fintech's launch and broad acceptance have upended established banking paradigms and give customers and companies creative, effective options. The goal of this shift in the financial services industry is to improve client satisfaction in general, cut expenses, and make financial services more accessible. Fintech is positioned to influence the direction of finance and add to a technologically sophisticated, more linked global financial environment as it develops. Fintech creates accessible, intuitive, and effective financial services by utilizing advances in fields like blockchain technology, analytics of data, AI, and mobile computing. Fintech has a lot to offer the financial industry in terms of innovations, advances, and benefits, but it also has a "dark side" that includes risks, obstacles, and moral dilemmas. This dark side illuminates the possible drawbacks and unfavourable effects linked to the quick development and uptake of financial technology. According to (*Puschmann, T. 2017)*, financial services are impacted greatly by

[1] Ex-Student, Department of Business Administration, Vidyasagar University, India. E-mail: sampritidey2819@gmail.com

[2] Ex-Student, Department of Business Administration, Vidyasagar University, India. E-mail: souravggpme@gmail.com

[3] Assistant Professor, Department of Business Administration, Vidyasagar University, India. E-mail: dipa.2003@gmail.com

digitalization. The fact that financial goods are nearly entirely information-based is one of the main causes. As an illustration, credit agreements or payment transactions, which, in contrast when buying an automobile, generally don't include any tangible elements. Another factor is that the majority of procedures like online payments, for instance, are practically totally carried out devoid of any human contact. Relief from investing in stocks includes several tangible types of engagement like consumer advisement.

Shifting the way that consumers behave in the past few years, consumer adoption of digital engagement mediums has increased, forcing numerous banking services suppliers to scale back their agency and subsidiary operations and rearrange their distribution administration in a way that dual relationship with customers and increased self-interest amenities (*Nueesch et al. 2015).* Financial technology is an emerging field that has grown during the past ten years from the lengthy trend of digitalization finance mixed with data collection and emerging technologies like online storage, blockchain technology, big data, and artificial intelligence (AI). This trend of data collection and digitalization mixed with technological advances occurs in established worldwide marketplaces, sometimes much more quickly in developing and expanding markets. This study is done over thorough research of literature, challenges related to technology and cyberattacks are now developing into significant hazards to national security and economic health. Combining literature review from many sources and fields, such as technology, ethics, and finance, to create a comprehensive picture of the many problems that the shadowy side of fintech presents.

Even while financial technology has possibilities, it's feasible to overlook the alleged hazards related to certain potential Fintech remedies. These incidents may increase the hazards associated with working digitally. Additionally, there aren't a few coordinated global laws governing the implementation of fintech. The provision of financial products and services has led to a notable expansion in financial technology. The widespread acceptance of fintech is significantly hampered by the rising hazards. The hazards associated with using financial technology to provide financial assistance were identified by this study. The data demonstrates that the fintech movement causes the development of numerous hazards, including operational risk, cyber risk, strategic risk, and regulatory risk. This research looked into whether there is an adverse association among the desire to embrace fintech and the ongoing fintech revolution. It impacted as a result of new hazards. People are hesitant to adopt because they are afraid of the hazards involved. Auditors in fintech organizations can lower these risks considerably by using strong security measures (*Saleem, 2021*).

Objectives of the Study

- To create a comprehensive picture through a review of literature of the many problems that the shadowy side of fintech presents.

- To identify areas that need extra attention in the creation and implementation of financial technology.
- To understand unintentional consequences.

Problem Statement

Identifying the challenges or risk factors of fintech through a review of literature by the authors of this paper.

Fintech

Fintech is a term that comes from combining the words technology and finance. It is a multidisciplinary field that mixes technology administration, innovation, and finance to describe the relationship between internet-related technology and financial services business service operations like banking trading and lending of funds (*Giglio, 2021).*

Elements of Fintech

These are some of the elements of fintech:

Digitalized Payments, by offering digital payment options, fintech has completely changed the way we conduct business. Peer-to-peer communication payment apps, electronic payment technologies, and mobile wallets have grown in popularity because they provide consumers with easy and safe ways to handle their finances.

Internet Banking, without physical locations, digital-only or online banks offers a comprehensive variety of banking services. These organizations use technology to provide clients with a banking experience that is more flexible, affordable, and accessible.

Insurance technology is the application of technology to improve and expedite the insurance sector in a number of ways. This covers usage-based insurance, electronic settlements, and risk evaluation using data analytics.

Artificial Intelligence (AI) and Machine Learning (ML), these two technologies are vital to the fintech industry because they enable chatbots that assist customers, improve fraud detection, and offer sophisticated data analytics that reveal market trends and consumer preferences.

Big Data Analytics, by using big data to evaluate enormous databases, fintech organizations may provide more precise risk evaluations, individualized financial services, and informed choices.

In landscape of fintech is evolving continuously there are numerous elements involved in financial technology.

Comparison of Fintech Adoption Globally

	Money transfer and payments		Financial planning		Savings and investments		Borrowing		Insurance	
1	China	83%	China	22%	China	58%	China	46%	India	47%
2	India	72%	Brazil	21%	India	39%	India	20%	UK	43%
3	Brazil	60%	India	20%	Brazil	29%	Brazil	15%	China	38%
4	Australia	59%	US	15%	US	27%	US	13%	South Africa	32%
5	UK	57%	Hong Kong	13%	Hong Kong	25%	Germany	12%	Germany	31%

Figure 1: Comparison of Fintech Adoption Globally
(*Source:* ey-fintech-adoption-index-2017)

The above figure shows the average proportion of respondents in each market who stated they have used one or more FinTech services falls into each of the following figures as per the EY fintech adoption index 2017. According to the EY fintech adoption index 2017, the fintech service money transfer and payments are mostly used by China that is 83% then India used 72%, Brazil 60%, Australia 59% and lowest UK 57%. The fintech service financial planning are mostly used by 22%, then Brazil 21%, India 20%, US 15% and lowest Hong Kong 13%. The fintech service savings and investments highest used in China that is 58%, then India 39%, Brazil 29%, US 27% and Hong Kong 25% lowest. The fintech service borrowings highest used in China 46%, then India 20%, Brazil 15%, US 13% and Germany 12% lowest one to use this fintech service. The fintech service insurances are mostly used by India that is 47%, then UK 43%, China 38%, South Africa 32% and lowest by Germany 31%.

From the EY fintech adoption index 2017, the chart shows the highest fintech adoption done by China, in second position India, third position Brazil, UK, Australia, US, Germany, Hong Kong and South Africa accordingly.

Technology advancements, especially artificial intelligence (AI), are transforming businesses as they adapt to the financial sector's volatility, uncertainty, complexity, and ambiguity—a world known as a VUCA (*Millar et al., 2018*). Financial services are impacted greatly by digitalization. The fact that financial goods are nearly entirely information-based represents an important factor. As an illustration, consider credit agreements or financial transactions, which, unlike automobile purchases, typically don't have any tangible elements. A further advantage is that, with a few exceptions like client advice, the majority of processes—such as electronic payments and trading in stocks, for instance—are performed essentially without any human contact. Both the successful implementation of monetary policies by the central bank and the smooth operation of markets have depended heavily on currency and its payments (*S. Agarwal et al., 2020).* They discover that most consumers utilize ATMs inside the kilometre of their residence and that when local ATMs close, they utilize online banking more frequently. By lowering the possibility of paying, the growing use of FinTech also results in financial rewards costs for penalties (*Choi & Loh, 2019).*

Challenges or Risks of Fintech

Problems with ethics bring attention to matters like bias within algorithms, the confidentiality of information, and the possible misuse of weaker demographics. Due to fintech's heavy reliance on enormous volumes of personal and financial information, worries about user security and the moral application of analytics tools have gained traction. Furthermore, if left unchecked, the ingrained biases in programs have the potential to worsen already-existing societal injustices.

Given the stringent rules and regulations of financial services, the government is essentially the driving force behind the achievement or demise of fintech. The goal of the Indian ecosystem to transition to a paperless electronic economy is being actively supported by the government of India and its authorities. Economy and develop into a robust fintech ecosystem through investment and marketing campaigns (*Dr. C. Vijai 2019*).

Regulatory obstacles that the fintech industry must overcome. Technological development frequently advances faster than regulatory structures, creating gaps that can be used for manipulating markets and fraudulent activity. The lack of a cohesive worldwide regulatory framework exacerbates the situation by resulting in a disjointed and uneven environment that presents difficulties for companies as well as consumers.

Cybersecurity Risk

When we talk about security concerns in fintech, we're talking about the possible risks and weaknesses that come with integrating digital into financial services. Fintech's ongoing transformation in the financial sector presents new potential and problems for security breaches due to its dependence on electronic platforms and informed by data technology. Important details about clients, including economic and personal data, are being accessed or disclosed without permission. Financial loss, harm to one's reputation, fines from the authorities, and possible legal repercussions are all risk impacts.

The factor of cyber risk in this study outcomes show a strong negative path coefficient, which indicates that cyber risks have an impact on banks' performance. Consequently, when cyber dangers rise, bank performance drops. These risks can lead to bank disasters, including data breaches and information trickery they pulled. Cybercriminals and hackers are the source of this. There are two possible ways this may happen: either through security flaws that could expose banking systems, or through hacking and breaching client data, breaching the confidentiality of their information when they transact financially online. Providing FinTech may expose a significant quantity of underlying data to abuses. Financial data, financial transaction numbers, client account numbers, quantities, fees, and other financial information are all provided by banks. Therefore, it is believed that the biggest risks affecting banks' performance are cyber hazards (*Al-Shari et al., 2023*).

Operational Risk

In the fintech industry, operational risk is the possibility of suffering a loss as a result of subpar or unsuccessful internal systems, personnel, procedures, or outside circumstances such as fraud or fraudulent activities. It includes a broad range of hazards associated with a fintech company's daily operations, and these risks have the potential to seriously affect the company's capacity to meet its goals. Fintech organizations use risk management frameworks, put strong internal controls in place, regularly review risks, and keep up with changing regulations in order to efficiently manage operational risk. In order to guarantee the robustness and sustainability of fintech operations in a dynamic and demanding environment, proactive monitoring and mitigation techniques are crucial. It also causes financial losses business disruption and many more.

Bank performance will rise when operational risk is managed and prevented. This explains why banks that implement fintech run the danger of experiencing operational issues, which are exemplified by, faults in technology or digital this could affect bank systems while they're at work, such as operational errors made by bank staff or because internet services and technologies are so current errors that technicians may make and technicians. Errors may happen while handling client financial transactions using digital technology. These mistakes, which present dangers when using FinTech services in banks, negatively affect banks' performance, whether through clients or staff (*Al-Shari et al. 2023*).

Systemic Risk

This demonstrates that systemic risks, or the hazards associated with software and information technology in the banking industry, have no effect on banks operational performance. However, the anticipated and required preparation might be ready to prevent various hazards, which could not have an impact on banks' performance. Furthermore, modern tools like Blockchain use advanced technology to protect and secure data secrecy. Artificial intelligence methods support risk detection and identification as well as expected hazards, as well as big data technologies, which assist in identifying any data or information by analysing data that could put the organization at risk (*Al-Shari et al. 2023*). Because large databases manage a lot of confidential data, they are appealing targets for attackers. Extensive breaches of information may have structural consequences that impact several companies and people. It might result in monetary losses, harm to one's credibility, and a decline in trust in the general security of electronic systems.

Process Control Risk

Some third parties that provide services to regulated financial institutions are examples of entities that provide financial services but are not subject to the same regulatory framework or standards as those that fall inside them. Equally monitored or examined in terms of their corporate and operational management procedures that apply to financial firms that are governed. This could develop into a risk that these expanding companies provide to the financial system. private virtual money, for example, is only successful if the incentive system incorporated into their design supports converse in a setting where individuals lack mutual trust. These rewards up until now, buildings have only been tested under a small number of conditions, but they have done fairly well overall (*FSB 2017*). Like any coin, the fintech industry in India has its share of difficulties. However, with additional government assistance, these difficulties may be turned into opportunities (*Gupta P. 2018*).

Cyber Singularity

Since most major institutions utilize identical technological components like applications, infrastructure, and cloud services, there is an extra risk from cyberspace resulting from the lagging of cyber diversity. This is because hacks against one institution have the potential to work against another. An organization that utilizes comparable IT infrastructure. Thus, the consistency as well as the usage of technology new hazards are brought about by tech programs, which are fundamental to the digital economy (*Ross P. Buckley, 2019*).

Biasedness of Algorithms

Incredibly also clear that adding non-technical personnel to the ranks of individuals who work on AI will help to prevent biases from entering the AI factory. Employing authors, social scientists, language experts, and designers should be a consideration for businesses creating AI. Unsupervised AI stands out in particular since it continuously learns and so altering once it is released from the AI factory. The issue at hand is that the creation cycle of AI goods is not being tested to identify any potential damages that the technology could pose to humanity once they're on the market, either morally or psychologically. Bias screening would assist in addressing the blind spots brought about by the lack of diversity in the engineering community about the people who develop AI (*Herrmann et al., 2021*). It is important to take precautions to guarantee that data integrity is preserved and that it is accurately captured, particularly when the amount and diversity of data grow. Researchers in data science require choosing sample data sets, processing the data, and integrating present understanding to stop bias from developing (*Pozen et al., 2019*). In particular, bias exists in US banks' rejection of a disproportionately high number of loan applications from Black Americans and Hispanics. Since algorithms learn from historical data, the things we want to modify are reproduced this is also biasness of algorithms or lack of clarity (*Yale, 2018).*

Conclusion

In conclusion, this study focuses on the dark side of fintech through a review of literature. As of increase the adaptation rate of fintech the risks should be minimized at the lowest accordingly it will gain customer trust to the peak. The hazards and unfavourable effects of financial technology's quick development are referred to as the "dark corners" of fintech. Fintech has significantly advanced and benefited the financial sector, but it also includes risks and disadvantages that need to be carefully considered. In spite of these obstacles, it is critical to recognize that the negative aspects of fintech are a call to action rather than an inevitable consequence. To guarantee that fintech keeps making a beneficial contribution to financial inclusion, efficiency, and availability, it is imperative to strike the right equilibrium among invention and managing risks. Through improvised the financial literacy of consumers will help to cope with those challenges more efficiently and also develop a culture of ethical responsibility, and put in place strong regulations. There appears to be a ray of hope that could transform fintech into a more inclusive to all through utilizing fintech's advantages for the betterment of the lives of persons and societies worldwide.

References

[1] Agarwal, S. and Zhang, J. (2020). FinTech, Lending and Payment Innovation: A review. *Asia-Pacific Journal of Financial Studies*, 49(3), 353–367. https://doi.org/10.1111/ajfs.12294

[2] Al-Shari, H.A. and Lokhande, M.A. (2023). The relationship between the risks of adopting FinTech in banks and their impact on the performance. *Cogent Business & Management*, 10(1), 2174242. https://doi.org/10.1080/23311975.2023.2174242

[3] Ashta, A. and Herrmann, H. (2021). Artificial intelligence and fintech: An overview of opportunities and risks for banking, investments, and microfinance. *Strategic Change*, 30(3), 211–222. https://doi.org/10.1002/jsc.2404

[4] Buckley, R.P., Arner, D.W., Zetzsche, D.A. and Selga, E. (2019). The dark side of digital financial transformation: The new risks of fintech and the rise of tech risk. *UNSW Law Working Paper*, (19–89). https://doi.org/10.2139/ssrn.3478640

[5] Choi, H.S. and Loh, R.K. (2019). The Geography of FinTech. *SSRN Electronic Journal.* https://doi.org/10.2139/ssrn.3333636

[6] EY Fintech Adoption Index (2017). *The rapid emergence of FinTech.* Report of the Ernst & Young Global Limited, 2017. https://www.ey.com/en_gl

[7] FSB (2017). Financial Stability Implications from FinTech, Supervisory and Regulatory Issues that Merit Authorities' Attention. Report of the Financial Stability Board, 27 June 2017.

[8] Giglio, F. (2021). Fintech: A literature review. *European Research Studies Journal,* 24(2B), 600–627.

[9] Gupta, P. (2018). Fintech Ecosystem in India: Trends, Top Startups, Jobs, Challenges and Opportunities, July. Accessed through https://stoodnt.com/blog/fintech-ecosystem-in-india-trends-top-startups-jobs-challenges-and-opportunities/

[10] Millar, C.C., Groth, O. and Mahon, J.F. (2018). Management innovation in a VUCA world: Challenges and recommendations. *California Management Review,* 61(1), 5–14.

[11] Nüesch, R., Alt, R. and Puschmann, T. (2015). Hybrid customer interaction. *Business & Information Systems Engineering,* 57, 73–78. 10.1007/s12599-014-0366-9.

[12] Pozen, R.C. and Ruane, J. (2019). What machine learning will mean for asset managers. Harvard Business Review Digital Articles, December. Accessed through https://hbr.org/2019/12/what-machine-learning-will-mean-for-asset-managers

[13] Puschmann, T. (2017). Fintech. Business & Information Systems Engineering, 59, 69–76. https://doi.org/10.1007/s12599-017-0464-6

[14] Saleem, A. (2021). Fintech revolution, perceived risks, and Fintech adoption: Evidence from Financial industry of Pakistan. *International Journal of Multi-disciplinary and Current Educational Research,* 3, 191–205.

[15] Vijai, C. (2019). Fintech in India-opportunities and challenges. *SAARJ Journal of Banking and Insurance Research,* 8(1). https://doi.org/10.5958/2319-1422.2019.00002.x

[16] Yale, A. (2018). Black Home Buyers Denied Mortgages More Than Twice as Often as Whites, Report Finds. Forbes, May. https://www.forbes.com/sites/alyyale/2018/05/07/mortgage-loan-denials-more-common-with-minorities-new-report-shows/?sh=278878d4509a

Impact of ESG Attributes on the Corporate Risk Proposition: A Review of Extant Literature

Sudipta Chakraborty[1] and Abhijit Sinha[2]

ABSTRACT: Corporate social responsibility (CSR) initiatives played a formal role in developing environmental, social, and governance (ESG) attributes, which in recent times have become a vital point for reporting sustainability issues in corporate finance. Numerous studies have examined the connections between ESG factors and a variety of outcomes, including the characteristics of the market in which a company operates, ownership of the company, the capital structure of the company, the nature, political leanings, and gender dimension of leadership and management, as well as the financial performance and value of the company. The current study, on the other hand, is a review of the literature that has already been written about the connection between ESG and a company's risk profile. It has been suggested that ESG can influence many different types of risk, such as systematic risk, regulatory risk, supply chain risk, product and technology risk, litigation risk, reputational risk, and physical risk, through a variety of different channels. While numerous studies have looked at bond credit ratings as an indicator of a company's risk, various theoretical models, many of them quite recent, have examined the impact of investor preferences for ESG attributes on a company's capital costs. Several studies also suggest that ESG practices may serve as insurance against company-specific legal risk. With a few notable exceptions, the empirical evidence generally supports the idea that higher ESG attributes lower both risk and capital cost. These divergent findings highlight the gaps in the previous research works and open the window for future in-depth studies in this area.

Keywords: Company, Environmental, ESG, Governance, Risk, Social.

Introduction

In today's world, the value of non-financial activities of the business also impacts the price of its shares. Thus, the horizon of corporate stakeholders' interests has now transcended beyond mere financial incentives. Different stakeholders are now equally interested in knowing how much well-being or

[1] Ph.D. Research Scholar, Department of Commerce, Vidyasagar University, India. E-mail: chakrabortysudipta1993@gmail.com

[2] Professor, Department of Commerce, Vidyasagar University, India. E-mail: abhijitsinha_091279@rediffmail.com

harm the business is causing to society and the environment as a whole along with the financial performance of the same. According to the Governance and Accountability Institute's reports, there has been a significant 66% increase in the disclosure of sustainability or corporate responsibility reports among the S& P 500 firms in 2018 compared to that in 2011, demonstrating corporate interest in the areas of environment, society, and governance. In addition, 300 mutual funds with reporting requirements for Corporate Social Responsibility (CSR) and sustainability received a net inflow of $5 billion in 2018, which quadrupled the following year. Assets Under Management (AUM) for more than 3,000 institutional investors and service providers that have ratified the Principles of Responsible Investment (PRI) agreement have grown significantly by $79.5 trillion over thirteen years, starting in 2006.[2]

There has been a great buzz globally for quite some time now regarding triple-bottom-line reporting. The corporates are also reporting their sustainability achievements in conjunction with financial performance for the sake of their stakeholders' interest. Though it was voluntary initially, now in many countries, mandates have been made under various laws for compulsory disclosure of sustainability performances of specific classes of businesses. Sustainability reporting in a formalised manner started initially with CSR initiatives which primarily focused on corporate philanthropy to place companies as good social citizens. Thus, being a part of society, it was important for the corporates to take initiatives that would positively impact the environment, which would be able to compensate for the pollution and overall environmental degradation caused by such businesses. Moreover, history has witnessed several cases of corporate failures worldwide as a result of white-collar frauds due to misgovernance within the companies causing a loss of a huge amount of wealth for the investors. Thus, the laws are now much more stringent about corporate governance. Investors are the backbone of any firm, and such business organisations are the lifeblood of the economy of any country. Though profit maximisation continues to be the primary objective of most businesses, that cannot be at the cost of the environment and society at large. Moreover, the investors are also more aware and thus, want the companies to disclose their environmental and social attributes along with the governance measures taken besides the traditional financial reporting, making the idea of CSR enter into the realm of ESG. ESG stands for Environmental, Social, and Governance and was created by a report of 20 financial institutions at the request of the UN Secretary-General Kofi

[2] https://www.unpri.org/pri/about-the-pri. However, it needs to be noted that it does not yet appear to be the case that all of these assets were invested according to the PRI principles. (https://www.morningstar.com/articles/961765/sustainable-fund-flows-in-2019-smashprevious-records)

Anon in 2004.[3] As the name suggests, ESG is all about how companies and investors integrate these issues into their business models.

India is going through a paradigm shift in the same way as other countries in terms of reporting. Investors are increasingly requesting reporting on qualitative issues. There are numerous factors to be considered before investing wisely today besides taking into account the conventional risk, return, maturity period, etc. to maximize returns and ensure holistic well-being. It is crucial to understand that the money we invest in businesses or other organizations also affects social change. Depending on the company or sector in which it is invested, this change could be either positive or negative. Socially conscious investing is now a reality rather than a pipe dream. By incorporating Social, Environmental, and Ethical considerations, investors now have options for building portfolios with profit and beneficial social and environmental impacts. They can now take action to make their demands heard by corporate management and boards of directors, bringing about change within their organizations. ESG issues have come to the forefront of discussion in light of the evolving reporting landscape. Thus, there is a need for the study due to the significance of socially responsible investing, especially in the context of developing nations like India where it is still in its infancy. This study will aid in understanding the progress in studies across the globe concerning the relationship between the ESG performance of the firms and their risk propositions.

Gaps in the Existing Research

While studying the extant literature, it was found that most of the research works are limited to the areas of the relationship of ESG attributes with different outcomes such as characteristics of the market of operation, ownership of the firm, the capital structure of the firm, nature, political inclinations and gender dimension of the leadership and management etc. In fact, the area of analysis of the relationship between ESG attributes and the financial performance of the firm was found to be over-researched. Though, quite some impactful research works are available relating to ESG performance and firms' risk in developed countries, particularly in the U.S.; there remains a dearth of research works encompassing this area in developing economies like India. Thus, there lies the impetus of the present study to unravel the existing literature on ESG attributes and their impact on the corporate risk proposition across the globe.

Objective of the Study

The sole objective of the present study is to explore the existing literature on the impact of ESG attributes on the corporate risk proposition across the globe to provide some suggestions for paving areas of future research in this regard.

[3] Refer to "Who Cares Wins": https://www.ifc.org

Methodology Used in the Study

The present study is purely a work of descriptive research which tries to analyse the extant literature available worldwide on the relationship between ESG performance and the firms' risk by reviewing and arranging them thematically.

ESG and Corporate Risk—The Theoretical Underpinning

Starks (2009) suggested that ESG influenced various types of risks, namely, systematic risk, regulatory risk, litigation risk, reputational risk, physical risk, risk relating to product, technology and supply chain etc. Benabou and Tirole (2010) proposed that the firms having strong ESG profiles were less affected during the period of crisis and they had a specific ESG-related risk factor. Thus, their exposure to systematic risk was different from that of the other companies. Beloskar and Rao (2022) conducted a comparable study in the Indian context by analysing the investment performance, trading volumes and return volatility of ESG-rated firms listed in the BSE during the COVID-19 period. Observing the event study revolved around the COVID crisis, the authors concluded that ESG information could be treated as an indicator of future stock performance and hence could save the investors from downside risk. Further, it was observed to be useful for the investors not only by reducing the volatility of stock return during the crisis period but also by maximising shareholders' wealth during normal times. Lins *et al.* (2017) did not indulge in an extensive study of the relationship between ESG and firm risk; however, in consistency with the findings of Benabou and Tirole (2010), they concluded that firms with better ESG profiles performed well as compared to their counterparts during the financial crisis of 2008-09, which is in tandem with the resiliency proposition. Roy and Saurabh (2022) analysed the impact of ESG factors on the systematic and idiosyncratic risks of environmentally sensitive firms from manufacturing and energy sectors in India using CAPM Beta and the Fama-French 3-factor model. Using a balanced panel data set from 2010 to 2021 and employing fixed, dynamic and panel quantile regression models the authors concluded though ESG disclosures were able to reduce the idiosyncratic risk modestly, it could cause a substantial decrease in the systematic risk of the firms. The authors argued in favour of stakeholder, legitimacy, and resource-based view theories, experiencing a pronounced effect of firms' environmental disclosures on their performances. Further, they added that idiosyncratic risks were not homogeneous under varied market conditions. Thus, such arbitrary disclosures reduced the risk perception of Indian investors during periods of market uncertainty. Similar to this, Saini *et al.* (2023) aimed to analyse the impact of ESG risk level on the financial performance of 57 selected samples of Indian firms using the stakeholder theory. Prowess IQ and Sustainalytics databases were used by the authors to obtain the financial performance and ESG risk data for fiscal year 2021. The study used ordinary least squares regression to determine the impact of ESG risks on a company's return on assets and equity. The findings were consistent with stakeholder theory, which suggested that a company's financial performance had a strong negative correlation with ESG risks, indicating that companies need to reduce their ESG risks to increase profitability. Albuquerque *et al.* (2019) observed that firms with better ESG profiles faced lower systematic risk. They proposed a theory whereby the strong ESG firms were found to be facing a relatively inelastic price elasticity of demand while adopting a product differentiation strategy. Based on the evidence they concluded that firms with high product differentiation faced a stronger effect of ESG on their systematic risk. Gupta and Aggarwal (2023) aimed to empirically examine ESG as an effective strategy to reduce the hurdles for firms in the forms of cost of capital and systematic risk using beta, particularly concerning emerging markets like India. They used a sample of a total of 114 firms selected from eight different prominent Indian industries based on the Thomson Reuters classification and carried out a panel regression with industry-fixed effects. It was found to have a significant inverse relationship between ESG performance with the cost of capital and systematic risks of the firms. While analysing the relationship of cost of capital and beta with each pillar of ESG individually, it was revealed that while only governance performance is significantly adversely related to the cost of capital of the firms, the relationship of all three pillars with beta is negative and statistically significant. Analysing the performance of NIFTY 100 Enhanced ESG & NIFTY 100 Sector Leaders Index, Sharma (2023) analysed the return behaviour of better ESG risk-managed stocks and calculated Value at Risk to predict the return for post-COVID time. She concluded that the performance of the ESG index had proven to be relatively stable and resilient even in turbulent market conditions signalling the firms to indulge more in sustainable activities not only to stabilise the market and the economy, vis-à-vis, also to fetch more profits. Sudha (2015) not only compared the performance of the sustainability index of India—the S&P ESG India Index with two broad market indexes, viz., the Nifty and the S&P CNX 500 using daily index data but also analysed the inherent conditional volatility using generalised autoregressive conditional heteroscedasticity models. The results depicted that while the compounded daily returns of the ESG India index were not statistically different from the compounded daily returns of the Nifty or the CNX 500, the annualised returns of the ESG India index outperformed the returns of the other two indices. Focusing on environmental and social sustainability was therefore a win-win situation for companies, investors and society as a whole. All three indices were seen to have a significant volatility clustering. The ESG India index was less volatile compared to the Nifty index during this period. El Ghoul *et al.* (2011) hypothesised that firms with stronger ESG profiles attracted investments from a wide range of investors. Thus, they faced a lower risk than the others. In sync with their view, Hong and Kacperczyk (2009) further opined that such a diverse investor base caused lower litigation risk for the firm, which in turn reduces the cost of capital. The findings of Oikonomou *et al.* (2012) further supported this notion. According to them, several reasons were responsible for the ESG-intensive firms to have lower risk. In their study, though no relationship was found with the KLD social strength, they observed that the systematic risk is higher for the firms having higher concerns for ESG.

Multiple studies have considered the bond credit rating as the proxy for measuring the riskiness of the firms. Using a three-digit zip code for measuring ESG scores, Jiraporn *et al.* (2014) concluded that favourable credit ratings were achieved for the companies having better ESG profiles. They found that a company's credit rating depended highly on its neighbours through investor clientele effects, local competition, and/or social interactions. Stellner *et al.* (2015) had similar findings in their study. However, they opined that the credit ratings of the companies greatly depend on the countries they are located in as the concern for such countries towards ESG played a pivotal role in this regard. They could not find any systematic relationship between the ESG performance of the firms and their credit ratings statistically, examining a sample of corporate bonds from 12 European Union countries. However, it was observed that companies with better ESG performance tend to benefit from better credit ratings if they were situated in countries having above-average ESG profiles in general. Similar conclusions were arrived at by Di Giuli and Kostovetsky (2014); and Jha and Cox (2015), who tried to examine the relationship between ESG performance and bond ratings in the light of social capital and political inclinations. The study by Seltzer *et al.* (2020) successfully established a relationship between environmental scores and climate regulatory risk with the bond credit ratings and yield spreads of the companies. Using the Paris Agreement as a shock, the authors depicted a causal relationship between climate regulatory risk and bond risk and pricing. It was observed that a firm generally had lower credit ratings and higher yield spreads when it showcased a lower ESG performance. They portrayed that such results were more evident in the states having stricter regulations relating to the environment.

Several literature pointed out the relationship between bond credit risk and the ESG performance of the firm to indicate the default risk of the firms. Highlighting environmental politics as an important factor, Jagannathan *et al.* (2018) provided evidence that a firm's downside risk could be caused by ESG-related risks of the firm as these are large enough, non-diversifiable and rare in nature. Ilhan *et al.* (2019) shared the view that the firms' carbon intensity may increase due to the risk of equity downside, which is reflected in their option pricing. Donald Trump's being elected caused a lowering in the cost of the firms for protecting against such downside risk as the uncertainty relating to the climate policy reduced, they argued. In support of a similar argument Hoepner *et al.* (2019) found out that a firm's downside risk could be lowered if ESG issues, particularly environmental matters were actively peddled in.

Studies pointed out that indulging in intensive ESG activities could safeguard firms against their firm-specific legal risks. Hong and Liskovich (2015) used the enforcement of the Foreign Corrupt Practices Act to test if ESG performance could act as insurance against the litigation risk of the companies. They concluded that more lenient settlements are received from the prosecutors for the firms with better ESG scores. It, in turn, caused a higher market valuation of such firms. Further, corporate clients having better social and environmental policies impregnated a relatively lower probability of socio-environmental legal hassles to their suppliers, Schiller (2018) added.

Contrary to most of the studies providing evidence of the inverse relationship between ESG ratings and various types of risks to the firms, Becchetti *et al.* (2015) argued that though ESG activities reduced the shareholders' risk, it is positively related to the idiosyncratic risk of the firms. They opined that such a result is caused by the existence of rigidity in generating responses to the adverse productivity shocks augmented by the firms' ESG activities. It, as a result, caused a significant reduction in the welfare of the stakeholders. The returns from higher ESG stocks became less predictable because of the existence of such a relationship, in the opinion of the authors. However, comparing the UK firms with varied ESG ratings, Humphrey *et al.* (2012) did not find any significant differences in the idiosyncratic risk of such firms. Nasreen and Sreejith (2022) chose a sample of 2302 Indian companies for 8 years (i.e., 2014-21) to assess the impact of ESG performance on the default risk of the firms. They found ESG to have a direct relationship with the firm's default risk. In their opinion, firms might use greenwashing techniques to inflate their ESG performance. Furthermore, the need for calibration in Refinitiv was inevitable to suit the computational needs of ESG performances of various firms in emerging economies like India.

Limitations of the Study

Sustainability reporting in a formalised manner started initially with the concept of Corporate Social Responsibility (CSR) initiatives which primarily focused on corporate philanthropy to place companies as good social citizens. Though CSR directly addresses important sustainability issues, namely the environment and society; governance issues are not focussed on explicitly. To address sustainability matters broadly, the concept of CSR has now started entering the realm of environmental, social and governance (ESG) initiatives, which address all three important dimensions of sustainability and focus equally on environmental protection, Society and Governance (ESG). Thus, ESG is more expansive than CSR as terminology. Since, ESG is comparatively a new concept and is in a nascent stage in many countries, in this study, we, however, have used both terms interchangeably. We have not reviewed the vast literature solely focused on corporate governance, however, our focus on the literature concerning environmental and social aspects of ESG/CSR allowed us to examine the interrelationships between a company's governance structure and its environmental and social activities. Although closely related and important, we have not reviewed the extensive investment literature on ESG-Investing or Socially Responsible Investing (SRI) nor the extensive culture, trust, social capital and climate finance literature.

Further, in this paper, we have reviewed the research works in corporate finance on ESG/CSR issues with a primary focus on their relationship with various types of corporate risks. To keep this review to a manageable length, we have confined our attention primarily to the corporate finance literature that dealt with the questions we were addressing. In doing so we acknowledge the omitting of a wide and influential literature on ESG/CSR that exists in other disciplines.

Areas for Future Research

Concerning risk, with a few exceptions, the empirical evidence from the existing literature generally supports the view that higher ESG attributes lower it. However, for calculations of ESG performances and firm risk, different studies have considered different aspects. Moreover, most of the studies are confined within a geographical territory, particularly in developed countries, failing to establish a universality in the findings and statistical results obtained thereby. Neither there is any standard ESG rating method nor a universally accepted method of calculating firm risk worldwide; hence, results may differ from one study to another in their modalities of calculating these ratings[4]. Thus, the empirical finding of the relationship between ESG attributes and firms' risk proposition may differ dramatically with changes in the choice of ESG rating agencies and method of risk calculation. Hence, standardisation of the rating procedure is the need of the hour.[5] Again, there lies an issue with the consistency of the rating procedure, as over the years almost all the rating agencies have been modifying their ESG measurement scale by adding and dropping various indicators, posing a serious question about the basis of comparison.[6] Last but not the least, existing literature reveal that sufficient research work concerning

[4] https://www.sirc-icai.org/images/cabf/Corporate%20Governance%20in%20India.pdf

[5] Globally consistent ESG reporting; Deloitte, March 2022.

[6] See "Scoring Model Changes": Corporate Governance Scores Increasing Expectations Based on the Indian Corporate Governance Scorecard Framework Developed by IFC-BSE-IiAS; March 2023.

the relationship between ESG performance and corporate risk is inadequate, particularly in emerging economies. Further, the contradictory results of some of the studies from the general notion clearly point out the need for future research in this area.

Conclusion

Researchers have proposed and documented several connections between ESG activities and different firm attributes in both descriptive and empirical studies. While some results are mixed, some are quite robust. Thus, there remains the need to address this gap by reconciling them to add to the furtherance of knowledge. Additionally, various other drivers impacting the risk of the firms and their relationship with the ESG attributes need to be studied in further detail. The contradictory results of literature on this topic make the central issue that necessitates further discussion, even though the majority of evidence points to a positive relationship between ESG attributes and the risk of the firms. The expansion of ESG initiatives and their extensive implementation across the globe along with more transparency in reporting making easy data availability wakes hope for the development of new dimensions and empirical designs opening up the gateway for a rich bouquet of research offerings in a while.

References

[1] Albuquerque, R., Koskinen, Y. and Zhang, C. (2019). Corporate social responsibility and firm risk: theory and empirical evidence. *Management Science,* 65 (10), 4451–4469.

[2] Becchetti, L., Ciciretti, R. and Hasan, I. (2015). Corporate social responsibility, stakeholder risk, and idiosyncratic volatility. *Journal of Corporate Finance* 35, 297–309.

[3] Beloskar, V.D. and Rao, S.N. (2023). Did ESG save the day? Evidence from India during the COVID-19 crisis. *Asia-Pacific financial markets,* 30(1), 73–107.

[4] Benabou, R. and Tirole, J. (2010). Individual and corporate social responsibility. *Economica,* 77 (305), 1–19.

[5] Di Giuli, A. and Kostovetsky, L. (2014). Are red or blue companies more likely to go green? Politics and corporate social responsibility. *Journal of Financial Economics,* 111(1), 158–180.

[6] El Ghoul, S., Guedhami, O., Kwok, C.C. and Mishra, D.R. (2011). Does corporate social responsibility affect the cost of capital? *Journal of Banking & Finance,* 35(9), 2388–2406.

[7] Gupta, S. and Aggarwal, D. (2023). Shrinking the capital costs and beta risk impediments through ESG: study of an emerging market. *Asian Review of Accounting.*

[8] Hoepner, A.G.F., Oikonomou, I., Sautner, Z., Starks, L.T. and Zhou, X.Y. (2019). ESG Shareholder Engagement and Downside Risk. Working paper.

[9] Hong, H., Kacperczyk, M. (2009). The price of sin: the effects of social norms on markets. *Journal of Financial Economics,* 93(1), 15–36.

[10] Hong, H. and Liskovich, I. (2015). Crime, Punishment and the Halo Effect of Corporate Social Responsibility (National Bureau of Economic Research working paper).

[11] Humphrey, J.E., Lee, D.D. and Shen, Y. (2012). Does it cost to be sustainable? *Journal of Corporate Finance,* 18(3), 626–639.

[12] Ilhan, E., Sautner, Z. and Vilkov, G. (2019). Carbon tail risk. Working paper.

[13] Jagannathan, R., Ravikumar, A. and Sammon, M. (2018). Environmental, social, and governance criteria: why investors should care. *Journal of Investment Management,* 16 (1), 18–31.

[14] Jha, A. and Cox, J. (2015). Corporate social responsibility and social capital. *Journal of Banking & Finance,* 60, 252–270.

[15] Jiraporn, P., Jiraporn, N., Boeprasert, A. and Chang, K., 2014. Does corporate social responsibility (CSR) improve credit ratings? Evidence from geographic identification. *Financial Management,* 43 (3), 505–531.

[16] Lins, K.V., Servaes, H. and Tamayo, A. (2017). Social capital, trust, and firm performance: the value of corporate social responsibility during the financial crisis. *Journal of Finance,* 72(4), 1785–1824.

[17] Nasrin, S. and Sreejith, R. (2022). Impact of ESG Performance on Firms Default Risk. In Conference on Contemporary Economic Issues in Asian Countries. pp. 39–48. Singapore: Springer Nature Singapore.

[18] Oikonomou, I., Brooks, C. and Pavelin, S., 2012. The impact of corporate social performance on financial risk and utility: *A longitudinal analysis. Financial Management,* 41(2), 483–515.

[19] Roy, P. and Saurabh, S. ESG Disclosure and Financial Risk: Firm-Level Evidence. Available at SSRN 4149263.

[20] Saini, M., Dhingra, B. and Yadav, M. (2023). ESG risk and financial performance of the Indian financial firms. *International Journal of Governance and Financial Intermediation,* 1(4), 304–314.

[21] Schiller, C., 2018. Global Supply-Chain Networks and Corporate Social Responsibility. Working paper.

[22] Seltzer, L., Starks, L.T. and Zhu, Q., 2020. Climate Regulatory Risk and Corporate Bonds. Working paper.

[23] Sharma, S. (2023). Does ESG risk management ensure better risk management? Evidence from India. *Procedia Computer Science*, 221, 912-919.

[24] Starks, L.T., 2009. EFA keynote speech: corporate governance and corporate social responsibility: what do investors care about? What should investors care about? *Financial Review,* 44(4), 461–468.

[25] Stellner, C., Klein, C. and Zwergel, B. (2015). Corporate social responsibility and eurozone corporate bonds: the moderating role of country sustainability. *Journal of Banking & Finance,* 59, 538–549.

[26] Sudha, S. (2015). Risk-return and Volatility analysis of Sustainability Index in India. *Environment, development and sustainability*, 17, 1329–1342.

Journey of Indian Fintech Industry during Last Decade

Baitali Paul[1] and Atanu Ghosh[2]

ABSTRACT: Major events like Global meltdown of 2008, Demonetization of 2016 associated with Covid-pandemic could not thwart the mushrooming growth of Fintech Companies in India. Starting its operations way back through Fintech 2.0, Indian Fintech's successfully traversed several years having more than 3085 Fintech Companies in their kitty as of August 2023.

Following the footsteps of global leader India is also becoming a Global Fintech Industry Hub. NASSCOM report stated that from turnover of $33 billion in 2016 the market is expected to touch a valuation $84 billion by 2025 with a CAGR of around 22%–25%. By 2030 Indian Fintech is projected to generate $200 billion revenue which will contribute 13% of global Fintech industry's revenue. The growth of India's Fintech may have been fueled by increasing smart phone adoption, digital literacy, open banking, API based services, secured digital easy payments, simple partnership between Fintech and corporates, simple management of personal wealth, extensive use of cloud services using artificial intelligence. India houses the second largest digital population in the worlds as of January 2023.

It is further expected that Indian Fintech industry startup are going to operate in different diverse segment creating huge revenue pools. The sectors where the Indian Fintech companies operating are mainly digital lending, digital payments, Insurtech, Wealthtech, Blockchain. Digital lending has grown enormously in the last few years on account of a booming funding environment, growth of venture capitalist interest. It may be worth mentioning over here that GDP downfall during pandemic necessitated the use of digital currency and recovery of GDP during 2021 facilitated the setting of startup and unicorns.

The paper tries to identify the growth of Fintech industry in India during the last five years. Authors have also tried to identify the factors which fueled this growth in two digits. Emergence of digital ecosystem for tackling the challenge of the pandemic through use of high speed 4G and 5G internet services has no doubt reduced the time and increased efficiency of data transmission in the villages through use of optical fibers. AEPS based micro – ATMs at CSCS (Central Secretariat Clerical Service) and post offices no doubt boom the banking system but are not devoid of frauds, which

[1] SACT-I, Department of Commerce, New Alipore College, Kolkata, India.
E-mail: baitalipaul@newaliporecollege.ac.in

[2] Associate Professor, Department of Commerce, New Alipore College, Kolkata, India.
E-mail: atanughosh@newaliporecollege.ac.in

may affect overall financial stability and market integrity. Growth of Fintech is a part of inclusive growth commensurate with Digital India's moto of "Power to Empower" through participation of Government sectors and private sectors. Thus Fintech in its growth ladder act as a promoter for innovation through self-regulation.

Keywords: API based Services, NASSCOM, Power to Empower, Revenue by Fintech.

Introduction

Financial Technology which aims to improve the delivery and use of financial services come under the purview of Fintech. The technological partners try to provide better services to the business entities and consumers of financial services through improved financial operations and processes Globally Fintech have been operating for more than three decades. Fintech bring customers online for different financial services. It has been observed that Global Fintech Investment has risen during the last five years starting from 2018. Startups are important constituent of Fintech. Use of artificial intelligence, modern technology is spurring the growth of Fintech. Companies like Ant Group, Paytm, Stripe, Adyen, Coinbase, Robinhood, Square, Klarna are operating globally as successful Fintech companies.

Table 1: Number of Fintech Startups which Grew Globally

Year	*Americas*	*EMEA (Europe, the Middle East, and Africa)*	*APAC (Asia Pacific Region)*
2018	5,686	3,581	2,864
2019	5,779	3,583	2,849
2020	8,775	7,385	4,765
2021	10,755	9,323	6,268
2023	11,651	9,681	5,061

Source: https://www.statista.com/statistics/893954/number-fintech-startups-by-region, accessed on 18.12.2023 at 11 pm

With 11,651 Fintech startups as of May 2023, America leads the world in the number of Fintech startups. Comparatively, the Asia Pacific region had 5,061 Fintech startups, while the EMEA region had 9,681 startups. As of 2023, United States was the country with the highest number of Fintech. The number of unicorns in USA was the highest in the world. In USA the number of unicorns is five times when compared to that of United Kingdom.

Table 2: Investment in the Fintech Industry

Year	*Amount of Investment (US $)*
2010	9 billion
2011	6 billion
2012	4 billion
2013	18.9 billion
2014	45.4 billion
2015	67.1 billion
2016	63.4 billion
2017	59.2 billion
2018	148.6 billion
2019	216.8 billion
2020	138.8 billion
2021	247.2 billion
2022	209.3 billion
2023 (upto first half i.e. June 2023)	52.4 billion

Source: https://www.statista.com/statistics/719385/investments-into-fintech-companies-globally, accessed on 18.12.2023 at 11.30 pm

Starting from the year 2010 till 2014 it can be seen that there was a downfall in the amount of investment in two consecutive years in 2011 and 2012. Thereafter an uptrend in the amount of investment is noticeable till 2016. 2017, 2018 and 2019 were years where global investment in Fintech sector increased but with the advent of Covid pandemic the global investment in Fintech industry flattened. Decrease in economic activities boosted the use of digital currency in pandemic and post-pandemic period. A massive recovery was located in global investment in Fintech industry in the year 2021 which could not be retained in 2022.

Table 3: Global Fintech Net Revenue Share by Region, Level of Development, %

Year	*North America*	*Europe*	*Asia-Pacific*	*Latin America*	*Africa*	*Middle East*
2022	48	11	34	5	2	<1
2028	41	14	30	9	4	2

Source: Dealroom.co; McKinsey analysis

Net Revenue: Revenue after risk minus direct costs.

Fintech industry is expected to grow almost three times faster than in the traditional banking sector between 2022 to 2028. From the above table it appears that in 2028 level of development with respect to net revenue will be lower in case of North America, Asia Pacific while level of development percentage will be more in Europe, Latin America, Africa and Middle East as forecasted in Mckinsey Report. For the Asia Pacific region projection shows that level of revenue is expected to grow at a CAGR percentage of around 12. In 2022, for Asia Pacific region revenue was in the range of US $55 billion to US$65 billion. In the year 2028 the revenue is expected to touch US $110 billion to US $130 billion. India operates in the Asia Pacific region and in this analysis the authors have tried to focus on the activities of Fintech in India during the last few years of its operation in India.

Objective of the Study

In pursuing the objectives of the study the authors have tried to identify the growth of Fintech industry in India. An effort was also been made to identify the factors which favoured the growth of Fintech industry in India.

Research Methodology

The study is "exploratory" in nature. This "exploratory" section is based on the most recent available literature on this particular topic that is currently available in books, journal articles, research projects, websites, and other materials.

India's Fintech Industry

Indian Fintech industry has been growing since the first few years with reference to funding, product launches etc.

Investment in India's Fintech Industry

Table 4: Investment in the Fintech Industry in India

Year	*Amount of Investment (US $)*
2014	401.8 million
2015	107.8 billion
2016	700.1 million
2017	3.1 billion
2018	1.9 billion
2019	3.6 billion
2020	2.0 billion
2021	9.6 billion
2022	6.0 billion
2023	2.1 billion

Source: https://bfsi.economictimes.indiatimes.com/news/fintech/how-indian-fintech-funding-fared-in-last-10-years/106261047

Barring the year 2015 amount of investment in Indian Fintech Industry was in million dollars till 2016. Thereafter, excluding 2020 and 2018 amount of investment in Indian Fintech Industry was above 2 billion in every year till 2022. A projection shows in 2030 Indian Fintech is to generate US $200billion revenue which will contribute 13% of global Fintech industry's revenue. It may be noted that despite slowdown in economic activity due to pandemic in 2020, Fintech continued its unabated growth in India on various parameter. Investment in 2020 dropped to $2 billion in comparison to that of 2019 which was $3.6 billion. India was topper in Asia-Pacific (APAC Countries) in Fintech investment creating 121 deals during Covid. Phonepe's $ 788 million was one of the notable contributors. It may be observed that in APAC Fintech investment dipped in 2020 but considering aggregate value of investment India stood well ahead of China, South Eastern Asia, Australia and Japan during the Covid pandemic. A glimpse through Fintech funding with reference to Equity Investment excluding Debt, Grant, Post-IPO funding for Fintech industry in India has been on the rise from 2014 to 2015, thereafter it dropped in 2016 but reach again a high in 2017. The year 2018 witnessed a downfall in investment followed by a record high in investment in 2019. Thereafter, a dip in Fintech investment was noticed in India in 2020 and 2021. Private funding from the large players were supported by IPOs. Massive investment from large venture capital and private Equity firms was available in the Fintech sector.

Below is enumerated the sectors where Indian Fintech Industry is operating successfully:

Table 5: Areas of Operation of Indian Fintech Industry

Pay Tech	*Lend Tech*	*Digital Banking*	*Insur Tech*	*Wealth Tech*
Consumer	Consumer	Digital Subsidiary of banks	Insurance Comparison Platforms	Expense Management
		Retail Neobanks	Digital Insurers	Robo Advisors
		SME Neobanks	Electronics Insurance	Discount Brokers
			Employee Insurance	Mutual Fund Investment Platform
				US Equalities investment
				Research Platforms Alternative Investment Platform
				White-label Robo Advisor

Pay Tech	*Lend Tech*	*Digital Banking*	*Insur Tech*	*Wealth Tech*
TRAP Prepaid card/Wallet Bill Payment QR code Payment Payment aggregator POS	BNPL Personal Loan Salary Loan Gold Loan Auto Loan Education Loan P2P Lending			
Business	SME			
Corporate card B2B Payment Invoice payment	Corporate Card Fixed term loans Trade Finance			

Source: ey-winds-of-change-india-fintech-report-2022.pdf

The Fintech sector is now replacing the sectors which required human capital. These activities namely are Real Time Payments, Faster disbursal of loans, Investment Advisory, Transparent Insurance Advisory and Distribution, Peer to Peer lending, Personal finance, Gold lending etc. Other sectors in which Indian Fintech are operating are enumerated below:

- *Pay Tech:* It operates through consumer centric services including third party application provider, prepaid card/wallet, bill payment, QR code payment, payment aggregator. Regarding business centric services B2B payments, invoice payments, use of payment gateway, Application Programming Interface (API) are other services. The major players in this PayTech sectors are Paytm, Phonepe, Mobikwik and GooglePay. Big bank technology company are joining Fintech startups for offering financial services.
- *Lend Tech:* Buy Now Pay Letter (BNPL), Personal Loan, Salary Loan, Gold Loan, Auto Loan, Education Loan are areas where Fintech operate at personal level. Corporate Card, fixed term finance, trade finance are some of the business centric services attached to Fintech activities. All these services of Fintech include collection management, credit bureau, Alternate Credit Scoring, Loan Organisation System (LOS), Loan Management System (LMS). Lending platforms like GooglePay, M-Swipe, RazorPay are emerging as leading players both at personal and business level.
- *Digital Banking:* As an initiative of Digital India, Fintech services employed in digital banking involve conversational platforms, account aggregator, API

provider, core banking etc. Some Fintech firms which operate in digital banking areas are Yono, Kahatabook, Crazybee.

- ***Insurtech:*** Enable services like Insurance Comparison Platforms, digital insurers, electronic insurance, employee insurance. Fintech manages services like claims management, sales platform, underwriting risk management, insurance infrastructure, API, Insurance Product Configurator, Policy Admin System. One major player in this segment is Policy Bazar.
- ***Wealth Tech:*** Firms like Zerodha, Smallcase functioning in this sector helps in portfolio management and Cap Table Management. These firms performed the activities of Discount Brokers, Mutual Fund Investment Platforms, Research Platforms, Alternative Investment Platforms, Wealth & expense management through Robo Advisors. Fintech participating Wealth Tech building startups and operating in upstart segment like crypto currency, block chain.
- ***Finance Tech:*** In this segment, a range of services can be offered, such as:
  (a) *Accounting:* Services are offered to micro, small, and enterprise-sized businesses.
  (b) *Procure to Pay (P2P):* The process of requesting, acquiring, receiving, paying for, and accounting for goods and services is known as "procure to pay." Though there is software specifically made to handle the entire procure-to-pay process, certain parts of it, like invoicing, or associated processes, like inventory management and financial accounting, it is a process rather than a technology.
  (c) *Quote to Cash (Q2C):* The term "Q2C" refers to the complete set of business processes associated with the sales lifecycle. The procedure includes presenting an offer to a potential customer as well as collecting, allocating, and recording revenue. Businesses utilise the information to enhance ensuing sales cycles.
  (d) *Taxation:* Under Sections 2(22A) and 2(23A) of the ITA, FinTech companies are either classified as Domestic Companies or Foreign Companies and are therefore liable to Corporate Income Tax. Foreign FinTech companies are only liable for Corporate Income Tax on income generated within India, while Indian FinTech companies must pay Corporate Income Tax on income both inside and outside of the country.
  (e) *Reconciliation:* Financial reconciliation is a critical process for businesses of all sizes to ensure the accuracy and reliability of their financial records. Financial reconciliation presents certain difficulties, such as the time and labour involved in manually comparing records, but there are practical solutions that can be put in place to make the process go more quickly. Using automated tools like Nanonets is one such tactic.

- ***Regulation Tech:*** In the financial services industry, technology is also being used to meet regulatory and compliance requirements. Examples of these include risk management and banking compliance, fraud detection, digital onboarding, KYC, and anti-money laundering (AML).

Off late India has been producing the largest number of Unicorns with entrepreneurs, incumbent institutions, big tech firms being the major players. Digital payment Fintech has been the highest fund tech and pioneer of Fintech revolution in India. In 2021, payment startups attracted $3.5 billion recording a growth of 169% as compared to overall funding in 2020. During the period from 2014 to 2022 startups like JAM trinity were pioneers in creating the list of more than 550 startups functioning with a total funding of $22 billion.

Challenges for Fintech Industries in India

Some of the major barriers for Fintech industry of India are enumerated below:

1. ***Data Security and Privacy risk:*** Security of database is of utmost importance for both the service providers and the clients, in these days of cyber frauds and digital India.
2. ***Varied Options:*** India's business environment is filled up with different types of business entities. In most cases small entrepreneurs do not have the desired digital infrastructure required by Fintech. In such situation for expansion of Fintech business, business model needs dynamism and is expensive.
3. ***Regulatory Infrastructure:*** Fintech businesses need to comply with Investment, Crypto Currency, Payment, Data Security, Infrastructure regulations. These regulations are ever changing and dynamic. Indian regulators are concerned with transparency and safety of investors. Adoption to such an ever changing regulatory framework is no doubt a challenge for Indian Fintech Industry.
4. ***Lack of Investor Education:*** Indian investors living in non-metro cities and rural are not always aware of financial literacy programmes of Government of India. Moreover, the issue of internet connectivity and uninterrupted power was another challenge for Indian Fintech. To remove this financial illiteracy blockade education blogs, videos on streaming platform channels, digital pocket money apps for younger audience (like Junio), online seminars, virtual training stimulators was introduced to educate investors.

Factors Responsible for Fintech Growth in India

Factors Responsible for Fintech Growth in India can be enumerated under three headings:

1. *Macro Driven:*

(a) ***Government and Regulatory initiatives:*** Favorable government initiatives like Jan Dhan Yojana, Jan Dhan Aadhar Mobile, Startup India, License for payment banks, Digital India Programme through robust public digital infrastructure (Aadhar linking, UPI, Account aggregation, OCEN etc.), recognition of P2P lenders as NBFCs and National Common Mobility Card through initiatives of RBI, IRDAI and SEBI favored the growth of Fintech. Scheduled banks have to set up 75 digital banking units in 75 districts in India. For easy registration for potential startups a dedicated portal was also started.

(b) ***Funding environment:*** Growth of VC (Venture Capitalist) and PE (Private Equity) firms along with expansion of Insur tech and Wealth tech sectors has made easier availability of funds for the Fintech sectors.

(c) ***Demographic opportunities and Public Infrastructure:*** 1180 million wireless subscribers were in India as in March 2021. The figure touched 1143.93 million at the end of March 2023. By 2030 India is expected to add 140 million middle income and 21 million high income household as wireless subscribers. Expansion of Digital India Initiatives is also in Tier-II and Tier-III cities in India.

Linking of Aadhar through KYC and introduction of OCEN (Open Credit Enablement Network) Network is further expanding the market for Fintech sector. Thus, increase in connectivity, use of smart phones and Government initiatives may have acted as stimulators to the growth of Fintech sector. This expansion may have been possible due to increased use of smart phones with high speed 4G and 5G internet services.

2. *Technology Driven*

(a) ***Strong technical and human resource pool:*** Use of Artificial Intelligence, Machine Learning, Biometric Identity Verification Technologies (Voice, Face recognition, IRIS scanning) e-KYC, Video-KYC, Big Data Analysis, Intelligence Robotic Process Automation (IRPA) are helping Fintech startups to reduce cost. These services create collaboration with Fintech and banks, financial service providers and in certain cases Fintech act as Back Offices for banks.

India has strong technical team with respect to Engineering, Technology, Management and Competitive human resource making India one of the low cost working destination. All these factors favored the growth of Fintech sector in India. A table given below provides information about the steady growth in adopting and deepening of digital payments across the country.

Table 6: DPI Index

Quarter Ending	*DPI Index*
Sep-20	217
Mar-21	270
Sep-21	304
Mar-22	349

Source: RBI

The sub-parameters against which the digital payment index is measured are:

- Payment enablers (mobile, Aadhar, bank accounts, merchants).
- *Payment infrastructure—demand side:* Debit cards, credit cards, prepaid payment instruments, FASTags.
- *Payment infrastructure—supply side:* Bank branches, business correspondents, ATMs, PoS terminals, QR codes, intermediaries.
- *Payment performance:* Volume, value, unique users, currency in circulation, cash withdrawals.
- *Consumer centricity:* Awareness, declines, complaints, frauds, system down-time.

As we migrate from September 20 to March 22 it may be observed that DPI Index as increased by 129%

3. *Customer Driven*

(a) *Highly tech savvy consumer base looking for low cost services:* Tech savvy Indian masses are adopting to more and more smart phone usage along with mobile-first product services. Use of digital currency wire transfer is being processed in India at low cost due to technical factors as stated above. These factors favored the growth of Fintech industry.

Some Initiatives Taken by Fintech in India

For SME Sector- to bring cost effectiveness Fintech are helping in different ways. Below are examples of such ways:

(a) *Implement Bring Your Own Device (BYOD) policy:* Through use of own device and providing of reimbursement of employee's service plans in case of IT and IT enabled services the business entities are not only monitoring the activities of employee but also controlling cost as only recurring expenses are being borne. Creation of virtual workplace with access to various software applications stored in cloud further reduces infrastructural cost.

(b) *Outsource non-critical tasks to experts:* For cost effectiveness outsourcing has been one of the manufacturing strategies in the global village in the last few decades Outsourcing of low level maintenance task and specialized knowledge services through a professional pool of experts provided by Fintech through various IT and digital enabled services no doubt reduces cost and is also good for the company's health.

(c) *Boost worker efficiency:* Use of back end processes supported by Artificial Intelligence and Process Automation reduces workload on individuals. This in turn act as motivators and in certain cases may boost up worker's productivity.

Conclusion

Financing through IPOs as initial investment for Fintech may have been a positive incentive but performance of Fintech stock lost sheen in the recent market. The reason behind the Fintech stock loosing sheen may be due to rising borrowing rates in the global market and increasing demand for finance with increase in total size of banking, lending, trading, investing and insurance sector.

It may be worth mentioning over here that for sustainability of Fintech sector Asset Light Model are being introduced but availability of Fintech talent with ever changing regulation enabling customer interest protection, transparency and collaboration is another obstacle for Fintech growth in India. As we move towards Digital India's moto of "Power to empower" through participation of government sector and private sector we need to build World's most comprehensive Digital Public Good Infrastructure to create more OCEN and ONDC (Open Network for Digital Commerce) facilities. Optimisation of all these negative and positive forces will no doubt increase the growth of Fintech industry in India.

References

[1] The Winds of Change: Trends shaping India's Fintech Sector (September 2021) retrieved fromhttps://www.iamai.in/sites/default/files/research/EY%20FCC-%20The%20Winds%20of%20Change%20-%20India%20FinTech%20Report%20-%20Final%20%281%29_0.pdf, accessed on 17.12.2023 at 10.30 pm.

[2] The Winds of Change: Trends shaping India's Fintech Sector: edition II (September 2022) retrieved from ey-winds-of-change-india-fintech-report-2022%20.pdf, accessed on 17.12.2023 at 11.00 pm.

[3] 15 Cost-Cutting Ideas and Spend Optimization Tips for your SME retrieved from https://www.fujifilm.com/fbhk/en/insights/article/15-spend-optimization-tips-for-your-sme , accessed on 20.12.2023 at 12.30 pm

[4] What Trends are Driving the Fintech Revolution in India? (June 2022) retrieved from https://www.india-briefing.com/news/what-trends-are-driving-the-fintech-revolution-in-india- 23809.html/#:~:text=In%202020%2C%20India%20topped%20among,almost%20double%20that%20of%20China, accessed on 23.12.2023 at 11.30 pm.

Dividend Policy and Its Liaison with Firm Performance

Debasish Bera[1], Mrinal Maity[2] and Sanjib Das[3]

ABSTRACT: The basic aim of this study is to examine whether dividend policy impacts firm performance in the Indian Oil & Gas sector. Data have been collected from the published annual reports, and money control.com from the period 2014 to 2023. According to market capitalization, the top two companies in the Indian oil and gas industry are selected. Firm performance is represented by Return on Equity (ROE) and Return on Assets (ROA). On the other hand, dividend policy is measured by the Dividend pay-out ratio (DPOR), Earnings per Share (EPS), Price to Earnings Ratio (P/E), Price/Book Value Ratio (Price BV). Moreover, the debt-equity ratio, current ratio, and Ln_firm size are taken as control variables. Panel data regression model is used in the study. The study finds that firm performance is positively affected by Earning per share and negatively affected by dividend payout ratio and Debt equity ratio.

Keywords: Dividend Policy, Firm Performance, Return on Assets, Return on Equity.

JEL Classification: G35, G32, L25.

Introduction

The term dividend refers to the part of the profits of a company that the company distributes among its shareholders. Distribution of dividends out of current earnings is crucial in the financial management decision-making process. Since there is no statutory obligation on a company to pay dividends, therefore it depends upon the company's policy to pay or not. The distribution of dividends has two sides of financial importance. First, from the investor's perspective, and second from the company's viewpoint. From an investor's point of view, every shareholder wants to increase their current returns on investment thus, they prefer more dividends in order to increase their wealth. The more logical standpoint of shareholders may be of the time value of money, i.e.,

[1] Research Scholar, Department of Commerce, Vidyasagar University, Midnapore, West Bengal-721102, India. E-mail: mcomdb2014@gmail.com

[2] Assistant Professor, Department of Commerce, Tamralipta Mahavidyalaya, Tamluk, Uttar Chara Sankarara, West Bengal-721636, India. E-mail: mrinalcom19@tmv.ac.in

[3] Assistant Professor, Department of Commerce, Egra Sarada Shashi Bhusan College, Egra, West Bengal-721429, India. E-mail: sanjibdas.egra@gmail.com

receipt of a dividend today has more value than receiving the same later or time of liquidation of the company. But, from the side of the company's management, the earnings may be retained for future purposes instead of paying dividends. In case of a higher amount of earnings is paid to shareholders, a dividend, may reduce cash in hand as well as retained earnings of the company. On the contrary, if less or no amount is paid to shareholders then a substantial amount of earnings may be used in the future for business growth, or diversification purposes as ploughing back profits. Since retained earnings bear less cost of capital therefore may be proven as an economic source without incurring extra efforts and diluting shareholder's rights in a company.

As we have learned there are two views of dividends, similarly there are two sets of approaches to dividend policy, one approach treats dividend policy as an irrelevance and the other treats it as relevant for firms. The relevance of dividend policy is described by famous theories i.e., Walter's model and Gordon's model, and the irrelevance theory is concluded in the MM model. Therefore, the dividend policy of a firm plays a crucial role in determining its financial performance and attractiveness to investors.

Financial performance serves as a fundamental indicator of how a company can utilize assets from its primary business mode to generate revenue. Numerous stakeholders are keen on monitoring the financial performance of the company. The financial performance of a company indicates how well it generates revenues and manages its assets, liabilities, and the business interests of its stakeholders (Shiranthi, A.A., & Perera, I.N.D.I.K.A., 2020).

The purpose of this research is to determine how the firms' financial performance is impacted by their dividend policies. The study will also attempt to draw conclusions from various theories and research arguments regarding the causes of and connections between dividend policies and the financial performances of the firms, as well as identify the key variables influencing the dividend policies of the companies.

The oil and gas companies operating in a capital-intensive industry with significant financing needs, often face unique challenges and considerations in formulating their dividend policies. The Indian Oil & Gas industry plays a vital role in fuelling the rapid growth of the Indian economy and influencing decision-making for all the other important sections of the economy. It is the third largest consumer of petroleum products, after US and China. Indian Oil & Gas industry always has an increased focus on gas and renewables, oil demand, and it is estimated to grow at least until 2040. As per the report published by India Brand Equity Foundation (IBEF), India's energy demand is expected to double to 1,516 million tonnes of oil equivalent (Mtoe) by 2035 from 927 Mtoe in 2021.

The Government has taken many initiatives to fulfil the increasing demand. It has allowed 100% Foreign Direct Investment (FDI) in many segments of the sector, including natural gas, petroleum products, and refineries, among others. Today, it attracts both domestic and foreign investment as attested by the presence of Reliance Industries Ltd. (RIL) and Cairn India. This study aims to examine the relationship between dividend policy (represented by ratios) and firm performance in the context of selected oil and gas companies in India. For the purpose of the study, we have systematized the entire paper into five parts. Section I consists of an Introduction. The rest of this paper is organized as follows: Section II covers an overview of the existing literature and research gap. Section III describes the objectives of the study and its hypotheses. the research methodology used for this study presents the research framework and methodology and analysis, findings whereas section V discusses the conclusion, limitations, and future scope of the study.

Review of Literature

For the purpose of the study, we have reviewed some relevant literatures which are briefly mentioned below.

Mohammed Amidu (2007) in their study found a positive relationship between return on assets, dividend policy, and growth in sales from 1997 to 2004 through OLS model of regression equation. Surprisingly, the study revealed that bigger firms on the GSE performed less with respect to return on assets. The results also revealed negative associations between return on assets and dividend payout ratio and leverage. Priya, & Nimalathasan (2013) analyzed dividend policy ratios and firm performance using correlation and multiple regression analysis during the period 2008 to 2012 of selected hotels & restaurants in Sri Lanka. The results showed that dividend policy ratios had a great impact on all firm performance ratios except Return on Investment (ROI) and Return on Equity (ROE). Further EPS, P/E and PB are significantly correlated with ROA at 5 percent level of significance. At the same time, P/E is significantly correlated with ROE at 5 percent level of significance. Finally, EPS and PB are significantly correlated with ROE at 1 percent level of significance. Anton (2016) investigated the impact of dividend policy on firm performance of non-financial firms listed on the Bucharest Stock Exchange. The study used panel data constructed from the financial statements of sixty-three non-financial firms listed on the Bucharest Stock Exchange over the period 2001–2011. The result showed that dividend payout ratio, firm size, the degree of indebtedness and firm value (TQ) were positively correlated but negative correlation between debt ratio and dividend payout ratio indicated that leveraged firms were likely to pay lower dividends. Employing a fixed effects model, we found that dividend payout ratio positively influenced the firm value after the control of other firm-specific variables. Farrukh, Irshad, Shams Khakwani, Ishaque, and Ansari (2017) pointed out the influence of dividend policy on firm's performance and shareholders' wealth of a sample of 51 companies from Pakistan stock exchange for the period of 2006–2015 by employing common constant effect model. The result showed that dividend policy positively and significantly influenced the EPS, share price and ROA. Therefore, it was concluded that the study supported dividend relevance theory, signalling effect theory, bird in hand theory and clientele-effect theory. Israel. Odion E. Idewele and Bein A. Murad, (2017) analysed the relationship between financial performance and dividend policy for a sample of fifteen deposit money banks quoted on the Nigeria Stock Exchange from 2009 to 2014. Panel data regression analysis was used as the method of analysis and the model was estimated using the Pooled Least Squares estimation technique. The study revealed that there was a positive and significant relationship between dividend payout ratio and financial performance. On the contrary, there was a negative and insignificant relationship between dividend yield and financial performance. The study recommended that since there was a positive and significant relationship between dividend payout ratio and financial performance, firms should strive to maintain healthy and a stable dividend policy. N Suresh & Pooja M (2020) studied the determinants of dividend policy and its impact on financial performance of 60 NSE listed Indian firms for the period 2009-2018 using correlation and panel OLS regression analysis model. The result revealed a positive and significant relationship between dividend policy and return on assets. This result indicated the enhancement of profitability of the organisation and attracted investors. This will also encourage the investors to invest in the organisation because of positive NPV. Muhammad, Abdul, & Khali (2023) examined that impact of dividend policy on firm performance within the context of non-financial firms of Pakistan. The study used descriptive statistics, correlation, and regression techniques for analysing the data during the period 2010-2021. The result showed that dividend policy and financial performance variables were positively correlated and all the independent variable was statistically significant to explain the dependent variable.

Research Gap

Based on the literatures as reviewed above, it is found that most of the studies are related to the dividend policy and financial performances which were conducted both at national and foreign context. However, no such studies are found on oil and gas industries. Hence, this study may act as a pointer to the existing literature.

Objectives of the Study

The key objective of the study is to examine the impact of dividend policy on firm performance of the selected sample companies in Indian oil and gas industry. To attain this key objective, the following secondary objectives are required to be achieved:

- To identify the factors that significantly contribute to the firm performance.
- To examine the relationship between dividend policy ratios and firm performance.

Hypotheses of the Study

In compliance with the above stated objectives, the following testable hypotheses have been formulated as follows:

- H_{01}: Dividend policy has no impact on Return on Equity.
- H_{A1}: Dividend policy has impact on Return on Equity.
- H_{02}: Dividend policy has no impact on Return on Assets.
- H_{A2}: Dividend policy has impact on Return on Assets.

Basic Models and Research Methodology

We have considered the following variables so as to fulfil the objectives of the study.

Table 1: Variables Used

Dividend Policy Ratios	
Earnings Per Share (EPS)	Net Income/Total Number of Capita
Price to Earnings Ratio (P/E)	Market Price per Share/Earnings per Share
Dividend Payout Ratio (DPOR)	Total Dividends/Total Net Earnings × 100%
Price/Book Value Ratio (PriceBV)	Stock Price Per Share/Shareholders' Equity Per Share
Firm Performance Ratios	
Return on Asset (ROA)	Return/Total Asset × 100
Return on Equity (ROE)	Profit after interest & tax/Equity capital × 100
Control Variables	
Debt Equity Ratio (Debt Equity)	Long-term debt/Shareholders fund
Current Ratio (CR)	Profit after interest & tax/Equity capital × 100
Firm Size (Ln_FirmSize)	Ln_Total Assets

Source: Conceptualised by authors

Basic Models of the Study

Multiple regression analysis has been performed to investigate the impact of dividend policy ratios on firm performance of the selected sample companies in the Indian oil and gas industry. For this purpose, we have used the following model which is given below.

Firm Performance = f (ROA; and ROE) It is important to note that firm performance depends upon Earnings Per Share (EPS), Price to price-to-earnings ratio (P/E), Dividend Payout Ratio (DPOR), and Price/Book Value Ratio (PB). We consider the Current Ratio (CR), Debt Equity Ratio (Debt-Equity) and Firm Size (Ln_Firm Size) as control variables. Firm performance ratios are represented by Return on Asset (ROA) and Return on Equity (ROE).

The following two models are formulated to measure the impact of dividend policy ratios on firm performance:

$$ROA = \alpha + \beta1\ EPS + \beta2 P/E + \beta3 DPOR + \beta4 PriceBV + \beta5 CR + \beta6 DebtEquity + \beta7 Ln\_FirmSize + \varepsilon \quad \ldots (1)$$

$$ROE = \alpha + \beta1\ EPS + \beta2 P/E + \beta3 DPOR + \beta4 PriceBV + \beta5 CR + \beta6 DebtEquity + \beta7 Ln\_FirmSize + \varepsilon \quad \ldots (2)$$

Where, α is constant,

$\beta1$, $\beta2$, $\beta3$, $\beta4$, $\beta5$, $\beta6$ and $\beta7$ are coefficients of variables, and $\in$ is the error term of the models.

Sample Companies: Two leading companies in Indian Oil and Gas industry are selected for the study, namely: Bharat Petroleum Corporation Limited (BPCL) and Hindustan Petroleum Corporation Limited (HPCL).

Study Period: The present study spans a total of 10 years i.e., beginning in 2014 and ending in 2023 in order to examine the impact of dividend policy ratios on firm performance of the selected sample companies in Indian oil and gas industry.

Data Source: The study is solely based on secondary data which are collected from the published annual reports of the selected companies. Moreover, data from the websites like money control.com and topstockresearch.com are also used in this study.

Tools Used for Analysis: For the analysis of each of the nature of the variables, we have used descriptive study. We have also conducted a panel data analysis (both fixed and random effect) model to examine the impact of dividend policy ratios on the firm performance of the selected sample companies in the Indian oil and gas industry.

Data Analysis and Discussion

Multicollinearity

A correlation matrix is used in order to determine the presence of multi-co linearity among the independent variables in the study. These methodologies involved calculation of a tolerance test and Variance Inflation Factor (VIF). The results of this analysis are presented in Table 2.

Table 2: Test of Multicollinearity

Variable	*Tolerance*	*VIF*
Ln_FirmSize	0.333461	3.00
CR	0.276025	3.62
PriceBV	0.336333	2.97
P/E	0.276442	3.62
EPS	0.454088	2.20
DebtEquity	0.363817	2.75
DPOR	0.779051	1.28

Source: Authors' own calculation

According to Table 2, all the tolerance level is above 0.25 and also VIF values are perfectly which is below 5. Therefore, there is no presence of multi co linearity among the independent and control variables.

Table 3 describes the correlation between dividend policy ratios and firm performance. It indicates that Earnings per Share (EPS), Price-earnings ratio (P/E), price-to-book value ratio (Price BV), and equity ratio (Debt Equity) are significantly correlated with Return on Assets (ROA) at 5 or 10 percent level of significance.

But in the case of Return on equity (ROE), only the Price-to-book value ratio (Price BV) and the debt Equity ratio (Debt equity) are significantly correlated at 5 or 10 percent level of significance. The rest of the other variables are not correlated. Hence, multiple regression analysis is performed to identify the predictors of firm performance variables as hypothesized in the models. A step-wise variable selection is used in the regression analysis and Table 3 provides the summary measure of the models.

Table 3: Correlation Matrix

	ROE	*ROA*	*DPOR*	*EPS*	*P/E*	*PriceBV*	*DebtEq~y*	*CR*	*Ln_Fir~e*
DPOR	–0.391 (0.087)	–0.096 (0.684)	1.000						
EPS	0.383 (0.094)	0.760* (0.000)	–0.006 (0.978)	1.000					
P/E	0.305 (0.190)	0.5798* (0.007)	0.154 (0.515)	0.584* (0.006)	1.000				
PriceBV	0.513* (0.020)	0.547* (0.012)	0.067 (0.777)	0.280 (0.231)	0.589* (0.006)	1.000			
DebtEq~y	–0.572* (0.008)	–0.695* (0.000)	0.062 (0.793)	–0.351 (0.128)	–0.406 (0.075)	–0.475 (0.034)	1.000		
CR	–0.050 (0.833)	0.150 (0.527)	–0.118 (0.619)	0.426 (0.060)	0.350 (0.129)	0.185 (0.434)	0.325 (0.161)	1.000	
Ln_Fir~e	–0.314 (0.177)	–0.299 (0.199)	0.325 (0.160)	–0.235 (0.316)	–0.016 (0.944)	–0.389 (0.089)	–0.051 (0.830)	–0.572 (0.008)	1.000

Source: Authors' own calculation
Correlation is significant at 0.10 level (2-tailed)
* Correlation is significant at 0.05 level (2-tailed)

Panel Regression Model

Regression model is a statistical tool which used to establish association among variables. It helps in establishing fact that how the particular value of a dependent variable will change with any change in one of the independent variables; while keeping other independent variables fixed. It helps in conducting multi-dimensional analysis over a period.

For panel regression, first we will try to know which method is best for our model. In this context, two methods are available: Fixed effect model and Random effect model. It is tested to ascertain whether fixed effects or random effects would be required to develop the model. In this respect, it can be checked by Hausman test.

Table 4 exhibits the result of Panel Data Analysis under both Fixed effect and Random effect models. The Hausman test accepts the Random Effect Model as the expected model for panel data analysis. The p-value (0.004) of the Chi^2 (20.69) of the random effect model shows that the model is a good fit for the study. The value of R^2 indicates that the model is explaining 63% variation of ROE. The p-values of the coefficients Earning per share (EPS) (0.104), Debt Equity ratio (–1.709), Ln_ Firmsize (–13.983), Current Ratio (CR) (–1.709), Price to Book Value Ratio (5.373) and Price Earnings Ratio (P/E) (0.043) are

Table 4: Regression Analysis (Dependent Variable: ROE)

Model/ Independent Variable	*Fixed Effect Model Coefficients (p-value)*	*Random Effect Model Coefficients (p-value)*	*Hausman Test Chi² (p-value)*	*Preferred Model*
Constant	–59.931 (0.729)	104.760 (0.374)	1.78 (0.9710)	Random Effect Model (As the p-value of Chi² >.05)
DPOR	–.072 (0.196)	–.099 (0.047)		
EPS	0.066 (0.442)	0.104 (0.203)		
PriceBV	9.122 (0.111)	5.373 (0.241)		
DebtEquity	–3.075 (0.456)	–1.709 (0.666)		
CR	–4.433 (0.856)	–23.421 (0.235)		
Ln_FirmSize	13.975 (0.642)	–13.983 (0.505)		
P/E	.261 (0.446)	.043 (0.882)		
R^2	0.43	0.63		
F/Chi²	3.39 (0.034)	20.69 (0.004)		

*Significant at 5% level.

ROE: Return on Equity, DPOR: Dividend Payout Ratio, EPS: Earnings Per Share, Price BV: Price/Book Value Ratio, Debt-Equity: Debt Equity Ratio, CR: Current Ratio, Ln_FirmSize: Firm Size, P/E: Price to Earnings Ratio.

Source: Authors' own calculation

lying above the significance level at 0.05. So, all the above variables are insignificant and are not contributing to the firm performance in terms of Return on Equity (ROE). However, the coefficient of DPOR (–0.099) and the p-value is 0.047 which is lies under the significance level, it means 1% change in dividend payout ratio will change the return on equity negatively at 9.9%.

Table 5 shows the result of panel data analysis under both Fixed effect and Random effect models. The Hausman Test accepts the Random Effect Model as the expected model for panel data analysis. The p-value (0.000) of the Chi^2 (63.58) of the Random effect model shows that the model is a good fit for the study. The value of R^2 indicates that the model is explaining 84 % variation of ROA. The p-values of the coefficients of Dividend Payout ratio (DPOR) (–

0.003), Earning per share (EPS) (0.070), Ln_ Firmsize (–6.058), Current Ratio (CR) (–3.509), Price to Book Value Ratio (0.627) and Price Earnings Ratio (P/E) (0.034) are lying above the significance level at 0.05 except Earnings per Share (EPS) and Debt Equity ratio. ROA is significant positively affected by Earning per share and significant negatively affected by the equity ratio.

Table 5: Regression Analysis (Dependent Variable: ROA)

Model/ Independent Variable	*Fixed Effect Model Coefficients (p-value)*	*Random Effect Model Coefficients (p-value)*	*Hausman Test Chi^2 (p-value)*	*Preferred Model*
Constant	–21.256 (0.619)	37.389 (0.229)	3.82 (0.8008)	Random Effect Model (As the p-value of Chi^2>.05)
DPOR	0.0057 (0.665)	–.003 (0.770)		
EPS	.0571 (0.019)	.070 (0.001)		
PriceBV	1.962 (0.158)	0.627 (0.604)		
DebtEquity	–2.534 (0.025)	–2.047 (0.050)		
CR	3.252 (0.591)	–3.509 (0.500)		
Ln_FirmSize	3.897 (0.599)	–6.058 (0.274)		
P/E	0.111 (0.197)	.034 (0.661)		
R^2	0.70	0.84		
F/Chi^2	11.08 (0.0003)	63.58 (0.000)		

*Significant at 5% level.

ROA: Return on Assets, DPOR: Dividend Payout Ratio, EPS: Earnings Per Share, Price BV: Price/Book Value Ratio, Debt-Equity: Debt Equity Ratio, CR: Current Ratio, Ln_FirmSize: Firm Size, P/E: Price to Earnings Ratio.

Source: Authors' own calculation

Conclusion

This research has shed light on the complex connections between dividend policy and company success in India's oil and gas sector. Model I, focusing on Return on Equity, and Model II, focusing on Return on Assets, were both validated using the random effect regression framework as required. These models provide a strong analytical foundation for understanding the complicated relationship between dividend policy and financial performance measures. The study lays a solid groundwork for future research, offering valuable insights that can aid in making strategic decisions and forming policies across the sector. The results underscore the importance of the Dividend Payout Ratio in influencing profitability, particularly in its substantial impact on Return on Equity. On the other hand, Return on Equity was found to be unaffected by variables such as Earnings Per Share, Price-to-Book Value, Debt-Equity ratio, Current Ratio, Firm Size, and Price-to-Earnings ratio. The study also emphasizes the favorable influence of the Debt-Equity ratio and Earnings Per Share on improving asset efficiency, particularly on Return on Assets.

Limitations and Future Scope

The study has been conducted only on two Indian oil & Gas Companies for a period of 10 years i.e., from 2014 to 2024. Besides, the study is based on historical data. Other industry may have exhibits different result. Other important aspect that we have not captured in this study are government policies, tax rates, inflation, and economic condition of the country, that directly or indirectly affect the dividend payout ratio and firm performance.

Despite the limitations as stated above, further study may be carried out in this line of research by including more sample companies with a longer period of study, corporate governance variable and other important aspects.

References

[1] Amidu, M. (2007). How does dividend policy affect performance of the firm on Ghana stock Exchange? Investment management and financial innovations, 4(2), 103–112.

[2] Anton, S.G. (2016). The impact of dividend policy on firm value. A panel data analysis of Romanian listed firms. *Journal of public administration, finance and law. (10),* 107–112.

[3] Farrukh, K., Irshad, S., Shams Khakwani, M., Ishaque, S. and Ansari, N. Y. (2017). Impact of dividend policy on shareholders wealth and firm performance in Pakistan. *Cogent Business & Management.* 4(1), 1408208. doi:https://doi.org/10.1080/23311975.2017.

[4] Idewele, I.O.E. and Murad, B.A. (2019). Dividend policy and financial performance: a study of selected deposit money banks in Nigeria. *African Journal of Business Management, 13*(7), 239–255. DOI: 10.5897/AJBM2018.8667.

[5] Jaara, B., Alashhab, H. and Jaara, O.O. (2018). The determinants of dividend policy for non-financial companies in Jordan. *International Journal of Economics and Financial Issues, 8*(2), 198–209.

[6] Jatoi, M. Z., Rasheed, A. and Wahla, K. (2023). Impact of Dividend Policy on Firm Performance: Evidence from Non-Financial Firms of Pakistan. *Pakistan Journal of*

Humanities and Social Sciences, *11*(2). https://doi.org/10.52131/pjhss.2023.1102.0430.

[7] Priya, K. and Nimalathasan, B. (2013). Dividend policy ratios and firm performance: a case study of Selected Hotels & Restaurants in Sri Lanka. *Global Journal of Commerce & Management Perspective*, *2*(6), 16–22.

[8] Rahman, A. (2018). Effect of dividend policy on firm's performance: A case study of cement sector Pakistan. SEISENSE Journal of Management, 1(5), 6–15. doi:https://doi.org/10.5281/zenodo.1450462.

[9] Suresh, N. and Pooja, M. (2020). Determinants of Dividend Policy and its Impact on Financial Performances: A Panel Data Analysis for Indian Listed Firms. *Journal of Seybold Report*, *15 (8)*, 2791–2799.

[10] Retrieved from https://www.moneycontrol.com

The Impact of Green Finance on Sustainable Development in India

Amitabha Bhattacharyya[1]

ABSTRACT: Green finance is two-way relationship between the environment and finance and investment. The term green refers to human activities that should be environment-friendly. According to the 2030 plan, all financial activities including investment must be shifted from carbon and intensive resources to sustainable finance. It means that the green finance is closely connected with the economy in nature. The Green finance is defined as the monetary assistance provided for the projects which deals with environmental protection, investing in renewable sources of energy, increasing the green cover, mitigating the effects of climate change, and all other projects related to sustainable development. The government agencies and financial institutions should provide the fund to support the sustainable green finance implementation and continuously support for finding out the innovative ways to attain the goal of sustainability. The present study is conducted on the aspects of Green Bonds, Green Banking, and Green Insurance as a part of Green Financing and also evaluates the opportunities and challenges for Green Finance in India.

Keywords: Financial Market, Green Banking, Green Bond, Green Finance, Green Insurance, Green Investment, Investor, Stakeholders, Sustainable Development.

Introduction

Green finance is an economic system which is specifically use for economically sustainable projects that embrace aspects of climate change. Environmentally, sustainable project means which include the production of energy from renewable sources such as solar, wind, biogas, etc. The clean transportation includes low greenhouse gas emissions; waste management which includes recycling, efficient disposal, and conversion to energy, etc.; Energy efficient projects such as green buildings. The sustainable defined projects under disclosure requirements for green debt securities include sustainable waste, climate change adaptation, and water management. Uses of Sustainable land which includes sustainable forestry, agriculture and biodiversity conservation (SEBI 2017). To meet the financial needs of these types of projects, new financial instruments such as Carbon market tools (e.g. carbon tax); green bonds; and new

[1] Associate Professor of Commerce, Balurghat College, Dakshin Dinajpur, West Bengal, India. E-mail: amitabha.bhttchr@gmail.com

financial institutions (e.g. green banks) are being set up. These are made together the green finance. The Green finance is at the centre of the overall discussion on the sustainability of economic growth. To achieve the sustainable growth, green finance have been developed in major countries that include all stakeholders in economic development, such as governments, central banks and corporates. The need for protecting the environment and preserving natural resources from the increasing problems like ozone layer depletion, global warming, increasing pollution levels, cut-throat competition for scarce non-renewable sources of energy, and other environmental issues. Green finance is to create a balance between nature and economics. Monetary assistance provided for the projects which contributing to sustainability like the construction of green buildings, efficient management of energy, waste management, preservation of biodiversity, projects related to renewable sources of energy and other related projects can be termed as Green financing. The 2015 Paris agreement has considered the financial aspect on long-term goals i.e. limiting the rise of global average temperature and increasing the ability in adapting to the impacts of climate change. In this article, the attempt has been made to evaluate the emerging trends and challenges of green finance in India

Literature Review

Chowdhury and Datta *et al.* (2013) explained that green finance is a powerful instrument which will reduce the greenhouse gas emission, green building saves energy and keeps healthy environment. The author also explained that the green finance has the ability to generate equal return on investment compare to the traditional instrument. Keerti (2013) described that India's energy area is not at all capable to keep the peace with excessive financial boom fee inside the use which results the chronic energy cut and lack. He further defined that the Indian government targeted more at the renewable electricity area for minimizing the dependency on the import of power. The author also defined that Climate Change has a major reason which effect courting with agriculture and rural improvement activities, sports such as forestry, agriculture and different land use activities, like dairy, soil conservation, strength use practices, use of renewable energy which results incredible potential for decreasing the GHG emission. Dipika (2015) explained the tendency of the business organizations and the stakeholders and their importance on environmental protection and sustainable development. The researcher also concluded that the green banking helps to improve economic growth and protects the environment and so the green lending should be given priority for sustainable development. Soundarrajan *et al.* (2016) mentioned that Green finance is the core part of low carbon growth connecting with the financial industry, environmental improvement, and economic growth and also concluded that sustainable finance is the future. Indian banks should play an important role of change agent with the overall emphasis on three P's of People, Planet and Profit. Joseph (2017) described about the idea of green finance in an Indian context and the importance of green finance in exceptional ways. The author mentioned the steps to be taken by the authorities of India for application of inexperienced finance through diverse schemes. Green finance helps to improve the environment in the country like India. Mohd *et al.* (2018) studied the role played by the Green Finance between the environment and the economy to bring harmony and also mentioned the various Green financial instruments available for the sustainability initiatives in India. There is needed a great potential to create a green infrastructure for green finance in India. Sai and Reddy (2018) discussed about the current status of green finance in India. He said that the growth of green finance in India is at very low stage and the government of India has to take many steps for the promotion of green finance. The author also explained that the Government should bring stable policy framework for green finance for removing constraints and also encourages the private sectors for finance sustainable development programs. Bielinski and Mosionek *et al.* (2019) explained that EU leads the world's shift towards sustainable economy and more investment needed in the sectors such as renewable energy generation and transmission, renovation and energy efficient building, and low carbon transportation. Krozer (2019) explained that the global shift towards low-carbon economies needs five times larger annual investments in renewable energy and energy efficiency compared with the present and it can be done through public savings. The good condition like the cost-reducing technology helps in shifting towards low carbon economy. Al-Louzi and Busler (2021) discussed the status of green finance and sustainability in the Middle East region which has a main focus on Saudi Arabia, Qatar, and the United Arab Emirates. The authors pointed that there are significant potential in green finance for promoting sustainable development in this region if the challenges such as a lack of awareness, regulatory frameworks, and financial infrastructure is overcomes. Sharma and Mishra (2021), the researchers review the regulatory and policy frameworks for green finance and also the institutionalization of green finance and its effectiveness in promoting sustainable development. After critical analysis of the previous studies. it can be said that tremendous work has been done in the field of green finance. Some considered green finance as an emerging form of sustainable development, while some take green finance as a phenomenon that mixes the world of finance and commercial enterprise with environmentally pleasant behavior. Green finance can be expressed otherwise depending at the player, and it is able to be led by using monetary incentives, a desire to hold the planet, or a mixture of each. Contrary to the traditional monetary sports, green finance emphasizes more at the ecological environment gain and pays greater attention to environmental protection enterprise. Green banking is furnished to make sure the use of organizational resources for the environment and society.

After going through the previous studies, it can be stated that green finance is that branch of modern finance which focuses on environmental sustainability along with the profitability of the interested parties. It includes all the measures which have far reaching impact on the positive side of the environment and ensures the preservation and conservation of the environmental resources for the future generation. Green finance includes measures like granting loans at lower interest rate than market rate for environmental projects, raising money through green bonds, forestry securitization, weather derivatives, nature linked securities, using e- payment services, using electronic vehicles and all other practices which either reduces the use of natural resources or creates new sources which the help of financial activities.

Need of the Study

Green finance has made tremendous attention in modern financial market by issuing the instruments like green bonds, green equity and green debenture. World Bank has issued the first green bond on 2008 when the intergovernmental of climate change provided the data on climate change with its political and economic impact. In 2017, Indian Renewable Energy Development Agency (IREDA) has launched first Masala Bonds which raised $300 million for renewable energy (London stock exchange group, 2017). India set the target for reducing the carbon emission intensity of GDP 33 to 35% by the 2030 under the national determination goals. India also made the announcement that it becomes the first country in the world which will use only electronic vehicles by 2030.

India has set the following targets for the period 2021–2030:

1. To reduce the GDP emissions by 33% to 35% from 2005 levels by 2030.
2. To achieve approximately 40% of the accumulated electrical installation capacity of non-fossil gas-based energy assets by 2030 and transfer the Yuga and Coffee Fee Global Finance from the Green Climate Fund (GCF).
3. To create an additional carbon sink equivalent to 2.5 to 3 billion tons of CO_2 through the additional forest and tree protection by 2030.
4. To implement agriculture, forestry, fisheries infrastructure, water resources and ecosystem adaptation India preliminarily need about 6 206 billion (at 2014–15 prices) between 2015 and 2030.
5. To assess the cost of adapting to climate change in South Asia as suggests by the Asian Development Bank (ADB) that the estimated adaptation cost for India in the energy sector alone will be approximately 77.7 billion in 2030.
6. According to the National Institution for Transforming India (NITI) Commission estimates that mitigation measures for moderate to low carbon development will cost about 83834 billion by 2030 at 2011 prices.

7. A preliminary estimate over time suggests that at least 22 (2014–2015 fever) may be needed to complete India's climate change movement by 2030.

Objectives of the Study

1. To understand the concept of Green Finance.
2. To analyse the trend of Green Financing in India.
3. To study the various aspects of Green Finance that helps in attaining sustainability goals.
4. To analyse the benefits and limitations of Green Finance.

Research Methodology

This is an exploratory research where the existing literature available on green finance has been reviewed so that new research direction in this area can be enlightened. This study is of descriptive nature and is based on secondary data collected from various sources such as journals, research articles, government reports and websites.

Green Finance as an Effective Tool Towards Sustainability

Funding the projects through green financing which aim to achieving sustainable development and helps in creating harmony between the environment, finance, and development. It helps in protecting the natural resources, encourages the using of renewable energy resources, and attempts to reduce the exploitation of the environment by the human beings. Green financing works as an effective tool to attain the sustainable development goals for the country.

Carbon Tax: It is a form of Pollution Tax. It levies a fee on the production, distribution or use of fossil fuels based on how much carbon their combustion emits. It is a cost-effective tool to reduce greenhouse gas emissions in the atmosphere. Carbon tax is a pollution tax that is levied on the burning of carbon-based fossil fuels and it is paid by the consumers and producers. The tax levied on the basis of carbon emission from industry, number of employee hour and turnover of the factory is called carbon tax. This tax is paid by industries.

Carbon Credit: Carbon credits are part of national and international efforts to mitigate growth in concentrations of greenhouse gases (GHGs). These programs cap greenhouse gas emissions. Markets then allocate the emissions among the group of regulated sources. Carbon credits are a transparent, measurable and results-based way for companies to support activities, such as protecting and restoring irrecoverable natural carbon sinks, like forests or marine ecosystems and scaling nascent carbon removal technology that keep global climate goals within reach. Carbon credits are financial instruments where the buyer pays another company to take some action to reduce its greenhouse gas emissions, and the buyer gets credit for the reduction. As companies creep closer to their net zero target years, many have already begun purchasing carbon credits.

Global Green Finance

The City UK is an industry-led body representing UK-based financial and related professional services that made the following survey.

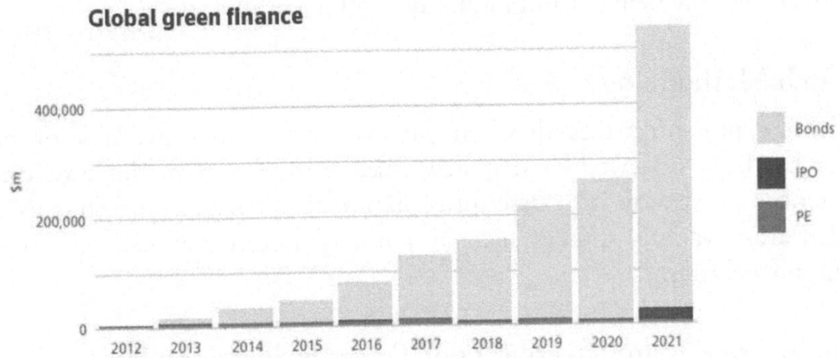

Source: TheCityUK analysis based on data from Refinitiv Workspace

Figure 1: Global Growth of the Green Finance Market

The data showed in figure 1, green bond accounted for 93.1% of total green finance globally between 2012 and 2021. In 2021, global green bond issuance stood at $511.5 billion, compared with $2.3 billion in 2012. The share of green finance in the total finance market was about 4% in 2021, compared with around 0.1% in 2012.

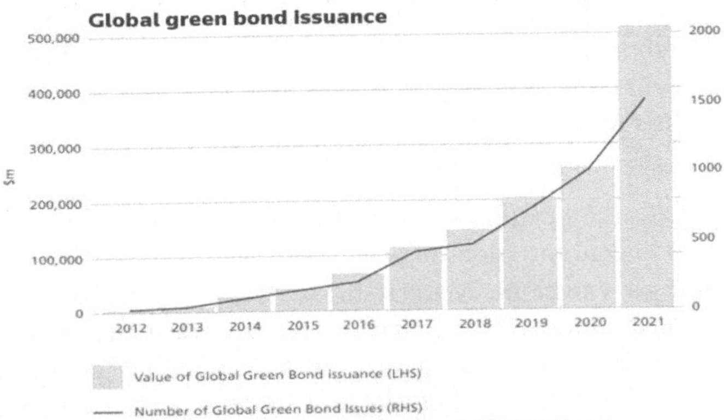

Source: TheCityUK analysis based on data from Refinitiv Workspace

Figure 2: Global Green Bond Issuance

China and the U.S. accounted for 13.6% and 11.6% of the green bond issuance between 2012 and 2021. They were followed by France and Germany, with about 10% each of the issuance of green bonds during the period (figure 2).

Source: TheCityUK analysis based on data from Refinitiv Workspace

Figure 3: Green IPOs

The number of publicly traded companies involved in green activities grew from 401 companies in 2012 to 669 in 2021, the data showed in figure 3.

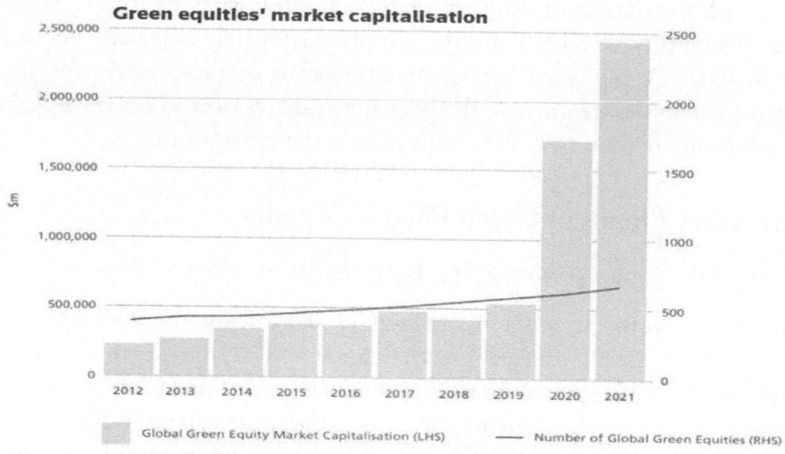

Source: TheCityUK analysis based on data from Refinitiv Workspace

Figure 4: Green Equalities Market Capitalisation

For assessing the awareness regarding green finance and sustainable development from the conventional sources, Google trends can be a powerful tool for understanding the pattern of Google searches made in different locations at different point in time (figure 4).

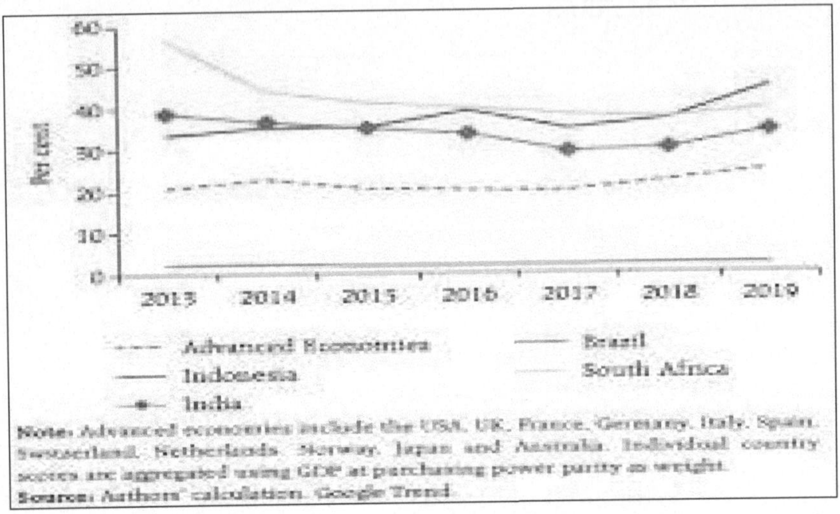

Figure 5: Green Finance: India's Comparative Score

Source: Google Search Related to Green Finance: India's comparative Score

Figure 5 (Chart 1) shows that climate change and green finance in India is no less than those in advanced and major emerging economies. The chart shows that India's comparative score is higher than the advanced economies and the country with the maximum value of the search intensity is set to 100, then later the search intensity of other countries are proportionately adjusted. The country scores in Chart 1 represent the weighted average of these scores for the five keywords, where the weights are the percentage shares of searches on a particular keyword in the total number of searches across these five words.

Progress and Trends of Green Finance in India

Growth of the Green Finance Market in India

Green finance flows in India are falling far short from the country's current needs. In 2019–2020, tracked green finance was INR 309 thousand crores (~USD 44 billion) per annum, approximately a fourth of India's need. According to the Paris Agreement, it is estimated that to achieve India's Nationally Determined Contributions (NDCs), the country requires approximately INR 162.5 lakh crores (USD 2.5 trillion) from 2015 to 2030, or roughly INR 11 lakh crores (USD 170 billion) per year. In 2021, India put forth enhanced ambitions on climate action and announced the Panchamrit targets, which include adding 500 GW of non-fossil fuel-based energy capacity and meeting 50% of its energy requirements through non-renewable sources and such enhanced ambition requires mobilization of green finance at a much faster pace. The green finance flows increased by 150% from FY2017-FY2018 to FY2019-FY2020 (figure 6).

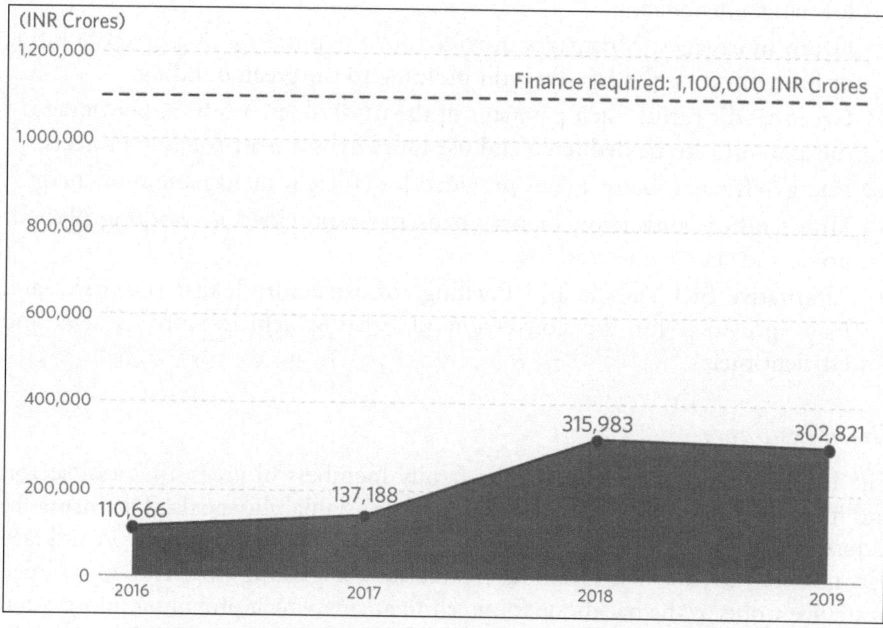

Figure 6: Tracked Green Finance Investments and the Estimated Finance Required to Meet Current NDCs

Source: The Landscape of Green Finance in India 2022- CPI

Areas Covered Through Green Finance

Green Banking

It deals with encouraging the eco-friendly practices with the help of banking activities and Green banking helps in protection of the environment and contributes to the welfare of nature and the financial sectors. Green banking operates by integrating technological improvements, changing stakeholders' expectations, and operational innovations. The different Indian banks are providing green banking services to their customers. State Bank of India, Punjab National Bank, Bank of Baroda, Canara Bank, ICICI Bank Ltd, DFC Bank Ltd, Kotak Mahindra Bank, Induslnd Bank, YES Bank, HSBC Group, IDBI, etc. used various practices as a part of green banking.

Green Banking practices

- **Online Banking:** Providing banking services to the customers with the help of internet for encouraging paperless and cashless transactions.
- **Green home equity loans:** Loans provided to purchase and install energy-efficient equipment at home.
- **Green car loans:** Offers low-interest rate loans for purchasing the non to low emission vehicles.
- **Green mortgages:** Mortgages provided for the purchase of a green building or for renovating the already built building to the green building.
- **Green credit cards:** Each payment of the cardholder, a certain percentage of the amount is to be deducted and used for environment-friendly projects.
- **Energy-efficient loans:** Loans provided for efficient management of energy.
- **Home office conversion loans:** Loans to be provided in working place at home and start home working.
- **Alternative fuel Vehicle and Fuelling Infrastructure loans:** Incentives and loans provided for the conversion of existing vehicles into cleaner and efficient fuels.

Green Insurance

The Insurance industry is one of the family members of green financial sector, and it plays an important role in attaining the sustainability goals. The insurance industry hasn't been directly involved in the environmental degradation and also has nothing to do with framing regulations regarding these issues. Green insurance works as the backbone for green financing which providing information for the risk management and tries to lower the risk involved with its various strategies and its business of underwriting. The Insurance Regulatory and Development Authority of India (IRDAI) recently announced that Third Party (TP) premium rates for insurance of private electric vehicles will be given at 15% discounted rates w.e.f. FY 2019–20.

There are various types of Green Insurance as given below.

1. **Green Life Insurance:** The Green life insurance company will donate a certain percentage of the insurance premium received for eco-friendly projects.
2. **Green Business Insurance:** Incentives to be given to the owners of the business for the renewal or reconstruction of the damaged buildings with environment friendly products.
3. **Green Travel Insurance:** The green travel insurance compensates for the effects of emission of carbon dioxide (CO_2) on the environment during travelling by donating part of the premium paid for the projects with the aim to reduce the carbon emissions.

4. **Green Car Insurance:** The amount of green car insurance premium will depend on the miles travelled by car and it will reduce the unnecessary use of private vehicles and thus it contributes to the environmental protection.
5. **Eco-friendly Home Insurance:** It provides technological and maintenance support for the renewable energy power systems along with insurance coverage.
6. **Carbon Insurance:** It provides insurance cover for the plantation of forests against the weather-related risks.

Green bonds

The Green bond proceeds to be utilised in the funding of energy-efficient products like reforestation, climate-related projects, and other assets or business activities aimed at the protection of the environment. A balanced approach is required for proper allocation of funds in eco-friendly projects and at the same time, it has to consider the risk and return involved with the bonds. Green bond helps the issuing companies or financial institutions in enhancing their goodwill among the stakeholders and helps in getting access to the investor base those are determined to invest only in green investment products. At the same time, it also helps those types of investors who want to invest in socially responsible projects and satisfies their urge to integrate investment and social responsibility. Green bonds were first issued by the European Investment Bank and the World Bank in the year 2007 after that, the private companies, banks, and financial institutions started issuing green bonds. Securities and Exchange Board of India (SEBI) has issued guidelines for listing and issuing of this type of debt securities in India and as per SEBI guidelines, the proceeds of such bonds should be invested in green projects such as renewable energy, initiatives of climate change action, preserving biodiversity, reducing pollution levels, management of waste, etc.

Types of green bonds:

1. Green "Use of Proceeds" bond: It is secured by assets.
2. Green "Use of Proceeds" revenue bond: It is secured by projects with income-producing nature.
3. Green project bond: It is secured by a project's assets and liabilities.
4. Green securitized bond: It is secured by a large asset pool.

Figure 8 show that India issued $6.11 billion in green bonds during the first 11 months of 2021, according to U.K.-based green bond tracking agency Climate Bonds Initiative. It was the strongest year since green bonds from the country were first issued in 2015. India's green bond issuance is set to reach a new record in 2022, following an exceptionally strong 2021.

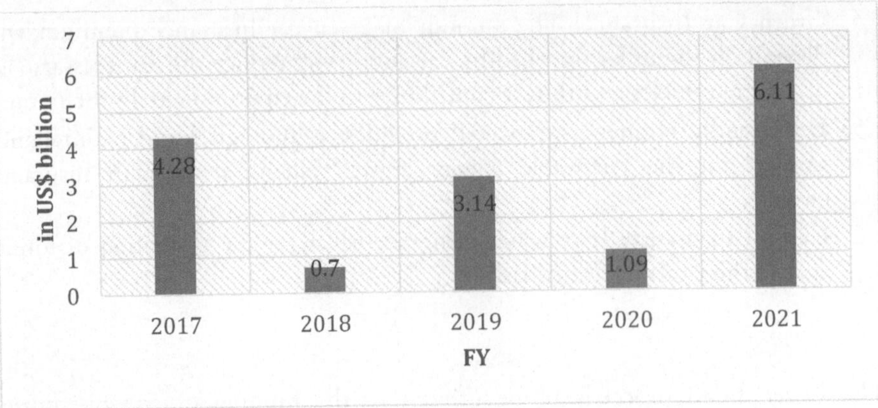

Figure 8: Volume of Indian Green Bond Issuance

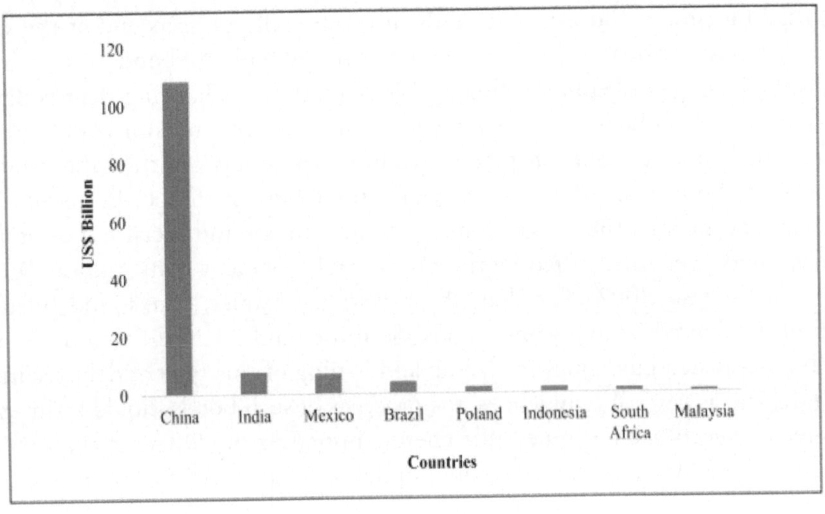

Figure 9: Major Emerging Markets for Green Bonds Issuance 2012–18 (US$ Billion)

Source: Emerging Market Green Bonds Report 2018

Economic Survey 2019–20 has reported that, India has emerged as the second-largest green bond market next to China with transactions amounting to $10.3 billion in the first half of 2019 (figure 9).

Benefits of Green Finance

Green finance made the harmony between the monetary aspect and nature. It will give benefit both environment and the economy of the country. The various benefits of Green Finance are mentioned here under:

- **Environmental protection:** One of the major aspects of green financing is to funding the projects aimed at sustainable development and environmental protection is an integral part of the funding. This concept helps to reduce the pollution levels, adapting to climate changes, mitigating depletion of the ozone layer, preserving biodiversity, etc which are very much needed for the survival of living organisms.
- **Helps in attracting FDI:** It helps for protection of the environment which is rising across the globe. The foreign investors are investing in domestic companies will evaluate the projects taking into consideration the social cost and the benefits. Issuing of green investment products will attract Foreign Direct Investment (FDI) to our country.
- **Efficient energy management:** Various incentives will be provided for installing and using renewable energy resources and funds also provided for projects aimed at reducing wastage of energy under Green financing through which efficient energy management can be achieved.
- **Enhances reputation:** The increasing number of stakeholders wants to contribute to the society through their investments and also to perform their social responsibility work. It will be giving priority to the companies that work towards benefiting the environment. The government provides incentives for eco-friendly projects and green financing helps the organizations to build and enhance their reputation in the long run.

Limitations of Green Finance

1. **Lack of awareness:** Few groups of people are opening up to eco-friendly investments as large number of stakeholders are not aware of the concept of green finance. Due to that lack of information and awareness, it results in less capital accumulation in green investment products than required which cause an imbalance in terms of demand and supply of funds.
2. **No proper regulatory framework:** There are no rules, regulations and specific laws related to the evaluation and growth of green projects. No particular policy actions exist regarding green investment. This type of regulatory gap acts as a hindrance for the growth and development of green investment.
3. **Ambiguity regarding definition:** There is no such standard uniform definition for green finance. The investors are facing difficulty to choose the right green projects as there is no clarity regarding the definition, which will lead to confusion among them, and thus it works as a barrier for investment in green projects.

Challenges and Public Policy Towards Green Finance

In India, emphasis was laid on Green finance as early as 2007. The Reserve Bank of India issued a notification in December 2007 on "Corporate Social Responsibility, Sustainable Development and Non-financial Reporting: Role of Banks" thereby mentioning the importance of global warming and climate change in the context of sustainable development. The National Action Plan on Climate Change (NAPCC) was formulated in 2008, with a vision to outline the broad policy framework for mitigating the impact of climate change. In 2011, the Climate Change Finance Unit (CCFU) was formed within the Ministry of Finance to work as a coordinating agency for the various institutions responsible for green finance in India. The major strategic move included for implementation of the sustainability disclosure requirements since 2012. However, the Security and Exchange Board of India (SEBI) made it compulsory for top 100 listed entities based on market capitalization at BSE and NSE to publish annual business responsibility reports since 2012 and therefore revised it from time to time.

The integrated policy approach of green finance is definitely a gaining momentum. Although in India, there have been improvements in public awareness and financing options, the major challenges could be high borrowing costs, plurality of green loan definitions, false claims of environmental compliance, and maturity mismatches between long term green investment and relatively short-term interests of investors. Generally, the cost of issuing green bonds has remained higher than the other bonds in India and most of the green bonds in India are issued by the public sector units or corporates with better financial health. In India, the higher borrowing cost of green bonds could be on account of asymmetric information, higher risk perception and other governance issues. From the existing information it is evident that green projects often have a high cost with some cost saving features only applicable in the long-term. Absence of universal definition of green finance and information asymmetry may result in "green washing", wherein the investors end up receiving false signals about the green bonds and the large domestic market and much smaller penetration of green instruments so far, thereby leave vast opportunities to be tapped. The significant challenges in the green finance market include deepening of corporate bond market, standardisation of green investment terminology, consistent corporate reporting, and removing information asymmetry between investors and recipients.

Climate change has been on the G20 agenda since the first summit in 2008, where focusing on the global Circular Carbon Economy (CCE) to tackle harmful emissions. Several major programs aimed at raising awareness around the world and promoting the funding for green initiatives in the world. These kinds of programs encourage financial and non-financial companies to incorporate environmental considerations into their financing. United Nations Environment Program (UNEP), Equatorial Principles (EP) and signatures on financial institutions' commitments on sustainable development suggest the ways to implement green finance and many organizations in India sign up for these events. With the help of reliable source of information about the overall management of environmental and social risk organizations, it is possible to ensure a good rate of return only if the track record of the organizations has a good rate of identification of opportunities.

There have been many fiscal and financial incentives taken in India and these incentives are in line with India's commitments under the 2015 Paris Agreement to reduce greenhouse gas emission intensity by 33% to 35% below 2005 levels, and to achieve 40% of installed electric power capacity from non-fossil sources by 2030. The Government of India (GOI) offers 30% of the installation cost of the rooftop solar panels as subsidy to the institutional, residential and social sectors in most states of the country. In case of special category states (which includes Uttarakhand, Sikkim, Himachal Pradesh, Jammu and Kashmir, Lakshadweep as of May 2019) the subsidy is up to 70% of the installation cost.

Recommendations and Suggestions

Implement sustainability initiatives: The businesses should implement sustainability initiatives such as, reducing greenhouse gas emissions, increasing energy efficiency, and sourcing renewable energy to attract green finance. These kind of initiatives can help to improve business reputation and potentially lower its cost of capital. Some of the key recommendations based on literature review and the way outlook is changing towards green finance are:

- **Creating awareness among the general public:** To protecting the environment and to aware the general people about the wide variety of green investment products available in the market, the Government, banks, financial institutions, and business organizations should come forward and take necessary steps in this regard. The Technology combined with finance should come up with innovative products which attract the investors and at the same time contributes to the development of the environment of the country.
- **Developing a proper regulatory framework:** A proper regulatory framework is needed for evaluating the projects related with green finance and also to protect the interest of the investors. The regulating authorities have to ensure about the funds raised for each project are to be used for the intended purpose only.
- **Engage with sustainable investors:** By engaging with sustainable investors and understand their specific criteria for investment the business can help to

tailor a business's sustainability strategy and reporting to meet the needs of these investors.

- **Monitor and report sustainability performance:** By tracking their sustainability performance and report it transparently to stakeholders the business can help to build trust with investors and customers, as well as demonstrate compliance with regulations.
- **Separate laws to be passed to regulate the misuse of funds:** It is needed to pass the Strict laws to punish those market participants who are taking unfair advantage of the growing demand for green projects. This law should also to concentrate on the use of raised funds and in case of violation of guidelines, proper actions have to be taken.
- **Providing support to research:** The proper initiatives to be taken to encourage the research in the field of green financing which will combine the technological developments with the financial sectors. This will help in bringing out the efficient green projects, the innovative green investment products, and proper policy actions needed for full development and also the growth.
- **Explore green bonds:** By exploring the use of green bonds which are debt instruments that are specifically designed to fund sustainable projects, the business can provide a lower cost of capital than traditional debt, and can also help to demonstrate a business's commitment to sustainability.

Concluding Remarks

Green finance is nowadays in the priority list for public investment policy. In the recent years, the developments of green finance in India have been made certain improvements in public awareness and financing options in India. For the sustainable long term economic growth, it is needed that a reduction in the asymmetric information regarding Green Projects through better information management systems and increased coordination amongst the stakeholders. At present, the green financing is an effective tool for sustainable development. The investors are thinking beyond the risk and returns and to be more responsible towards the society. In the present scenario, by raising awareness among the people about the need for protecting nature, increased funding in green projects will open wide varieties of opportunities in the area of green finance. The researchers, environmentalists, policymakers, government, investors, and financial institutions have to work together for raising the fund in green finance. In these circumstances, a proper regulatory framework should be set up for evaluating the green projects and to ensure that investors are not cheated in the label of green. India should concentrate on protecting natural resources, renewable energy generation, efficient energy management, climate adoption, and other ecological issues with the help of green financing. Hence, it is to be concluded that green finance if properly managed will work as an effective tool for sustainable development for any country.

Future Directions for Further Research

An analytical study can be done between Information Gap and Green Finance decisions.

Comparative analysis can be done between the two developed and developing countries about Green Finance.

Relationship analysis can be done between Green Finance and Investment Culture.

Impacts of psychological factors on Green Finance practices.

A study can be done on the feedback analysis of Green Finance Stakeholders.

The above mentioned are some of the emerging areas of green finance and working on it may become a major contribution in the area of Finance. The present study is based on secondary sources of data and no analysis had done on the perception of the investors about green financing. Further, the present study is not based on primary data, so future studies may be conducted on these issues also.

References

[1] Al-Louzi, O.A. and Busler, M. (2021). Green finance and sustainability in the Middle East. *Journal of Environmental Management*, 283, 111959.

[2] Ansari Md., K. and Anand, Y. (2022).Green Finance In India: Trend and Challenges. *Hans Shodh Sudha*, 2(4), 43–50.

[3] Berensmann, K. and Lindenberg, N. (2019). Green Finance: Actors, Challenges and Policy Recommendations. *Briefing paper.*

[4] Bielinski, T. and Mosionek-Schweda, M. (2019). Green bonds as the financial instrument for environmental project funding. *Unia Europijska*, 1.

[5] Chhaochharia, M. (2021). Green Finance in India: Progress and Challenges. *Research Journal of Humanities and Social Sciences*. 12(4), 223–226.

[6] Chowdhary, T.U., Datta, R. and Mohajan, H.K. (2013). Green Finance is Essential for Economic Development and Sustainability. *International Journal of Research in Commerce, Economics and Management,* 3(10), 104–108. https://mpra.ub.uni-muenchen.de/id/eprint/51169

[7] Dipika (2015). Green Banking in India: A Study of Various Strategies Adopted by Banks for Sustainable Development. *International Journal of Engineering Research and Technology (IJERT).*

[8] Dikau, S. and Volz, U. (2018). Central Banking, Climate Change and Green Finance. *Tokyo: Asian Development Bank Institute*. ADBI Working Paper 867.

[9] Ghosh, S., Nath, S. and Ranjan, A. (2021). Green Finance in India: Progress and Challenges. *RBI Bulletin, 1,* 61–72.

[10] Joseph, J. (2017). Viability of green finance and green growth in India; A study. *International conference on recent development in engineering and social science, Humanities and management,* 5. http://data.conferenceworld.in/ESHM5/P118-124.pdf.

[11] Jain, S. (2020). "Financing India's green transition". *ORF Issue Brief No. 338,* January 2020, Observer Research Foundation.

[12] Keerthi, B.S. (2013). A Study on Emerging Green Finance in India: Its challenges and Opportunities. *International Journal of Management and Social Sciences Research (IJMSSR),* 2(2), 49–53.

[13] Mohd, S. and VK, K. (2018). Green Finance: A Step towards Sustainable Development. *Journal Press of India*, 5(1), 59–74. https://doi.org/10.17492/mudra.v5i01.13036

[14] Soundarrajan, P. and Vivek, N. (2016). Green finance for sustainable green economic growth in India. *Agric.Econ,* 62(1), 35–44. https://doi.org/10.17221/174/2014-AGRICECON.

[15] Dikau, S. and Volz, U. (2020). Central Bank Mandates, Sustainability Objectives and the Promotion of Green Finance.

[16] Sachs, J.D., Woo, N., Yoshino, N. and Hesary, T. Hesary (2019). Why is Green Finance Important? ADBI working paper 917. https://www.adb.org/publications/why-green-finance-important.

[17] Sharma, R. and Mishra, A.K. (2021). Institutionalizing green finance for sustainable development: A review of regulatory and policy frameworks. *Journal of Cleaner Production*, 311, 127503.

[18] Shen, C. Zhao, K. and Ge, J. (2020), "An Overview of Green Building Performance Database", *Journal of Engineering.*

[19] Wang, K., Tsai, S.-B., Du, X. and Bi, D. (2019). Internet Finance, Green Finance, and Sustainability. *Sustainability*, 11(14), 3856. https://doi.org/10.3390/su11143856

[20] Krozer. Y, (2019), Financing of the global shift to renewable energy and energy efficiency, Green finance, *University of Twenty and Sustainable Innovations Academy*, Amsterdam, Netherlands, 1, 264 – 278.

Websites

1. https://www.ceguide.org/Strategies-and-examples/Finance/Green-bonds
2. https://www.ifc.org/wps/wcm/connect/9e8a7c68-5bec-40d1-8bb4-a0212fa4bfab/Amundi-IFC-Research-Paper2018.pdf?MOD=AJPERES
3. https://energy.economictimes.indiatimes.com/news/renewable/india-becomes-second-largest-market-for-greenbonds-with-10-3-billion-transactions/73898149
4. https://environmental-conscience.com/green-insurance/
5. https://www.iisd.org/about-iisd/sustainable-development
6. https://www.iii.org/article/green-insurance
7. https://www.scotsmanguide.com/browse/content/green-financing-benefits-business

Central Bank Digital Currency (e₹): The New Financial Landscape of the Indian Economy

Tushar Kanti Das[1]

ABSTRACT: Central Bank Digital Currency (CBDC) is a digital form of currency notes issued by a central bank. At present most central bank across the globe are exploring the issuance of CBDC, but the key motivations of its issuance are specific to each country's specific requirements. The Reserve Bank of India (RBI) has recently launched the country's first pilot project for digital currency known as digital rupee or e-rupee (e₹). This is significantly advancement in "Digital India" revolution. The objective behind it is to have a "more efficient and cheaper currency management system" by using block chain and other technologies. The digital currency, e₹, will provide an additional opportunity to the currently available forms of money. It will also have all the transactional benefits of other forms of digital money. But if it is poorly designed, it would lead to increase cyber security risks or be subject to fraud and other types of crime. This paper tries to understand the concept of digital currency (e₹), its relevance, how does it will work and the challenges and prospects associated with it.

Keywords: Block Chain, Digital Currency, Digital India, e-Rupee (e₹).

Introduction

Management of currency is one of the core central banking functions of Reserve Bank of India (RBI). Along with the Government of India (GOI), RBI is responsible for the design, production and overall management of the nation's currency, with the goal of ensuring an adequate supply of clean and genuine notes in the economy, India has made impressive progress towards innovation in digital payments. The present state of the art payment system are affordable, accessible, convenient, efficient, safe, secure and available 24 × 7 × 365 days a year are a matter of pride for the nation. The striking shift in payment preference has been due to the creation of robust round the clock electronic payment system such as RTGS (Real Time Gross Settlement) and NEFT (National Electronic Funds Transfer) that has facilitated seamless real time or near real time fund transfers. In addition, the launch of IMPS

[1] Assistant Professor in Commerce, Naba Ballygunge Mahavidyalaya, India.
E-mail: tusharkantidas.wb@gmail.com

(Immediate Payment Service) and UPI (Unified Payments Interface) for instant payment settlement, the introduction of mobile based payment systems such as BBPS (Bharat Bill Payment System) and NETC (National Electronic Toll Collection) to facilitate electronic toll payments have been the defining moments that has transformed the payment ecosystem of the country and attached international recognition. The convenience of these payment systems ensured rapid acceptance as they provided consumers as alternative to the use of cash and paper for making payments. With the development in the economy and the evolution of the payment system, the form and function of money has changed over time, and it will continue to influence the future course of currency. The concept of money has experienced evolution from Commodity to Metallic Currency to Paper Currency to Digital Currency (Figure 1). The changing features of money are defining the new financial landscape of the economy. Advancement of technology has made it possible for the development of new form of money viz. Central Bank Digital Currencies (CBDCs).

Recognizing the global development in the field of CBDC, the RBI has set up an Internal Working Group in October 2020 to undertake a study on appropriate design/implementation architecture for introducing CBDCs in India. The working group highlighted the need for a robust legal framework to back the issuance of Digital Currency (e₹) as another form of currency. After careful consideration, GOI has announced in the Union Budget (placed in the parliament on February 01, 2022), the launch of the Digital Rupee – Central Bank Digital Currency (CBDC-e₹) from financial year 2022–23 onwards.

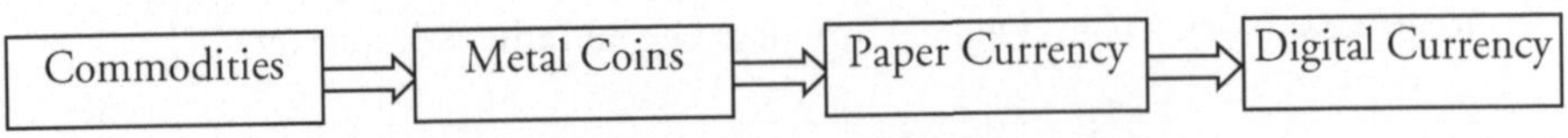

Figure 1: The Evolution of Payment System

Objectives of the Study

The following are the main objectives of the study:

- To know the concept CBDC and its importance in Indian Financial System.
- To understand how CBDC will works and its national and international scenario.
- To know the opportunities and challenges associated with CBDC in India.

Methodology of the Study

This study is based on mainly secondary data. A descriptive and analytical research methodology has been used for this research paper. The secondary data has been collected from various government reports, journals, newspapers etc. In order to enrich the study, the related websites and articles have been searched as and when required. Editing, classification and tabulation of the data collected from the above mentioned sources have been done as per requirement of the study.

Central Bank Digital Currency (Digital Rupee-e₹)

Digital currencies are a type of currency that exists solely in digital form, without a physical counterpart like paper money or coins. They are often used for online transactions and can be transferred electronically between parties. Digital currencies continue to gain popularity and are increasingly being adopted by businesses and consumers around the world. Digital currencies can be broadly divided in to two categories-Central Bank Digital Currency (CBDC) and Crypto currency. CBDCs are digital versions of traditional fiat currencies issued and backed by central banks. It can be implemented using a variety of technological approaches. Block chain technology is one possible approach for implementing CBDCs. Crypto currencies is digital or virtual currencies that use cryptographic techniques to secure transaction and control the creation of new units. Most Crypto currencies are built on block chain technology. According to RBI, "CBDC is a legal tender issued by a central bank in digital form. It is the same as a sovereign currency and is exchangeable one-to-one at par (1:1) with fiat currency. Only its form is different." In other words, CBDC is a digitized or virtual version of domestic currency that is equal to physical cash. Though CBDC is a virtual or digital currency, it is different private crypto currencies, as it satisfies the key requirements of definition of currency being backed and issued by central bank. CBDC is same as money issued by a central bank, except it doesn't come in paper form. It is a sovereign currency in electronic form and would appear as a liability (currency in circulation) on the balance sheet of the central banks. It is essential to understand the difference between CBDCs and crypto currencies. Not all digital currencies are crypto currencies, but all crypto currencies are digital currencies. Digital currencies may not be encrypted, but crypto currencies operate in an encrypted format through block chain technology. Since there is no issuer, private virtual currencies do not represent any person's debt or liabilities.

The important features of CBDCs are as follows:

- CBDC is sovereign currency issued by central banks in alignment with their monetary policy.
- It appears as a liability on the central bank's balance sheet.
- Must be accepted as a medium of payment, legal tender, and a safe store of value by all citizens, enterprises and government agencies.
- Freely convertible against commercial bank money and cash.
- Fungible legal tender for which holders need not have a bank account.
- Expected to lower the cost of issuance of money and transactions.

Why CBCD?

The majority of central banks throughout the globe are experimenting with digital currency to combat the current wave of virtual currencies or crypto currencies. Private or decentralized money is not something that the central bank can regulate, and it also poses a challenge to the sovereignty of their national currencies as the public is responsible for both the creation and upkeep of these virtual currencies. The central bank can prevent these misdeeds by regulating the digital currency. That is why most central banks including those in Sweden, China and the EU, are developing their own CBDC.

Another issue with crypto currencies is that their value is based on speculations because they are not linked to any assets or currencies (demand and supply). As a result, the value of crypto currencies like bit coin has fluctuated greatly. As CBDCs are issued by central banks, their demand and supply can be regulated and they can be used as a monitoring tool. If CBDCs are designed prudently, they can potentially offer more resilience, more safety, greater availability, and lower cost than private forms of digital currency.

In addition, CBDC would also allow for greater financial inclusion by expanding across of financial services to those who are currently excluded from the formal banking system. At present, there are around 1.2 billion people in India who do not have access formal banking services. CBDC could address this by providing a safe and convenient way for people to store and use money without going through a bank.

CBDC could help to reduce the cost of printing and circulation paper currencies in physical cash management. As per report of RBI, the total expenditure incurred on security printing during April 1, 2021 to March 31, 2022 was Rs. 4,984.80 crore against Rs. 4, 012 crore in the previous year. CBDC affects the overall value of the money issuing function to the extent that it reduces operational costs e.g. cost related to printing, storage, transportation and replacement of banknotes and cost associated with delay in payments and settlements.

Working of CBDC

As CBDCs are electronic form of sovereign currency, it should imbibe all the possible features of physical currency. The design of CBDC is dependent on the functions it is expected to perform, and the design determines its implications for payment systems, monetary policy as well as the structure and stability of financial services. The key design choices to be considered for issuing CBDCs are based on-1) Type of CBDC. 2) Forms of CBDCs and the 3) Models for issuance and management of CBDC.

Type of CBDC: CBDC can be classified into two broad types; viz. General Purpose or Retail CBDC (e₹-R) and Wholesale CBDC (e₹-W). Retail CBDC would be potentially available for use by all entities viz. private sector, non-financial consumers and businesses while wholesale CBDC is designed for restricted across to select financial institutions. Wholesale CBDC is intended for the settlement of interbank transfer and related wholesale transactions, Retail CBDC is the electronic version of cash primarily meant for retail transactions.

Forms of CBDCs: CBDC can be structured as "token-based "or "account-based". A token-based CBDC is a bearer–instrument like banknotes, meaning whosoever holds the token at a given point in time would be presumed to own them. In contrast, an account–based system would require maintenance of records of balances and transactions of all holders of the CBDC and indicate the ownership of the monetary balances. In token-based CBDC, the person receiving a token will verify that his ownership of the token is genuine, whereas in account-based, CBDC, an intermediary verifies the identity of an account holder. Considering the features, a token-based CBDC is viewed as a preferred mode for CBDC-R as it would be closer to physical cash, while account-based CBDC may be considered for CBDC-W.

Models for Issuance and Management of CBDC: There are three models for issuance and management of CBDC across the globe. These are:

(a) **Single Tier Model:** This model is also known as Direct CBDC Model. This system would be one, where the central bank is responsible for managing all aspects of the CBDC system including issuance, account-keeping, transaction verification etc. In this model, central bank operates the retail ledger and therefore the central bank server is involved in all payments. In this model, CBDC represents the direct claim on the central bank, which keeps a record of all balances and updates it with every transaction. It provides an advantage of a very resilient system as the central bank has complete knowledge of retail account balances.

(b) **Two-Tier Model (Intermediate Model)**: Under this, there is two models—Indirect Model and Hybrid Model.

- *Indirect Model:* In indirect CBDC model, consumers would hold their CBDC in an account or wallet with a bank or service provider. The obligation to provide CBDC on demand would fall on the intermediary rather than the central bank. The central bank would track only the wholesale CBDC balances of the intermediaries and must ensure that the wholesale CBDC balances are identical with all the retail balances available with the retail customers.
- *Hybrid Model:* In this method, a direct claim on the central bank is combined with a private sector messaging layer. The central bank will

issue CBDC to other entities which shall make those entities then responsible for all customer-associated activities. Under this model, commercial intermediaries (Payment Service Providers) provide retail service to end users, but the central bank retains a ledger of retail transactions. This architecture runs on two engines: intermediaries handle retail payments, but CBDC is a direct claim on the central bank.

Table 1: Comparison between Three Models

	Direct Model	*Indirect Model*	*Hybrid Model*
Liability	Central Bank	Central Bank	Central Bank
Issuer	Central Bank	Central Bank issues and Intermediaries distribute it	Central Bank issues and Intermediaries distribute it for retail use.
Operations	Central Bank	Intermediaries	Intermediaries
Ledger	Central Bank	Intermediaries	Intermediaries as well as Central Bank
Settlement Finally	Yes	No	Yes

Source: Compiled by the author

Considering the merits of different models, the indirect model may be the most suitable architecture for introduction of CBDC in India.

Recent Developments: National and Global Scenario

In India, the first pilot in the Digital Rupee- Wholesale segment (e₹-W) commenced on November 1, 2022 for the settlement of secondary market transactions in government securities. The use of e₹-W is expected to make the interbank market more efficient. Other wholesale transactions and cross-broader payments will be the focus of the pilot in future. RBI has identified nine banks for participation in the digital rupee's wholesale pilot project. These are: State Bank of India, Bank of Baroda, Union Bank of India, HDFC Bank, ICICI Bank, Kotak Mahindra Bank, Yes Bank, IDFC Bank, HSBC. After that, on December1, 2022, the RBI has announced the launch of first pilot for retail digital rupee (e₹-R).The pilot would cover select location in Closure User Group (CUG) comprising participating customers and merchants. The e₹-R would be in the form of a digital token that represents legal tender. It would be issued in the same denominations that paper currency and coins are issued. It would be distributed through intermarries, i.e., banks. Users will be able to transact with e₹-R through a digital wallet offered by the participating banks and stored on mobile phones/devices. Transactions can be both Person to Person (P2P) and

Person to Merchant (P2M). Payments to merchants can be made using QR codes displayed at merchant's locations. Eight banks have been identified for phrase-wise participation initially in selected cities.

Across the globe, more than 60 central banks have expressed their interest in CBDC, with a few implementations already under pilot across both retail and wholesale categories and many others reaching, testing and /or launching their own CBDC framework. Around there are 114 countries in the process of exploring CBDC. 10 countries have launched CBDC, the first of which was the Bahamian Sand Dollar in 2020, and the latest was Jamaica's JAM-DEX. Countries that have already launched retail CBDC (R-CBDC) are the Bahamas, Cambodia, East Caribbean Union, Nigeria, China and Jamaica. Central Banks which are exploring wholesale CBDC (W-CBDC) include Singapore, Australia, Saudi Arabia and European Union. South Korea, Thailand and Russia have started testing their R-CBDC's in 2021 and2022. China has started in April 2020, to pilot a CBDC and their intentions for widespread domestic use of the e-CNY by 2023. The European central bank has outlined plans to implement digital euro in 2023.

In addition, the various authorities across the globe are justified the adoption of CBDC for different reasons. Some of them are:

- The central bank of various countries challenged with decreasing use of paper currency, and seeks to popularize a more acceptable, safe legal tender electronic form of currency (example-Sweden).Sweden's central bank has already tested two phrases of its R-CBDC starting in 2020.
- The various authorities in the world with significant physical cash usage are in search to make issuance of more well organized currency system (example-Denmark, Japan, Germany, or even with US Economy).
- The countries with geographical barriers of limiting the physical movement of cash had the inspiration to go for CBDC (example-The Bahamas and Caribbean with small and large numbers of Islands).

Opportunities and Challenges

Digital Rupee will offer several advantages over physical currencies .The following arguments are in favor of digital currency in India.

- **Centralized and Secured:** As CBDCs is backed by GOI and will issue by RBI, it will be regulated centrally. A digital rupee can potentially offer greater security compared to traditional physical money by leveraging advanced cryptographic protocols, multi-factor authentication, decentralized ledger technology, and reduced susceptibility to physical theft. A digital currency leaves a digital trial that can be traced and audited more easily compared to physical cash.

- **Easy Accessible:** Digital currency can be used anytime and anywhere, without the need of physical cash or physical bank. This can make transactions more convenient and efficient, especially for people who live in remote and rural areas. We may purchase digital rupee from the bank in the form of tokens. In general, it would be similar to cash withdrawn from bank account, but instead of giving us cash, banks would credit our electronic wallets, allowing us to use it just like regular currency. The transactions via e₹-R will provide real-time account settlements.
- **Reduction in Cost Associated with Physical Cash Management:** CBDC will reduces the operational cost associated with physical cash management, Costs related to printing, storage transportation and replacement of banknotes and costs associated with delay payments and settlements are not required in using CBDCs.
- **Global Acceptance in Cross-Broader Transactions:** Many Transfers across borders and currency exchange are time consuming and costly. If CBDCs are used for cross border transfers and payments, it can greatly contribute transparency, speedy and cost efficiency.
- **Improved Government Payment System:** CBDC could provide a very effective mechanism to facilitate the payments of all government agencies across in a single platform and it enables the government to reach every agent everywhere in the economy at any time. It would especially valuable during certain types of disasters.

Challenges

The following important points are to be consider very carefully before introduction of CBDC in India.

- **Digital Literacy:** The digital literacy position on India is not satisfactory as compared to other countries where already launched CBDC. The main reason is that there are many rural areas in India where high speed internet facilities are not available. People have to face problem to avail the facility. In India, out of nearly 140 crore population, 82.5 crore people have access internet. So the infrastructure facilities are to be developed first so that everyone in remote area can access the facilities of CBDC and to ensure the widespread use CBDC.
- **Privacy and Security Concern:** Under CBDC, the RBI keeps central records of every transaction. Authorities may use centralized data for official purposes. If CBDC is poorly designed, it would lead to increase cyber security risks or be subject to fraud and other types of crime. One of the key risks is the potential for CBDC to be used for money laundering and terrorist financing. The cyber security considerations need to be taken care of both for the item and environment. For example, while the token

creation process should insure the highest levels of cryptography to ensure security at the item level, the transaction of tokens also needs to be secured to ensure a trusted environment.

- **Banking Disintermediation:** Banks in India have also raised their disintermediation concerns over RBI"s digital currency plans. Banks worry about the potential long term effects if central bank takes on the role of keeping and dispersing digital currency, eliminating banks as an intermediately between customers and RBI. This could lead to a decrease in deposits, and if banks start to lose deposits over time, it will limit their ability to extend credit. Additionally, when banks loose sizable amounts of low-cost transaction deposits, their interest margin may be put under pressure, raising the cost of loan. RBI has to takes all these concerns into perspective and has to move solely and steadily.

Concluding Remarks

CBDC is one of the biggest innovations in the financial sector. With a wide range of benefits, it is the next milestones in the first developing digital economy. It is a new concept and based on complex technology. Many countries across the globe are showing their interest in using CBDCs, some countries have launched the CBDC in experiential stage and a few countries already launched their digital currency. CBDC is proposed to match rather than to replace the current forms of money and it is predicted to provide an additional payment system to users of the country and not to substitute the existing payment system. Like other central banks, RBI has been exploring the pros and cons of introduction of CBDCs for some time. The introduction of CBDC (e₹) in India is expected to offer a wide range of benefits, such as less dependency on cash, lesser overall currency management cost, and reduce settlement risk. It could provide general public and businesses with a convenient form of central bank money with safety and liquidity and provide entrepreneurs a platform to create new products and services. The introduction of CBDC, would possibly lead to a more robust, efficient, trusted, regulated and legal tender-based payments options including cross-border payments. But at the same time, CBDC could also pose certain risks that may have a bearing on the important public issues, such as risk to financial stability, monetary policy, financial market structure and the cost of availability of credit. If CBDC is poorly designed, it could need to increase cyber security risks. So these are to be carefully evaluated against the potential benefits.

References

[1] Haque, A.M. and Shoaib, M. (2023), e₹—The digital Currency in India: Challenges and Prospects, Bench Council Transactions on Benchmarks, Standards and Evaluation.

[2] Katyal, I. (2022). Central Bank Digital Currency-Way Forward, *The Journal of Indian Institute of Banking & Finance*, April–June, 35–46.

[3] Kaur, J. (2023) Central Bank Digital Currency-The Digital Rupee in India, *Economic and Political Weekly* (https://www.epw.in).

[4] Bank for International Settlements (2021). Central Bank Digital Currencies-Financial Stability Implications, September (accessed through https://www.bis.org)

[5] Ministry of Finance (2022). Central Bank Digital Currency (Digital Rupee e₹)-India, one of the pioneer in introducing CBDC, Report of the Ministry of Information and Broadcasting, GOI, PTI, December.

[6] Reserve Bank of India (2022). Concept Note on Central Bank Digital Currency, Report of Indian's Central Bank, October.

Financial Intelligence: A Study of Artificial Intelligence's Evolving Role in Finance

Sourav Misra[1], Sampriti Dey[2] and Dipa Banerjee[3]

ABSTRACT: The paper investigates the dynamic interplay between financial services and artificial intelligence (AI) in the context of evolving financial landscapes. With an aim to comprehend the unfolding paradigm of Financial Intelligence, the study scrutinizes key components of AI and financial services. The rationale stems from the transformative impact of AI on the finance sector. Objectives include outlining the current state via literature review, identifying technologies shaping future finance, and assessing AI applications in financial services. Examining benefits, threats, and potential pitfalls of AI, the paper delves into its role in enhancing financial literacy. A strategic approach is proposed for harnessing AI's potential, with a focus on its revolutionizing impact on India's financial landscape. Through transformative case studies, the paper offers insights into the profound innovation AI introduces to financial systems.

Keywords: Artificial Intelligence, Financial Intelligence, Financial Services, Transformative Innovation.

Introduction

In an era characterized by rapid technological advancements, the financial landscape is undergoing a profound transformation, driven by the integration of Artificial Intelligence (AI). As financial markets become increasingly complex and data-driven, the intersection of finance and AI gives rise to what can be termed as Financial Intelligence. This research paper delves into the evolving role of AI in the financial domain, exploring its impact on decision-making processes, risk management, and overall market dynamics. Through a comprehensive examination of recent developments, challenges, and opportunities, this study seeks to unravel the intricate relationship between AI and finance, shedding light on how this synergy is reshaping the future of financial intelligence.

---

[1] Ex-Student, Department of Business Administration, Vidyasagar University, India. E-mail: souravggpme@gmail.com

[2] Ex-Student, Department of Business Administration, Vidyasagar University, India. E-mail: sampritidey2819@gmail.com

[3] Assistant Professor, Department of Business Administration, Vidyasagar University, India. E-mail: dipa.2003@gmail.com

Financial Services

Financial services encompass a broad range of economic activities that involve the management of money, assets, and financial transactions. These services are provided by institutions such as banks, insurance companies, investment firms, and others to meet the financial needs of individuals, businesses, and governments.

The concept of financial services has evolved over time with contributions from various economists, policymakers, and practitioners. However, modern financial systems have been significantly influenced by thinkers like Adam Smith, John Maynard Keynes, and more recently, by economists and policymakers shaping global financial regulations.

Intelligence

Intelligence refers to the ability to acquire, comprehend, and apply knowledge effectively. It involves problem-solving, learning from experience, reasoning, and adapting to new situations.

Intelligence is a complex concept, and its study spans various disciplines. In the realm of psychology, Alfred Binet is often considered a pioneer for his work on intelligence testing. However, the concept has been shaped by numerous psychologists, philosophers, and scientists over the years.

Artificial Intelligence (AI)

Artificial Intelligence is the simulation of human intelligence in machines, allowing them to perform tasks that typically require human intelligence, such as visual perception, speech recognition, decision-making, and language translation.

The term "artificial intelligence" was coined by John McCarthy in 1956, making him a key figure in the early development of AI. Other notable contributors include Alan Turing, Marvin Minsky, and Herbert Simon, among others.

Components of AI

- Data: The foundation of AI, as machine learning models learn from data.
- Algorithms: Mathematical instructions guiding the machine on how to learn from data and make decisions.
- Computing power: AI systems require significant computational resources, often provided by powerful hardware.
- Model training: The process of teaching the AI system using labelled data to make accurate predictions or decisions.
- Feedback mechanism: Iterative loops where AI models learn and improve over time based on feedback.

Components of Financial Services

- **Banking Services:** Core services provided by banks, including deposits, loans, and other financial products.
- **Investment Services:** Activities related to managing and investing funds, such as asset management and investment advisory.
- **Insurance Services:** Providing coverage and protection against financial losses.
- **Payment and Settlement Services:** Facilitating transactions and ensuring the smooth transfer of funds.
- **Financial Planning Services:** Advisory services for individuals and businesses to achieve their financial goals.

Rationale of Study

The study aims to explore and understand the transformative impact of artificial intelligence (AI) on the financial industry. As technological advancements continue to reshape traditional financial practices, it is crucial to investigate how AI, specifically in its latest iterations, is influencing financial intelligence. The rationale for this study lies in the growing importance of AI in financial decision-making, risk management, fraud detection, and overall operational efficiency. By examining the evolving role of AI in finance, the paper seeks to identify key trends, challenges, and opportunities associated with the integration of advanced technologies. Insights derived from this study can guide financial institutions, policymakers, and industry professionals in adapting to the dynamic landscape of financial intelligence, fostering innovation, and ensuring sustainable growth in the digital era.

Objectives of the study

(a) To encapsulate the concepts and analyse the role of AI in financial services.
(b) To study the impact of AI in financial services and financial literacy.
(c) To recognize the ways of implementation of AI in financial services.

Literature Review

Kalaivani and Saranya (2023) delve into the transformative potential of AI within the financial sector, underscoring its capacity to address contemporary challenges. They highlight the importance of executive managers and business owners in actively exploring AI applications, particularly in finance, to maintain a competitive edge. Their research emphasizes AI's role in optimizing sales, pricing, and fraud prevention, while also noting the unresolved issues faced by clients lacking financial knowledge. The study employs statistical software to analyze data from 2017 to 2022, examining AI's impact on task automation, cost savings, anti-hacking measures, and its broad application across various financial sectors. In a comprehensive study on AI's impact on the financial sector, Maple et al. (2023) explore the revolutionary potential of AI and Machine Learning (ML). They detail AI's significant contributions, from enhancing customer service to reshaping risk management and high-frequency trading. However, the study also addresses challenges such as transparency, interpretability, and the 'black box' nature of AI models, which pose systemic risks and market vulnerabilities. The authors advocate for proactive regulation, recommending a risk-based approach, ethical considerations, and collaboration between academia, industry, and regulators. They stress the importance of Responsible AI frameworks, human-in-the-loop systems, and international regulatory coordination to optimize AI integration while ensuring ethical practices and consumer protection. Iryani and Yulianto (2023) present a systematic mapping study on AI's role in the financial sector during the VUCA era. Using a quantitative approach and descriptive method, their study reviews 539 selected articles to identify key publishers, authors, and impactful works. The findings reveal a research gap, emphasizing the need for further exploration to understand AI's implications on financial systems in volatile, uncertain, complex, and ambiguous environments. The financial sector's critical role in economic development has led to a global focus on fostering financial literacy. In India, a nation known for its high savings rates, there is extensive literature examining the impact of financial literacy on income, savings behaviour, and the use of diverse financial products. However, a gap remains in understanding the relationship between financial literacy and the adoption of fintech products delivered via internet and mobile platforms. Murugesan and Manohar (2019) address this gap, focusing on developing countries like India and highlighting the transformative role of fintech companies in providing accessible and efficient financial services through AI-driven solutions. Umamaheswari et al. (2023) argue that the banking sector's reliance on legacy systems hampers innovation and efficiency in the current technological landscape. They advocate for a transformative shift through the implementation of AI and Virtual Assistants. Their research emphasizes the urgent need for banks to adopt modern technologies to automate processes, alleviate repetitive tasks, prevent fraud, and enhance decision-making. By embracing AI-driven solutions, banks can revolutionize their business models, improve profitability, performance, and reduce dependency on human resources, thereby enhancing speed, reliability, and efficiency across all banking operations. Bredt (2023) discusses AI's pivotal role in the financial sector, presenting opportunities for enhanced and personalized services, cost efficiency, and novel business models. Golic (2019) further explores AI's intersection with finance in the context of the fifth industrial revolution, emphasizing AI's transformative impact on the sector. The paper notes that a true AI system learns from data to perform tasks requiring human intelligence independently.

Recognizing AI as a strategic area within the European Union's approach, Golic contends that the financially advanced sector is an early AI adopter, expecting enhanced service delivery with reduced costs. The study aims to identify practical applications and business implications of AI in the global financial sector, addressing key aspects such as employment dynamics, regulatory challenges, and AI-related risk management. Truby et al. (2020) highlight the lag in regulatory translation of international AI governance principles into the financial sector. Financial regulators, seeking to maintain competitiveness in the global AI race, allow the introduction of experimental AI technologies with minimal controls, risking consumer and financial stability. The authors caution that unregulated AI software causing economic harm could lead to over-regulation, stifling innovation. The literature emphasizes AI's potential benefits in finance but advocates for a proactive regulatory stance with jurisdiction-specific rules aligned with international principles to foster sustainable innovation.

Vocke and Gangur (2022) examine key success factors for AI implementation in finance, focusing on cost reduction, process optimization, and risk management. They argue that companies investing in AI gain a competitive edge, particularly in maximizing profitability through efficient data handling and mathematical calculations. The authors anticipate future AI adoption challenges, including data repository quality, processing power, and evolving regulations. Machkour and Abriane (2020) explore the impact of Industry 4.0 on the financial sector, detailing the historical context of industrial revolutions and emphasizing the shift towards virtualization and interconnected intelligent objects. They argue that digitalization, driven by information technology and emerging technologies like Fintech, digital banking, and Blockchain, has significantly influenced the financial sector. Mavlutova and Volkova (2019) underscore the challenges of this transformation, emphasizing the need for competencies tailored to integrating ICT, AI, and robotics in financial business processes and product development. Their study highlights the relevance of new technologies in finance, stressing the demand for skills in computer science, big data analysis, predictive analytics, cybersecurity, and collaboration with virtual assistants. Bharadwaj's (2019) report assesses the current status, opportunities, and challenges of AI in India's financial landscape. The study explores key applications such as credit scoring, loan management, fraud detection, risk management, and financial transactions. Notable companies like Loan Frame and Capital Float use machine learning for small business lending, while institutions like the National Stock Exchange and Bombay Stock Exchange adopt AI for fraud detection and risk management. The review highlights challenges including the scarcity of trained AI data scientists, the importance of reliable data, multilingual considerations, and the need for robust data privacy and security measures. Han et al. (2023) emphasize AI's pivotal roles in investment management, risk assessment, fraud detection, and customer service, facilitating more accurate investment decisions, identifying patterns indicative of credit risks, and revolutionizing customer interactions through chatbots and virtual assistants. However, they note significant challenges such as data privacy, security, and ethical considerations due to AI's extensive handling of personal and sensitive information. Issues related to the opacity of AI decision-making, often attributed to the 'black box' nature of certain models, may lead to public distrust. Additionally, the potential automation of low-skilled jobs raises questions about AI's societal impact on financial services. Addressing these challenges requires comprehensive exploration across technological, policy, and ethical dimensions to maximize AI's benefits while minimizing risks. Future research opportunities lie in examining specific AI applications in finance and developing effective strategies for responsible AI implementation.

A recent KPMG survey reveals that 75% of financial services business leaders are apprehending AI's practicality, a 33% increase from the previous year. Despite accelerated interest in AI, organizations transitioning from experimentation to operationalization are seeing tangible progress, notes KPMG Advisory principal Agnel Kagoo. The study indicates that defensive AI strategies for cost savings may not yield leadership-level benefits, emphasizing the success of offensive strategies aimed at growth and customer-focused innovation. Despite concerns about AI adoption's rapid pace, 55% of leaders believe it is progressing appropriately, with 85% desiring more aggressive implementation. Cybersecurity and privacy concerns are identified as primary risks, but 93% are confident in AI's fraud detection capabilities. Based on insights from 950 executives, the study underscores the evolving landscape of AI adoption in the financial services industry (Settles, 2023). The adoption of AI by banks, driven by technological advancements and changing regulatory frameworks, enhances efficiency and customer experiences by providing 24/7 access to accounts and financial advice services (Insider Intelligence, 2023). AI in corporate finance proves beneficial for predicting and assessing loan risks, reducing financial crime, and contributing to long-term growth. The substantial benefits of AI implementation in finance, including frictionless customer interactions, task automation, and cost savings, highlight its transformative potential in the industry. The shift from traditional to online and mobile banking, accelerated by the COVID-19 pandemic, underscores AI's critical role in ensuring the success and competitiveness of financial institutions in this evolving landscape.

Key AI Technologies Shaping Future Finance

Artificial Intelligence (AI) technologies are significantly transforming the financial services industry, introducing innovations that enhance efficiency, accuracy, and decision-making. Several key AI technologies play pivotal roles in this transformation. Machine Learning (ML) algorithms, for instance, enable financial institutions to analyze vast datasets and identify patterns crucial for credit scoring, fraud detection, and risk assessment. By enhancing predictive modeling, ML helps organizations make informed decisions based on historical data and adapt to evolving market conditions. Natural Language Processing (NLP) is another transformative technology. It enables machines to understand, interpret, and generate human-like language, making it invaluable for sentiment analysis, customer service chatbots, and extracting insights from unstructured data sources like news articles and social media. This leads to improved communication with customers, real-time market sentiment analysis, and efficient processing of textual financial data. Robotic Process Automation (RPA) automates repetitive, rule-based tasks such as data entry, account reconciliation, and compliance checks. By streamlining operational processes, reducing errors, and enhancing workflow efficiency, RPA allows human resources to be allocated to more complex and strategic tasks, thereby increasing operational efficiency and reducing costs. Predictive analytics utilizes statistical algorithms and machine learning to forecast future trends and outcomes. In the financial sector, it is instrumental in predicting market trends, customer behaviour, and identifying potential risks. This technology enhances decision-making, enables proactive risk management, and helps capitalize on emerging opportunities. Blockchain technology, while not strictly an AI, complements AI in financial applications through its decentralized and secure nature. It is used for smart contracts, fraud prevention, and secure, transparent transactions, resulting in increased security, transparency, and efficiency in financial operations.

Computer vision technologies analyze visual data, such as images and videos, and are used in finance for document verification, facial recognition in biometric authentication, and monitoring physical security. These applications enhance security measures, improve customer authentication processes, and streamline document verification procedures. Generative Adversarial Networks (GANs) generate synthetic data, which is particularly useful for training AI models in financial fraud detection without compromising sensitive information. This leads to improved model training and accuracy without exposing real financial data to potential security risks. Chatbots, AI-driven conversational agents, interact with users in natural language formats. In financial services, they handle customer support, account inquiries, and transactional assistance, and aid in onboarding processes by providing real-time responses to customer queries. Chatbots offer 24/7 support, improve operational efficiency, and analyze customer data to provide personalized financial advice and product recommendations. The integration of these key AI technologies in financial services is ushering in a new era of efficiency, accuracy, and innovation. These advancements are fundamentally transforming how financial institutions operate and deliver services to their clients, paving the way for a more dynamic and responsive financial landscape.

Application of AI Technologies in Financial Services

The application of AI technologies in financial services offers numerous advantages, enhancing efficiency, customer experience, and risk management. One significant application is fraud detection and prevention, where AI algorithms analyze transaction patterns to identify and thwart fraudulent activities in real-time. In risk management, AI models predict market trends, aiding financial institutions in making informed investment decisions and effectively managing risks. Customer service and support benefit from AI-powered chatbots and virtual assistants, which provide instant responses to queries, handle routine tasks, and enhance overall customer experience. Algorithmic trading uses AI-driven algorithms to execute trades swiftly, leveraging real-time market data for optimal trading strategies. AI also revolutionizes credit scoring by analysing extensive data sets, including spending habits and social media activity, to create more accurate models. Personalized financial planning is another area where AI excels, analysing individual spending patterns, income, and financial goals to offer tailored advice on budgeting, saving, and investing. Furthermore, automated document processing streamlines tasks such as loan processing and regulatory reporting, while chatbot -assisted advisory services guide clients in investment decisions and financial planning.

Benefits of AI Technologies in Financial Services

AI technologies offer numerous benefits in the financial services sector. By automating repetitive tasks, AI enhances operational efficiency, minimizes manual errors, and accelerates processes. It significantly improves fraud detection through real-time transaction analysis, swiftly identifying and preventing fraudulent activities, thus protecting both institutions and customers. AI-driven chatbots and virtual assistants elevate customer experience by providing instant, personalized support, boosting overall satisfaction and engagement. Additionally, AI processes vast data to derive meaningful insights, enabling financial institutions to make data-driven decisions and better understand customer behaviour. Cost savings are achieved through task automation, increased efficiency, and reduced manual intervention. AI's advanced models analyze market trends and assess risks with greater accuracy, aiding in informed decision-making and reducing potential financial losses. Personalized financial services become possible as AI customizes products based on individual customer profiles. Furthermore, AI aids in automating compliance processes, ensuring adherence to regulations and robust security measures. Effectively leveraging AI gives financial institutions a competitive edge in the industry's evolving landscape.

Threats and Potential Pitfalls

AI technologies in financial services present various threats and potential pitfalls that require careful management. One significant risk is cybersecurity, as AI introduces new attack vectors and sophisticated algorithms vulnerable to hacking. Additionally, AI systems depend on vast amounts of sensitive financial data, raising concerns about data privacy and the severe consequences of mishandling or unauthorized access. Algorithmic bias is another issue, where biased training data can lead to unfair or discriminatory outcomes, exacerbating existing inequalities. This bias can extend to AI-driven credit scoring models, potentially affecting fair lending practices and inadvertently discriminating against certain demographic groups.

Legal and regulatory challenges also arise, as evolving regulations struggle to keep pace with rapid AI development, creating compliance challenges for financial institutions. The complexity and "black box" nature of many AI models, particularly deep learning, hinder explainability and transparency, complicating regulatory compliance further. Moreover, automation of financial tasks can lead to workforce disruption, displacing jobs and causing socioeconomic challenges. To address these issues, a multi-faceted approach is necessary, involving robust cybersecurity measures, ethical AI development, continuous monitoring, and collaboration among industry stakeholders, regulators, and technology developers.

Impact of AI in Financial Literacy

Artificial intelligence (AI) is revolutionizing the financial literacy landscape by providing personalized, accessible, and engaging learning experiences. AI-powered tools can tailor financial education to individual needs, learning styles, and risk tolerance, making it more effective and inclusive. Chatbots and virtual assistants can provide real-time support and answer financial questions in a convenient and conversational manner. Personalized budgeting apps and financial advisory platforms can help individuals manage their finances effectively, track spending, and make informed financial decisions. AI-powered gamification can make financial learning more engaging and interactive, encouraging participation and knowledge retention. As AI technology continues to advance, its impact on financial literacy is expected to grow even further, empowering individuals to make informed financial decisions and achieve financial well-being.

Strategic Approach to AI Technologies Shaping Future Finance

Artificial intelligence (AI) is swiftly revolutionizing the financial services industry, with financial institutions increasingly leveraging AI technologies to stay competitive. To fully utilize AI's capabilities, financial institutions must develop a strategic approach incorporating several key elements like firstly, clear

AI objectives need to be defined, aligning these specific goals with the overall business strategy. Identifying AI use cases is crucial, focusing on areas where AI can solve pain points, improve processes, and create new opportunities. A robust data foundation is essential, involving the establishment of a comprehensive data infrastructure to collect, store, manage, and analyze high-quality data for training and deploying AI models. Developing an AI governance framework is also vital. This framework should address ethical considerations, risk management, and regulatory compliance. Investment in AI talent and expertise is necessary to recruit, train, and retain individuals with the skills needed to develop, deploy, and maintain AI solutions. Additionally, fostering a culture of innovation is important. This culture should encourage experimentation, collaboration, and continuous learning in AI adoption. Monitoring and evaluating AI performance continuously ensures that AI models are delivering the desired outcomes and allows for informed adjustments as needed. By adopting this strategic approach to AI, financial institutions can effectively harness AI technologies to transform their operations, enhance customer experiences, and maintain competitiveness in the rapidly evolving financial landscape. AI has the potential to revolutionize the financial industry, positioning those institutions that strategically embrace it for future success.

Transformative Cases of Financial Innovation

In the Indian banking and financial services sector, AI implementation has led to transformative innovations among major providers. State Bank of India (SBI), the largest public sector bank in India, is leveraging AI to enhance customer experiences, improve operational efficiency, and mitigate risks. Their initiatives include the SBI Virtual Assistant, a 24/7 chatbot that addresses customer inquiries and resolves issues, the SBI Smart Scanner, an AI-powered app for document scanning and uploading, and an AI-based Fraud Detection System that analyses transaction data to prevent fraudulent activities. HDFC Bank, a leading private sector bank, uses AI to personalize customer experiences, automate processes, and bolster risk management. Their AI applications include HDFC Bank LIVA, a conversational AI platform offering personalized financial advice, AI-driven automation for back-office tasks like loan processing and account reconciliation, and predictive analytics to manage risks by anticipating customer behaviour and identifying potential risk factors. ICICI Bank, another prominent private sector bank, employs AI to enhance customer onboarding, streamline operations, and optimize risk assessment. Their initiatives feature the ICICI Video KYC, an AI-powered video-based customer verification system, Intelligent Document Processing for automating tasks like data extraction from invoices and contracts, and AI algorithms for assessing credit risk and making informed lending decisions. Axis Bank, a major private sector bank, utilizes AI to improve customer engagement, reduce operational costs, and strengthen regulatory compliance. Their AI applications include a personalized assistance chatbot for account inquiries and transactions, AI-powered customer segmentation for targeted marketing campaigns, and AI-driven regulatory compliance to monitor changes, identify risks, and automate compliance tasks. These cases illustrate how AI is transforming the Indian financial landscape, enhancing customer experiences, operational efficiency, and risk management. As AI technologies advance, further innovative applications are expected to revolutionize the sector even more.

Concluding Remarks

In conclusion, this paper sheds light on the dynamic intersection of artificial intelligence and financial services. It explores the components of AI and financial services, emphasizing the pivotal role of intelligence in reshaping the future of finance. With well-defined objectives and a comprehensive literature review, the study delves into key technologies influencing the financial landscape. The application of AI in financial services not only brings tangible benefits but also introduces potential threats and pitfalls. The impact of AI on financial literacy underscores the need for a strategic approach to harness its transformative potential. As exemplified by cases in India, the AI revolution is fundamentally reshaping the financial landscape, ushering in a new era of innovation and transformation.

References

[1] Bharadwaj, R. (2019, April 5). AI in the Indian Financial Sector – Current Traction, Opportunities and Challenges. *Emerj*. Accessed through: https://emerj.com/ai-sector-overviews/ai-in-the-indian-financial-sector-current-traction-opportunities-and-challenges/

[2] Bredt, S. (2019). Artificial Intelligence (AI) in the financial sector—Potential and public strategies. *Frontiers in Artificial Intelligence*, 2, 16.

[3] Elangovan, K. and Saranya, H. (2023). Study on Pros and Cons of AI in Financial Sector: A Review. *South India Journal of Social Sciences*, XXI, 135–142.

[4] Golic, Z. (2019). Finance and artificial intelligence: The fifth industrial revolution and its impact on the financial sector. *Proceedings of the Faculty of Economics in East Sarajevo*, 19, 67–81.

[5] Han, Y., Chen, J., Dou, M., Wang, J. and Feng, K. (2023). The Impact of Artificial Intelligence on the Financial Services Industry. *Academic Journal of Management and Social Sciences*, 2, 83–85. Accessed through: https://doi.org/10.54097/ajmss.v2i3.8741

[6] Insider Intelligence. (2023, January 02). Artificial Intelligence in Financial Services: Applications and benefits of AI in finance. Accessed through: https://www.insiderintelligence.com/insights/ai-in-finance/

[7] Iryani, I. and Yulianto, H. (2023). Artificial Intelligence (AI) of Financial in the VUCA Era: A Systematic Mapping Study. *Journal of Computer Networks,*

Architecture and High-Performance Computing, 5, 398-413. Accessed through: https://doi.org/10.47709/cnahpc.v5i2.2201

[8] Machkour, B. and Abriane, A. (2020). Industry 4.0 and its Implications for the Financial Sector. *Procedia Computer Science*, 177, 496-502.

[9] Maple, C., Szpruch, L., Epiphaniou, G., Staykova, K., Singh, S., Penwarden, W., Wen, Y., Wang, Z., Hariharan, J. and Avramovic, P. (2023). The AI Revolution: Opportunities and Challenges for the Finance Sector.

[10] Mavlutova, I. and Volkova, T. (2019, October). Digital transformation of the financial sector and challenges for competencies development. In *2019 7th International Conference on Modeling, Development and Strategic Management of Economic System (MDSMES 2019)* (pp. 161–166). Atlantis Press.

[11] Murugesan, R. and Manohar, V. (2019). AI in Financial Sector-A Driver to Financial Literacy. *Shanlax International Journal of Commerce*, 7(3), 66–70.

[12] Settles, P. (2023). Artificial Intelligence: Is it just hype or does it represent the future for the financial services industry? *KPMG Thriving in an AI World Study*. Accessed through: https://info.kpmg.us/news-perspectives/technology-innovation/thriving-in-an-ai-world/ai-adoption-financial-services.html

[13] Truby, J., Brown, R. and Dahdal, A. (2020). Banking on AI: mandating a proactive approach to AI regulation in the financial sector. *Law and Financial Markets Review*, 14(2), 110–120.

[14] Umamaheswari, S. and Valarmathi, A. (2023). Role of Artificial Intelligence in The Banking Sector. *Journal of Survey in Fisheries Sciences*, 10(4S), 2841–2849.

The Pathway to Inclusive Growth Through Banking Inclusion in India

Semanti Debroy Sen[1]

ABSTRACT: Ever since the globalisation and liberalisation of the financial markets, there has been a phrase going around called inclusive banking. It aims at extending the baking services to those who have so far not got any access to the banking system and was mainly depending on the organised and informal options for their financial requirements. The objective of this paper is to make an in-depth analysis of the progress of Inclusive banking in India. The study is basically and descriptive analysis to enumerate the growth of banks and its spread to rural and unbanked areas and the benefits received by those people who had no access to banking. As per the observations related to financial exclusion and its direct relation with poverty, Financial Inclusion gained significant success in the early 2000s. In India, the Reserve Bank of India (RBI) has taken various initiatives to achieve higher financial inclusion just like facilitating no-frills accounts and general credit cards for little deposits and credit. Some of these initiatives are Opening of no-frills accounts with nil or minimum balance, relaxation of KYC (know your customer) norms, engaging Business Correspondents (BCs) to address last mile issues, use of technology to provide facilities through BC model where account can be operated using biometrics, adoption of EBT (transfer social benefits electronically into the beneficiary's bank account), simplified branch authorization, opening of branches in unbanked rural centres. Some factors which are considered to evaluate the success of inclusive banking will be elaborated from secondary data. These include no of bank branches per 100000 adults, number of ATMS, number of depositors per 1000 branches, outstanding SME loans of commercial banks.

Keywords: Inclusive Banking, Financial Inclusion, Banking Spread, FI Index, RBI Initiatives.

Introduction

The new millennium ushered in several new strategies and paradigms for extending economic activities, benefits and facilities for people of every sphere of life and across all economic, social and cultural categories. An important issue in the strategies of development and economic progress was the concept of "inclusive growth", i.e. to extend the benefits of economic growth

[1] Assistant Professor, Department of Economics & Finance. Bhavan's Institute of Management Science, Kolkata, India.
E-mail: semantidr@gmail.com; semantidr@yahoo.co.in

across all sections of the population. One of the important pillars of inclusive growth is financial inclusion which implies including every member of the population into institutional financial services. The aim of financial inclusion is to extend financial, mainly banking and insurance services to those areas where they were hitherto unavailable and to include economically underprivileged people who reside in remote areas of the country. It also aims at providing affordable and accessible banking services to unbanked and underbanked areas which is stated as "inclusive banking".

Financial inclusion has been defined as "the process of ensuring access to financial services, timely and adequate credit for vulnerable groups such as weaker sections and low-income groups at an affordable cost". (Committee on Financial Inclusion—Chairman: Dr C Rangarajan, RBI, 2008). The Committee on Medium-Term Path to Financial Inclusion (Chairman: Shri Deepak Mohanty, RBI, 2015) has set the vision for financial inclusion as, "convenient access to a basket of basic formal financial products and services that should include savings, remittance, credit, government-supported insurance and pension products to small and marginal farmers and low income households at reasonable cost with adequate protection progressively supplemented by social cash transfers, besides increasing the access of small and marginal enterprises to formal finance with a greater reliance on technology to cut costs and improve service delivery."

Benefits of Financial Inclusion

There are several reasons why financial inclusion and inclusive banking have found much consideration in recent times:

- Financial inclusion reduces poverty and inequality. Financial inclusion provides opportunities for marginalized and low-income individuals to access formal financial services.
- Financial inclusion promotes economic growth. Increased financial inclusion leads to higher levels of savings, investment, and entrepreneurship, fostering economic growth and stability.
- Financial inclusion promotes small business. Small businesses often face challenges in accessing credit from traditional banking sources. This much-needed funding for small entrepreneurs can be provided through financial inclusion.
- Financial inclusion empowers otherwise marginalized demographics. Financial inclusion can promote gender equality and women's economic empowerment.
- Financial inclusion promotes innovation and digital inclusion. Financial inclusion drives innovation in the financial sector and also promotes access to and use of digital technology in delivering and use of financial services.

The Road to Inclusive Banking

In order to ensure banking and financial services reach every section of the society, some directed measures have been taken.

(a) Universal Access to Financial Services: to provide access to financial services for every village.
(b) Providing Basic Bouquet of Financial Services: like a basic savings account, loan facility, life and non-life insurance and several investment products.
(c) Access to Livelihood and Skill Development: by privding information and training about Govt. skill development and employment generation programs.
(d) Financial Education and literacy: to educate less informed people about financial services and products.
(e) Customer Protection and Grievance Redressal: by resolving their grievances and protecting the privacy of the customers
(f) Effective Co-ordination: which involves maintain coordination with all the stakeholders in the service delivery.

Literature Review on Inclusive Banking

In spite of many financial inclusion initiatives in last decades, those initiatives are accessible to few. Subbarao points out in his study that only 30,000 centres are covered by commercial banks out of the 600,000 inhabitations in India. There is a massive rural urban divide in terms of financial access indicators, as two thirds of the population resides in rural areas, it is therefore deprived of financial services and products. Empirical studies show that financial inclusion helps poor households—a majority of whom are employed in informal sector—to improve their standard of living and paves the way for higher economic growth (Rajan and Zingales 1998; Burges and Pande 2005; Bruhn and Love 2009; Bittencourt 2012). World Bank study for rural India found that about 40 per cent of households have deposit accounts, 20 per cent have outstanding loans and only 15 per cent have any insurance (Basu, 2006). Financial exclusion may be caused by (1) geographic limitations due to under provision of banking services in remote and scarcely populated areas, (2) socio-economic limitations when financial services appear inaccessible to specific income, socio or ethnic groups, or (3) limitations of opportunity when new or small firms with profitable projects are credit rationed because of lack of information and collateral (Beck/de la Torre 2006, Anderloni/Carluccio 2007, pp. 9). Some studies had attempted to find level of financial inclusion through surveys measuring proportion of households having access to bank accounts. However major difficulties of these type of studies is that these surveys are not regularly conducted and it becomes difficult to measure financial inclusion over time. Another problem with these surveys is that their methodologies varies and thus leading to inconsistencies in measure. Honohan (2008) has attempted to combine survey based information and secondary data on the number of bank accounts to econometrically estimate the proportion of households/adults having access to financial services for as many as 160 countries. Many existing literature uses financial indices computed solely on the basis of supply side information (like number of bank branches) and hence they fail to capture demand side dynamics (Dev, 2006). Focussing only on supply side leads to two issues- Overestimation of financial inclusion because one person can own multiple accounts. Secondly, merely owing account does not necessarily means usage of that account (Beck et al 2007). Kamath et al 2010 empirically showed that correlation between supply of institutional finance and demand for the same is low in India. Therefore, there is a need to study financial inclusion both from supply side and demand side to reflect ground situation on access and use of financial services (Beck et al 2009). Another interesting study points out that women are less likely to access formal borrowing than their male counterparts indicating gender bias (Jyoti, 2016). Also he pointed out that people with higher level of education are more likely to borrow from formal sources. This increase chances of vulnerable sections falling prey to informal agencies. As per Census2011, 58.7% households avail banking services in India. Documentary proofs required to meet KYC requirements as mandated by RBI pose serious impediments to access to banking services especially for poor migrants from rural India (Demirguckant and Klapper 2012). Even no frills account fail to reduce their woes as these account mostly remain dormant (Thyagarajan and Venkatesan 2008). High transaction costs in terms of account opening, account closing charges, minimum balance requirements, transportation charges, high opportunity cost of visiting bank branches, etc. also deters access to bank accounts in India (Beck et al 2009; Mowl and Boudot 2014).

Measuring Financial Inclusion

Quantifying financial inclusion progress is usually undertaken across the three dimensions of access, usage and quality. Access Indicators show the details pertaining to access points in the form of Banking Outlets (Bank Branches, Business Correspondent outlets), Automated Teller Machines (ATMs) and Point of Sale (PoS) terminals. The access parameters can be represented both in terms of geography (e.g number of banking outlets per 1000 sq km) as well as demography (e.g. number of banking outlets per 100000 adult population). Usage Indicators show how the products are being used by the target customers. Data for usage can be collected through primary and secondary sources. While data on number of accounts, products, etc. can be collected from financial service providers, insights into the usage of different financial products and services may be obtained through surveys/ feedback from customers. The Quality indicators describe the supporting pillars that ensure that the customers can use the financial services to their satisfaction.

Financial Inclusion Index

RBI had introduced the FI-Index in 2021 with the purpose of capturing the extent of financial inclusion across the country. The central bank had recognised that greater financial inclusion (FI) is crucial for a wider, inclusive and sustainable growth. RBI said that FI has been conceptualised as a comprehensive index, incorporating details of banking, investments, insurance, postal, as well as the pension sector, in consultation with government and respective sectoral regulators. CRISIL (2015) also develops similar index called Inclusix (for 2013) for India. It is a composite index consists of the indicators that measures the progress of financial inclusion in India. These include bank penetration, deposit penetration and credit penetration which are all combined together in one single metric. The CRISIL Inclusix indicate that there is an overall improvement in the financial inclusion in India. According to the study, deposit penetration is the main drive to attaining financial inclusion in India. The southern region is the most financially included with highest credit penetration while the eastern region is the least financially included. A plausible reason could be the higher literacy rate in the southern region as compared to the eastern and the north-eastern regions. However, it captured only supply side information and thus suffers from limitations. Sarma (2012) had constructed a multidimensional index of financial inclusion. This index is constructed similarly to that used by UNDP for constructing well known Human Development Index (HDI), Human Poverty Index (HPI), Gender development Index (GDI). Our study follows the methodology of Sarma (2012) because the composite financial inclusion index is methodologically improved, as it follows the distance-based approach, unlike the UNDP's methodology of average of dimension indices. The distance-based approach is suitable because it satisfies most of the properties like boundedness, monotonicity, etc. Also, this method captures financial inclusion from both demand side and supply side angles. For e.g. availability of bank branches captures the supply side story and usage of deposit and credit accounts captures the demand side story.

Objective of the Study

The objective of this paper is to make an in-depth analysis of the progress of Inclusive banking in India. The study is basically and descriptive analysis to enumerate the growth of banks and its spread to rural and unbanked areas and the benefits received by those people who had no access to banking.

Measurement of Inclusive Banking

The extent of financial /banking inclusion can be ascertained with the help of 3 key parameters; Access, Usage and quality of the service.

Access shows the reach the reach of banking services to the customers. Access is enumerated on the basis of the following facts:

(a) No. of bank branches per 100000 adults
(b) No. of ATMs per 100000 adults
(c) No. of POS machines per 100000 adults
(d) No. of business correspondents per 100000 adults

Usage shows how the banking products are being used by the customers or to what extent the services are useful to the beneficiaries. Usage is determined by:

(a) Percentage of adults with a savings account in a financial institution
(b) Percentage of adults having access to bank credit
(c) Percentage of adults having some insurance policy
(d) Percentage of adults having pension policy
(e) Percentage of SME having access to formal credit
(f) Percentage of MSME having access to formal credit

Quality indicator brings out the fact as to how satisfied the customers are upon the usage of the banking services. Quality can be expressed through:

(a) Financial literacy and capability which means basic knowledge about financial concepts like inflation, interest rates, purpose of insurance, meaning of risk diversification etc.
(b) Grievance redressal which is measured by no of complaints received and no. of complaints resolved by the respective institution.

Progress of Inclusive Banking in India

To provide greater and easy access to banking facilities, the Govt. of India undertook several measures. In India, the Reserve Bank of India (RBI) has taken various initiatives to achieve higher banking inclusion just like facilitating no-frills accounts and general credit cards for little deposits and credit. Some of these initiatives are:

- Opening of no-frills accounts with nil or minimum balance
- Relaxation of KYC (know your customer) norms
- Engaging Business Correspondents (BCs) to address last mile issues
- Use of Technology to provide facilities through BC model where account can be operated using biometrics
- Adoption of EBT (transfer social benefits electronically into the beneficiary's bank account)
- Simplified branch authorization
- Opening of branches in unbanked rural centres.

In addition to these, some other schemes introduced by the Govt are:

- Pradhan Mantri Jan Dhan Yojana (PMJDY)
- Atal Pension Yojana (APY)
- Venture Capital Fund for Scheduled Castes under the Social Sector Initiatives
- Varishtha Pension Bima Yojana (VPBY)

Current Status of Inclusive Banking in India

The access parameter of inclusive banking is evaluated on the basis of the following factors as expressed in the table below.

Table 1: Measure of Access of Banking Services

Year	*2009*	*2013*	*2017*	*2020*	*2021*
No. of bank branches per 100000 adults	9.5	11.8	14.5	14.7	14.6
No. of ATMs per 100000 adults	5.29	12.82	22	21.5	21.44
No. of POS per 100000 adults			2.5	5.1	4.72
No. of Business Correspondents (rural)		221341	543472	682651	1554212
No. of (urban)		27230	102865	538565	1059397

Source: RBI

Table 2: Measurement of Usage in Banking Operations

Year	*2011*	*2014*	*2017*	*2021*
% of adults with savings accounts	35.23	52.75	79.84	77.8
No. of accounts in commercial banks (per 1000 adults)		1337.41	1881.54	2023.67
Loan a/c with commercial banks	141.38 (2013)	175.81 (2017)	264.13 (2020)	285.22 (2021)
Insurance penetration				
% of people having life insurance		2.6	2.82 (2019)	3 (2022)
% of people with non-life insurance		0.7		1

Source: RBI

As on 31st March 2022, the total number of Central Govt pension holders were 6976240. Total number of pension holders under National Pension Scheme (NPS) were 22.84 lakh Central Govt employees, 55.77 lakh state Govt. employees and 14.05 lakh corporate employees. Needless to say, it is a negligible number compared to the total population. Also, this is mostly for the organised sector. The unorganised sector may still be outside the purview of the system.

Table 3: Institutional Credit Flow to MSME Sector

Year	*Amt. of Credit (Rs. crores)*
2015	1171026
2017	129398
2019	1510650

Source: RBI

Credit to MSME industries grew by 20% in 2021 and by 35 % in 2022. Total addressable credit demand is about $819 billion of which $ 289 billion has been fulfilled through the formal credit channels like NBFCs, public and private sector commercial banks (Source: Avendus Capital – Investment banking firm). Though there has been a substantial increase in credit lending to MSMEs, a large number is still outside the purview of bank credit mainly due to delay in loan sanction, lack of proper information, problem with collateral and procedural complications. So, based on the recommendation of Prime Minister's Task Force Committee, Bombay Stock Exchange (BSE) launched the SME Platform, where MSMEs can be listed and they will find a new source of finance. There is also the option of Angel funding for the MSMEs

The Future of Inclusive Banking

To achieve a financially inclusive society which can sustain inclusive growth, the citizens should be provided with education, basic financial services, affordable healthcare and ways of upgrading and applying their inherent skills. The disparity between rural and urban India must be eliminated. Digital payment system and rural infrastructure should be improved to ensure continual access to tele-networks with zero disruption. There should also be access to some line of credit. Inclusive banking has a multiplier in boosting GDP growth, reducing poverty and inequality. Progress of inclusive banking would involve some of the following efforts:

(a) There has to be a sustained effort so that people who have been included into the formal banking system do not get excluded due to some economic or social reasons.

(b) Digital penetration in rural areas has sometimes slowed down due to lack of financial awareness and cybercrimes which has created distrust in the minds of the rural population.

(c) There is a demarcation between urban, semiurban and rural areas because of the difference in tech savvy ness and the ease of handling electronic gadgets. There is a need for technical training to bridge this gap.

(d) Information regarding banking transactions sometimes does not reach the customers due the non-connectivity or non- availability of mobile device. This creates some confusion the the minds of service users.

(e) Govt. schemes have not fully penetrated into every corner of the society and high interest rate of local money lenders is still prevalent. Access to credit from financial institutions needs to be increased in a more organised manner. Banks can provide loans, insurance and other services based on the personalised data of each individual, for which they may take the help of AI & ML.

The Road Ahead for Inclusive Banking

Reserve Bank of India in its concerted efforts to ented banking services to every corner of the country came up with a Financial Inclusion Program (2020–2024) to provide banking access to every household. The target of the program is to provide a bank account, line of credit, insurance products, pension schemes and other suitable investment products to every eligible adult. The program focusses on:

- A financial transaction grievance redressal system to look ater the concerns and complaints of less tech savvy and less connected citizens.
- Increase digital penetration particularly among the rural population where it is visibly lower n compared to their urban and semi urban counterparts.
- With still 80% of the population having banks accounts, there is need to ensure account opening of the remaining 20%.
- Ensuring privacy of data and information of citizens.
- To provide easy and affordable digital payment options mainly for small businessman and unorganised sector workers.

India's National Strategy follows the broad indicators as suggested by the World Bank in its report on Universal Financial Access by 2020. Our country is continuously progressing on the road to achieve:

- Technology enabled financial inclusion. The technological initiatives under 'JAM Trinity', that is, PM Jan Dhan Yojana, Aadhaar and increased Mobile Phone & internet usage had led to 355 Mn accounts opened in the last 5 years.

"National Mission for Capacity Building" which is a measure by bankers essentially targeted towards the MSME sector.

The banking system has introduced several Regulatory Framework to protect customers, to promote fair business practices and prevent any unhealthy practices by market players. Also market development initiatives have been taken to ensure that beneficiaries can be accurately targeted. A strong action in this respect is to link all Govt. financial assistance schemes to DBT.

Several banking enabled digital payment schemes like UPI, NACH, CTS, AEPS etc have been initiated. Extent of online connectivity has been increased in rural areas by using real time Aadhar based authentication, micro ATMs, PoS machines, tablets and mobile phones. Last mile delivery to bridge the gap for remote connectivity and doorstep financial services is key to success. ICT based solution like business correspondents/ facilitators and IPPB are landmark steps in this area.

Concluding Remarks

In conclusion, we can say that a technological, multi-faceted & dynamic approach centred around enhancing financial literacy, social & education inclusion, improved cybersecurity & stricter laws, enhanced digital infrastructure is mandatory for wider coverage of next wave of financial inclusion in the country. Inclusive banking is not a standalone procedure. To bring about an overall improvement in the financial health of the country to foster inclusive growth it requires Social and Health Inclusion through improving skillset, education, physical and mental well-being to ensure a sustained livelihood. FI Ecosystem must aim to work in tandem with Healthcare Inclusion & Education Inclusion ecosystem to ensure well-being of people and educate the citizens financially.

References

[1] Mowl, J. and Boudot, C., "Barriers to Banking: Results from an Audit Study in South India," *NSE Working Paper Series* No. WP-2014-1 (2014).

[3] Dev, S.M. (2006). Financial Inclusion: Issue and Challenges. Economic and Political Weekly, 41, 4310–4313.

[4] Jamnani, J.T. (2020). Banking Sector and financial inclusion in India, *PRAGATI Journal of Indian Economy,* 6 (Special):13–24.

[5] Bruhn, M. and Love, I. (2013). The Real Impact of Improved Access to Finance: Evidence from Mexico, *Journal of Finance*, https://doi.org/10.1111/jofi.12091

[6] Burgess, R. and Pande, Rohini (2005). Do Rural Banks Matter? Evidence from the Indian Social Banking Experiment, *American Economic Review*, Vol. 95, No. 3, pp 780-795.

[7] Kamath, R. (2010). Financial Inclusion vis-a-vis Social Banking, *Economic and Political Weekly,* 42(15):1334-1335, DOI:10.2307/4419466

[8] Zingales, L. and Rajan, R.G. (2003). Banks and markets: The changing character of European finance (No. w9595). *National Bureau of Economic Research.*

[9] National Strategy for Financial Inclusion (NSFI: 2019-2024), RBI reports (2020).

[10] Report by Avendus Capital—Investment Banking firm.

A Study on the Financial Capability of Educated Middle Class in India

Debalina Chattopadhyay[1]

ABSTRACT: The capability of an individual to deal effectively with financial matters is known as Financial Capability. Financial capability is a combination of knowledge, attitudes, skills and behaviour necessary to manage personal finances and to choose and make appropriate use of financial products. Financial capability enables individuals to process financial information and make informed decisions about personal finance. A person's financial capability is best demonstrated by his/her behaviour. Financial capability is not only related with financial skills or financial numeracy but also it is a combination of financial attitudes, financial behaviour and financial knowledge. In this paper the researcher has attempted to test the financial capability of Indian educated middle class. It has been suggested that the Government of India should initiate steps for undertaking a national level financial capability study of Indian citizens, with special emphasis on financial capability of the educated middle class and initiate appropriate policy interventions to strengthen this capability.

Keywords: Financial Attitudes, Financial Behaviour, Financial Capability, Financial Knowledge.

Introduction

Financial Capability is one of the most essential factors contributing to financial well-being of the educated middle class. It is therefore one of the most discussed topics throughout the world in the recent times. (Lusardi and Mitchell, 2014; Sherraden, 2013; Xiao, 2015). Hence, the review of literature pertaining to this topic has increased manifold in the recent years. In general, financial capability can be considered human capital leading to life successes (Heckman and Mosso, 2014). Financial Capability has various meanings according to various researchers. Some researchers consider financial capability and financial literacy as interchangeable concepts and others consider it a synonym for financial access, an important concept regarding financial inclusion. Sometimes they are also used as overlapping terms. For example, financial literacy can narrowly mean financial knowledge or broadly financial capability to make effective decisions (Huston, 2010; Lusardi and Mitchell, 2014). Financial capability is also defined as an individual's ability to apply appropriate financial

[1] College Whole Time Teacher, Department of M.Com, The Bhawanipur Education Society College, Kolkata, West Bengal, India. E-mail: dchattopadhyay93@gmail.com

knowledge and perform desirable financial behaviours for achieving financial well-being (Xiao *et al.*, 2014) or refers to a combination of both personal ability and environment support (Johnson and Sherraden, 2007).

This paper sheds light on the four research themes of financial capability, namely (1) financial capability, financial knowledge and financial satisfaction, (2) impact of financial literacy and financial education on financial capability, especially among educated middle-class people, (3) impact of financial access on financial capability and (4) propensity to plan, financial advice, financial experience and financial capability. The paper also reviews the conceptualizations of financial capability and its underlying theoretical frameworks – the most prominent theory used in the literature is the capability theory. Actually, capability is the outcome of interactions among three components. The capability here refers to individual ability, which is a major difference from the concept of financial capability proposed by Sherraden (2013; see also Johnson and Sherraden, 2007).

Research Methodology

Data Sources

This research uses a systematic literature review process as a reliable, repeatable and scientific means of generating a knowledge base (Tranfield *et al.*, 2003; Kumar *et al.*, 2019). There are several types of systematic reviews such as structured review (Rosado-Serrano *et al.*, 2018), meta-analysis (Goyal *et al.*, 2022) and bibliometric review (Donthu *et al.*, 2021). A comprehensive review with content analysis depicts the state-of-the-art literature concerning the theories, concepts, factors and outcomes of financial capability (Goyal and Kumar, 2021). For the study, we have referred the largest platform of indexed articles i.e. Scopus. Scopus was referred because its scope is a proper balance between quality and diversity; compared to Web of Science, it is more inclusive; and when compared to Google Scholar, it is more selective (Donthu *et al.* 2021). We will follow the guidelines given by Mukherjee *et al.* 2022 for conducting the bibliometric analysis. We have limited the search to the documents published between 2007-March 2022. The starting year of the literature search was set to 2007 because it was the first year that the concept of financial capability was formally published in academic journals. Two influential papers on financial capability were published in 2007 (Atkinson *et al.* 2007; Johnson and Sherraden, 2007), followed by many studies applying the financial capability definitions proposed in these two studies. Only those articles were included in the review study which dealt with consumer financial capability or related concepts such as financial literacy and financial access as antecedents of financial capability; or financial behaviour, financial satisfaction and financial wellbeing as its outcomes. We have excluded those articles which did not focus on financial capability of individuals, consumers or the households but focussed on firms and banks. On reading the abstracts and the full papers, a total of 215 articles were selected for our review. The approach of Rashman (2009) was followed for the selection strategy.

Methods of Study

We have identified research trends of financial capability of educated middle class from the most prolific journals, prominent authors and most cited articles using the Scopus database and compiled those using MS-excel. Thematic arrangement shows scholarly work characteristics, and a knowledge structure analysis can reveal study referencing patterns between the knowledge of handling finances and expenditure-savings ratio (Donthu *et al.*, 2021). As a result, we used VOSviewer and Gephi software (Baker *et al.*, 2020) to perform a bibliographic coupling analysis (Kessler, 1963) to show the magnitude of intellectual associations among citing publications based on the degree of their standard references (Kessler, 1963). Bibliographic coupling is based on links; it identifies the level of overlap between citing texts, revealing the field's research fronts. This method is widely used in bibliometric analysis to explore the intellectual structures of the most influential documents in fields of research (Donthu *et al.*, 2021; Goyal and Kumar, 2021; Kumar *et al.*, 2017, 2022). The frequency with which two articles cite a typical article, the more similar they are considered in the research domain (Weinberg, 1974). Based on our in-depth analysis, we developed this that higher the knowledge of financial capability higher is the economic well-being of the middle-class people.

Here, we also refer to the economic model of human development proposed by Heckman and Mosso (2014). The core of the Heckman–Mosso model is skill formation (e.g. cognitive development), individual efforts (e.g. practices) and individual performance (e.g. test score). The Heckman–Mosso model includes cognitive skills, non-cognitive skills and health as three parts of individual skills, argues that individual skills are one key determinant of their efforts and further suggests that both skills and efforts affect individual performance (i.e. skills → efforts → performance). There are a variety of other factors affecting all these three concepts simultaneously. Parenting and public investment on skills, anticipated reward on efforts and environmental incentives on performance). While it does not intend to explain individual financial capability development directly, the Heckman–Mosso model is consistent with the conceptualization of financial capability in the knowledge, behaviour, knowledge-behaviour and outcome approaches. Applying this framework, financial knowledge can be considered part of individual skills, financial behaviours represent individual efforts and financial outcomes can be referred to as individual performance. The knowledge approach mainly addresses skill formation, and the behaviour approach solely emphasizes efforts. The knowledge-behaviour approach combines both skill formation and efforts, while the outcome approach is mainly interested in performance. This human development system proposed by Heckman and Mosso can incorporate all related constructs proposed in these four definitions.

Themes of Financial Capability Research and an Analysis of the same

Impact of Financial Literacy and Financial Education on Financial Capability, Notably of the Educated Middle Class

Articles in this sector, mainly focus on the effects of the interventions to improve financial capability particularly among the educated middle class. The most cited article in this cluster is by Sherraden *et al.* (2011). Another highly notable article by Serido *et al.* (2013) presents a developmental model of financial capability to understand the process by which young adults acquire the financial knowledge and behaviours needed to manage full-time adult social roles and responsibilities. Loke *et al.* (2015) examined the impact of the My Path Savings pilot process on economically disadvantaged youth and found that the program is highly relevant to youth as it resulted in significant increase in financial knowledge, financial self-efficacy, and the frequency with which positive financial behaviours were carried out.

Financial Capability and Financial Satisfaction

Articles in this sector, mainly focus on the relationship between financial capability and financial satisfaction. The sector also deals in the examination of the level of financial literacy and financial capability using NFCS and its impact on financial behaviour.

Propensity to Plan, Financial Advice, Financial Experience and Financial Capability

The articles in this sector, focus mainly on the propensity to plan, financial advice and financial experience as the indicators of financial capability that contribute to consumer financial satisfaction and well-being. The most cited article in this cluster by Xiao and O'Neill (2018b) demonstrates that the propensity to plan is positively associated with financial capability, and financial planning is a desirable financial behaviour to improve financial satisfaction.

Directions for Future Research

Backgrounds and Financial Capability

Consumer background differences in financial capability are still interesting topics. Some consumer attributes such as gender and age are always worthwhile to further explore with new dependent variables in terms of financial knowledge, behaviour, opportunity and capability. Future research could also explore more dimensions of consumer backgrounds such as psychological, social and cultural factors. International comparisons of financial capability are also important research topics to explore.

Financial Capability on Consumer Well-Being

Some research has been done to connect financial capability to consumer financial well-being and overall well-being. Future research could be more comprehensive to cover more dimensions of financial well-being such as earning, spending, and borrowing, insuring and saving/investing. More future research could also be conducted to explore how financial capability contributes to other life domain well.

Interventions on Financial Capability

Interventions offered by family, school, workplace, government and non-profit are important topics for future research. Interventions such as family financial socialization, financial education and other policy-supported initiatives for helping disadvantaged consumers should be described and evaluated in research papers. To make interventions more effective and efficient, more program evaluation research should be conducted. Various research methods including both qualitative and quantitative approaches can be used to collect rich information about these topics.

Financial Capability Interactions

A plethora of research has examined the association between knowledge and behaviour. Some research has also addressed the issue of endogeneity between financial knowledge and financial behaviour and provided approaches such as instrument variable, propensity score matching and difference in difference approaches to address this issue (Lusardi and Mitchell, 2014).

Conclusion

Financial capability initiatives are becoming increasingly important in the choice and responsibility for picking acceptable and advantageous financial goods and services. The goal of this research paper was to assess the current state of knowledge on financial capability of the young generation. The results also suggest that level of financial capability varies significantly among respondents based on various demographic and socio-economic factors. Overall, it can be concluded that financial capability level is not very high in our country and necessary measures should be taken by government to increase financial capability of individuals. This review paves a way forward for future researchers to undertake primary research and learn how retail banking providers are assisting consumers in improving their financial capability through their products and services, as well as how this is understood and regulated in the industry.

References

[1] Almenberg, J. and Save-Soderberg, J. (2011). Financial literacy and retirement planning in Sweden. *CeRP Working Paper,* No. 112.

[2] Al-Tamimi, H.A.H. and Kalli, A.A.B. (2009). Financial literacy and investment decisions of UAE investors. *The Journal of Risk Finance*, 10(5), 500–516.

[3] ANZ and AC Nielsen Research (2005). ANZ survey of adult financial literacy in Australia.

[4] Chen, H. and Volpe, R.P. (2002). Gender differences in personal financial literacy among college students. *Financial Services Review*, 11, 289–307.

[5] Cole, S., Sampson, T. and Zia, B. (2008). Money or Knowledge? What drives the demand for financial services in developing countries. *Harvard Business School Working Paper* No. 09–117.

[6] Hogarth, J.M. and Hilgert, M.A. (2002). Financial knowledge, experience and learning preferences: Preliminary results from a new survey on financial literacy. *Consumer Interests Annual*, 48, 1–7.

[7] Lusardi, A. and Mitchell, O.S. (2007). Baby boomer retirement security: The roles of planning, financial literacy and wealth. *Journal of Monetary Economics*, 54, 205–224.

[8] Monticone, C. (2010). How much does wealth matter in the acquisition of financial literacy? *The Journal of Consumer Affairs,* 44, 403–422.

[9] Volpe, R.P., Kotel, J.E. and Chen, H. (2002). A survey of investment literacy among online investors. *Financial Counseling and Planning*, 13(1), 1–13.

[10] Worthington, A.C. (2006). Predicting financial literacy in Australia. *Financial Services Review*, 15(1), 59–79.

Author Index